Amsterdam

WHAT'S NEW | WHAT'S ON | WHAT'S BEST

www.timeout.com/amsterdam

Contents

Published by Time Out Guides Ltd
Universal House
251 Tottenham Court Road
London W1T 7AB
Tel: + 44 (0)20 7813 3000
Fax: + 44 (0)20 7813 6001
Email: guides@timeout.com
www.timeout.com

Editorial Director Sarah Guy
Management Accountant Margaret Wright

Time Out Guides is a wholly owned subsidiary of Time Out Group Ltd.

© Time Out Group Ltd
Chairman & Founder Tony Elliott
Chief Executive Officer Aksel Van der Wal
Editor in Chief Tim Arthur
UK Chief Commercial Officer David Pepper
International Managing Director Cathy Runciman
Group Marketing Director Carolyn Sims

Time Out and the Time Out logo are trademarks of Time Out Group Ltd.

This edition first published in Great Britain in 2013 by Ebury Publishing
A Random House Group Company
Company information can be found on www.randomhouse.co.uk
Random House UK Limited Reg. No. 954009
10 9 8 7 6 5 4 3 2 1

Distributed in the US and Latin America by Publishers Group West (1-510-809-3700)

For further distribution details, see www.timeout.com

ISBN: 978-1-84670-241-9

A CIP catalogue record for this book is available from the British Library.

Printed and bound in Germany by Appl.

The Random House Group Limited supports The Forest Stewardship Council (FSC®), the leading international forest certification organisation. Our books carrying the FSC label are printed on FSC® certified paper. FSC is the only forest certification scheme endorsed by the leading environmental organisations, including Greenpeace. Our paper procurement policy can be found at www.randomhouse.co.uk/environment.

Time Out carbon-offsets all its flights with Trees for Cities (www.treesforcities.org).

MIX
Paper from
responsible sources
FSC™ C004592

Amsterdam Shortlist

The **Time Out Amsterdam Shortlist** is one of a series of guides that draws on Time Out's background as a magazine publisher to keep you current with what's going on in town. As well as Amsterdam's key sights and the best of its eating, drinking and leisure options, the guide picks out the most exciting venues to have opened in the past year and gives a full calendar of annual events. It also includes features on the important news, trends and openings, all compiled by locally based editors and writers. Whether you're visiting for the first time, or you're a regular, you'll find the *Time Out Amsterdam Shortlist* contains all you need to know, in a portable and easy-to-use format.

The guide divides central Amsterdam into seven areas, each of which contains listings for Sights & Museums, Eating & Drinking, Shopping, Nightlife and Arts & Leisure, with maps pinpointing all their locations. At the front of the book are chapters rounding up these scenes city-wide, and giving a shortlist of our overall picks in a variety of categories. We include itineraries for days out, plus essentials such as transport information and hotels.

Our listings give phone numbers as dialled within the city. The international code for the Netherlands is 31. To call from outside the country, follow this number with the code for Amsterdam, 020, dropping the initial 0.

We have noted price categories by using one to four euros signs (€-€€€€),

representing budget, moderate, expensive and luxury. Major credit cards are accepted unless otherwise stated. We have also indicated when a venue is NEW .

All our listings are double-checked, but places do sometimes close or change their hours or prices, so it's a good idea to call a venue before visiting. While every effort has been made to ensure accuracy, the publishers cannot accept responsibility for any errors that this guide may contain.

Venues are marked on the maps using symbols numbered according to their order within the chapter and colour-coded according to the type of venue they represent:

❶ Sights & Museums
❶ Eating & Drinking
❶ Shopping
❶ Nightlife
❶ Arts & Leisure

Map key	
Selected House Number	*463*
Major Sight or Landmark	▭
Hospital or College	▭
Pedestrianised Street	▭
Railway Station	▭
Metro Station	Ⓜ
Area Name	**LEIDSEPLEIN**

Time Out **Amsterdam** Shortlist

EDITORIAL
Editor Steve Korver
Copy editor Ros Sales
Researcher Floris Dogterom
Proofreader Marion Moisy

DESIGN
Senior Designer Kei Ishimaru
Guides Commercial Senior Designer
  Jason Tansley
Picture Editor Jael Marschner
Deputy Picture Editor Ben Rowe
Picture Researcher Isidora O'Neill

ADVERTISING
Sales Director St John Betteridge
Advertising Sales Charlie Sokol

MARKETING
Senior Publishing Brand Manager
  Luthfa Begum
Head of Circulation
  Dan Collins

PRODUCTION
Production Editor Dave Faulkner
Production Controller
  Katie Mulhern-Bhudia

CONTRIBUTORS
This guide was researched and written by Steve Korver and contributors to
Time Out Amsterdam.

PHOTOGRAPHY
Marie-Charlotte Pezek, except page 9 Jannes Linders; 13 (top) Elvis Vaughn/
Shutterstock; 13 (bottom) Jan Willem van Hofwegen/Shutterstock; 14 Matthew
Dixon/Shutterstock; 15, 54, 68 Shutterstock; 21 Alan Jensen; 24, 39 Dennis van
de Water/Shutterstock; 25, 26, 27, 42, 62, 67, 70, 90, 111, 125, 142, 143, 174
Michelle Grant; 32, 51, 73, 176 Wilmar Dik; 34 Denis Guzzo; 36, 37 Cassander Eeftinck
Schattenkerk; 40 Rob van Esch/Shutterstock; 45 Arthur de Smidt; 47 Vorm in Beeld;
48 Katarzyna Mazurowska/Shutterstock; 49 Anne Binckebank; 53, 80 Gemma Day; 55
Devy/Shutterstock; 57, 86, 93, 148, 175 Olivia Rutherford; 83 Shebeko/Shutterstock;
97 Thijs Wolzak; 102 Carolina Georgatou; 108 Christina Theisen; 112 (top) Luuk Kramer;
112 (bottom) Roos Aldershoff; 115 Floris de Ridder; 131 Gert Jan Van Rooij; 137 Erik
Smiths; 149 Eric Gevaert/Shutterstock; 154 (left) Axel Bueckert/Shuttestock; 154 (right)
Neirfy/Shutterstock; 155 Michael Bednarek/Shutterstock; 156 Jan Kranendonk/
Shutterstock; 159 (left) H. Tuller/Shutterstock; 159 (right) Desiree Walstra/
Shutterstock; 162 Kasia Gatkowska; 169 (top) Roel Ruijs; 172 Matthew Shaw.

The following images were supplied by the featured establishments/artists: 7, 18,
33, 52, 61, 76, 94, 103, 105, 106, 117, 123, 130, 140, 147, 161, 167, 168,
169 (middle and bottom), 170, 171, 177.

Cover photograph: Veronika Vasilyuk/Shutterstock.

MAPS
JS Graphics (john@jsgraphics.co.uk).

About **Time Out**

Founded in 1968, Time Out has expanded from humble London beginnings into
the leading resource for those wanting to know what's happening in the world's
greatest cities. As well as our influential what's-on weeklies in London, New York
and Chicago, we publish nearly 30 other listings magazines in cities as varied as
Beijing and Mumbai. The magazines established Time Out's trademark style: sharp
writing, informed reviewing and bang up-to-date inside knowledge of every scene.

Time Out made the natural leap into travel guides in the 1980s with the City Guide
series, which now extends to over 50 destinations around the world. Written and
researched by expert local writers and generously illustrated with original photography,
the full-size guides cover a larger area than our Shortlist guides and include many
more venue reviews, along with additional background features and a full set of maps.

Throughout this rapid growth, the company has remained proudly independent,
still owned by Tony Elliott four decades after he started Time Out London as a single
fold-out sheet of A5 paper. This independence extends to the editorial content of all
our publications, this Shortlist included. No establishment has been featured because
it has advertised, and no payment has influenced any of our reviews. And, for our
critics, there's definitely no such thing as a free lunch: all restaurants and bars
are visited and reviewed anonymously, and Time Out always picks up the bill.
For more about the company, see www.timeout.com.

Don't Miss

Rijksmuseum

Sights & Museums

Amsterdam's museum scene has officially awakened from a long slumber. After a full decade of renovation, the Rijksmuseum (see p134) has reopened to delirious acclaim – predictable since it houses some of the world's greatest arts treasures. The Stedelijk Museum of Modern Art (see p134) has reopened in the hopes of getting delirious acclaim some time in the future – but it's tricky if your budget keeps getting cut. The Scheepvaartsmuseum (see p118) has reopened to show the world the Dutch savvy with the sea. The EYE Film Institute (see box p124) has reopened in its eye-catching new building along the river IJ across from Centraal Station. Even the Van Gogh Museum (see p136) and the Royal Palace (see p67)

are open again after getting some speedy renovations. Feeling overwhelmed yet?

Even without this glut of freshness, there was always plenty to keep visitors amused in Amsterdam, whether they're inclined towards experimenting with vices or more cerebral, nobler pursuits.

In the city centre lies the old port and the fast-developing waterfront, along with its medieval buildings, the Red Light District, the grand 17th-century merchants' houses, the high spires of ancient religious institutions, the oldest and prettiest canals, as well as many of Amsterdam's most famous sights. Except to stroll to Vondelpark and Museumplein – where you can enjoy the sight of three major

museums and the world-class concert hall Concertgebouw – many visitors rarely go beyond the *grachtengordel*, that tranquil concentric belt of Golden Age canals that horseshoes round the fascinating and historic Old Centre. Make sure that you don't make the same mistake: venture to the newly gentrified, pretty residential areas of the Pijp and the Jordaan – or even Westerpark and the Westergasfabriek (see box p128) to discover the latest trends in cuisine and culture.

Most sights lie within half an hour's walk from one another, and the excellent network of trams provides back-up for those low on energy. You can join the slipstream of locals by saddling up on a bike (although beware of trams and cycle thieves); or, better still, beg or borrow a boat to absorb the city on a cruise down the canals – surely the angle from which it was meant to be viewed. There's also a bewildering array of other modes of transport: horse and carriage, rickshaws, interactive guides for mobile phones and Segways. You can even opt to get the seasoned photographers of Exposure Photo Tours (www.exposurephoto tours.com) to take you to the city's most photogenic spots.

Another shock to the system has occurred: there are now cheerful 'Welcome Teams' dressed in red, waiting at Centraal Station and other busy central locations, to help tourists with directions, transport and tips for events. This is part of a larger campaign aimed at making Amsterdam more hospitable for visitors. It includes encouraging shop assistants and bar/restaurant staff to raise their levels of service, as they're often accused of being indifferent (many locals attribute this lack of interest to poor levels of pay.)

Stedelijk Museum of Modern Art p9

Constant change

Unlike many nearby cities, Amsterdam was not devastated by bombing during World War II and much of its charm lies in how little it has changed, even though modern schemes remain in flux – especially the Noord-Zuidlijn metro line (see box p68), and the developments around Centraal Station and directly across the IJ in Amsterdam Noord. Most of the more appealing sights have been around for many decades or, more usually, for centuries.

Museum hopping

There's good news for under-13s: they have free admission to most of the nation's museums. Even for older visitors, prices are still reasonable; despite the fact that most museums charge for admission, prices are rarely more than €15. However, if you're thinking of taking in a few museums in one go, then the Museumkaart (Museum Card) is a steal, at €44.95 for adults and €22.50 for under-19s (plus a €4.95 administration fee for first-timers). The card offers users free or discounted admission to more than 400 attractions in the Netherlands, and is valid for a year from the date of purchase. The museums with discounted or free entry for card-holders are denoted in this guide's listings by the letters 'MK'. You can purchase the card at museums participating in the scheme.

The Amsterdam Tourist Board (see p186) also sells a savings pass, the I amsterdam Card, which gives you free entry to major museums, free rides on public transport and a complimentary canal trip, along with a hefty 25 per cent discount at certain tourist attractions and restaurants. It costs €42 for 24 hours, €52 for 48 hours and €62 for 72 hours.

Sights unseen

Much of Amsterdam's charm derives from what remains hidden to the untutored eye. For instance, there's an awful lot more to absorb than just sex and drugs in the Red Light District. A strange mix of prostitutes, clerics, schoolkids, junkies, carpenters and cops may offer you a peek at their strange brand of social cosiness. It's all pretty harmless, so long as you remember that window girls do not like having their pictures taken and you remain alert to drug dealers.

Then there are the local *hofjes* or almshouses, many of which are gorgeously peaceful, the most famous being the Begijnhof (see p81). Most are concentrated in the Jordaan. The best known are the Venetiae (Elandsstraat 106-136), the Sint Andrieshofje (Egelantiersgracht 107-114), the Karthuizerhof (Karthuizerstraat 21-31), the Suyckerhofje (Lindengracht 149-163), the Claes Claesz Hofje (1e Egelantiersdwarsstraat 3) and oldest by far, the Lindenhofje (Lindengracht 94-112). The art of *hofje*-hopping is a gamble, because entrances are sometimes locked in deference to the residents. But take a chance and you may be surprised by the delights inside. But don't leer inside the windows: the inhabitants are human and will feel violated.

Meanwhile, the major canals and radial streets are where the real Amsterdam exists. What they lack in sights, they make up for as places for scenic coffee drinking, quirky shopping and pleasant walks.

DON'T MISS

Begijnhof

De Waag

Neighbourhood watch

Of course, Amsterdam's infamous ground zero of consumerism, vice, entertainment and history is the Old Centre, which is bounded by Prins Hendrikkade to the north, Oudeschans and Zwanenburgwal to the east, the Amstel to the south and Singel to the west.

Within these borders, the Old Centre is divided into the New Side (west of Damrak and Rokin) and the Old Side (east of Damrak and Rokin). The Old Side, roughly covering the triangle formed by Centraal Station, the Nieuwmarkt and the Dam, is notorious for hosting the Red Light District. However, the area is also home to the epic Oude Kerk (p69) and the menacing De Waag (p66).

The New Side, on the other hand, is the Old Side's gentler sister, featuring a history entwined with the intelligentsia, thanks to its many bookshops, brown cafés and

the various buildings of the University of Amsterdam.

The *grachtengordel* ('girdle of canals') that guards the Old Centre is pleasant, idyllic and uniquely Dutch, and now boasts two of the most fascinating arrivals on the local sightseeing scene: canal museum Het Grachtenhuis (see box p97) and the Stadsarchief Amsterdam (City Archives, see p101). It is also home to Anne Frank Huis (see p90, the Westerkerk (see p93) and two rather intriguing photography museums: Foam (see p98) and Huis Marseille (see p93). For ease of use, we have divided the areas covered by canals into two sections: Western Canal Belt denotes the stretch of canals to the west and north of Leidsegracht, whereas Southern Canal Belt covers the area that lies to the east, taking in Leidseplein and Rembrandtplein. This split is historically justified by the fact that the western girdle

Westerkerk

Museumplein

was complete before work on the eastern half began.

The area around Waterlooplein, just east of the Old Centre, was settled by Jews four centuries ago, and so took its name, Jodenbuurt, from this rich culture. Now the heritage of Russia stands nearby at the Hermitage on the Amstel (see box p112) and oases of flora occupy the Plantage neighbourhood, east and south-east of Waterlooplein, among them the Hortus Botanicus (see p110) and Artis (see p108). Further east (Oost) lies the Tropenmuseum (see p113).

Once the gateway to prosperity, Amsterdam's Waterfront is now emerging as the setting for some of Europe's most inspired architecture. Traditional sights may be few, but the eastern stretch in particular is attracting thousands of new residents and developing as a boulevard of contemporary arts and nightlife.

Over in the other direction, the Westelijke Eilanden links up nicely with the charming neighbourhood of the Jordaan, bordered by Brouwersgracht, Prinsengracht, Leidsegracht and Lijnbaansgracht. Working-class stalwarts here rub shoulders with affluent newcomers in an area that, while lacking the grandiose architecture of the canals, wants for nothing in terms of character.

Spotlighted by its world-class museums and some incredibly sophisticated emporia of high-class fashion, Amsterdam's Museum Quarter is a mix of culture, in the form of the Museumplein, and couture, at the PC Hooftstraat. Against all the odds, the Pijp has remained a cultural melting pot, even though the area has been thoroughly gentrified for several years. It proves that the city is still full of charm – you may not even feel the desire to enter a museum.

wagamama

japanese inspired cuisine

wagamama amsterdam
amstelstraat 8 (rembrandtplein)
max euweplein 10 (leidse plein)
zuidplein 12 (wtc ı station zuid)

wagamama.nl

Barco p19

Eating, Drinking & Smoking

The hotel-restaurant-café business, or *horeca*, as it is often called here, is a crazy rollercoaster, with bars and eateries dropping like flies into the proverbial gazpacho. They are quickly replaced by an almost endless stream of new – and, considering the times, sometimes daring – ventures that might require diners to be willing to go further afield, both physically and with their taste buds.

Rising Dutch

It used to be that the term 'Dutch cuisine' inspired only the mirth of serious foodies; these days it's been reduced to the occasional chuckle. Well-travelled native chefs have returned home to apply their skills to fresh local and often organic ingredients (source your own at Noordermarkt's Saturday organic market; see p130). The land is most suited to growing spuds, cabbage, kale and carrots, but the nation is now employing its greenhouses to grow a startling array of ingredients, year-round. Things are looking so good that local restaurant critic – and infamous grump – Johannes van Dam continues to give out high ratings to local initiatives. He's even gone so far as to recently award his third perfect score, a 10, to &Samhoud Places (see p120). While some accuse him of becoming a softie in his old age, his generosity is not without

&Samhoud Places

good reason – Dutch restaurants have improved immensely.

In medieval days it was fish, gruel and beer that formed the holy diet. During the Golden Age, the rich indulged in hogs and pheasants. Then, with Napoleonic rule at the dawn of the 19th century, the middle classes were seduced by the Mediterranean flavours of herb and spices.

Only in the last century has Amsterdam taken to international cuisine. After World War II, the rich spicy food from Indonesia reawoke the Dutch palate (see box p105). Indonesian *rijsttafel* ('rice table'), along with fondue – a 'national' dish shamelessly stolen from the Swiss because its shared pot appealed to the Dutch sense of democracy – are both foods of choice for any celebratory meals.

Other waves of immigration helped create today's vortex of culinary diversity. But there's still nothing quite like the hotchpotch of mashed potato, crispy bacon and crunchy greens, holding a well of gravy and loads of smoked sausage, to prove that traditional Dutch food can still hit the spot. The most feverish buzz remains around places that combine

straight and honest cookery with eccentric ingredients and often out-of-the-way locations. Besides the watery ones (see box p120), there's De Kas (Kamerlingh Onneslaan 3, 462 4562, www.restaurantdekas.nl) in an old greenhouse and As (Prinses Irenestraat 19, 644 0100, www.restaurantas.nl) in a remodelled modernist church.

There's also a wave of specialisation occurring in various faraway locations: near Westerpark there's Worst (Barentszstraat 171, 625 6167, www.deworst.nl), which focuses on sausage and Holy Ravioli (Spaarndammerstraat 35, 681 8414, www.holyravioli.nl), which is wrapped up in, yes, ravioli. There's also much talk of a new 'nouveau rough' school of cookery that combines rough interiors, an obsession for fresh and responsible ingredients and reasonable prices. These establishments are exemplified by rotisserie specialists Rijsel (see p114), as well as the Italian Il Mattarello (Westerstraat 77, 688 7788, http://mattarello.nl) in the Jordaan, post-Dutch foodsters Wilde Zwijnen (Javaplein 23, 463 3043, http://wildezwijnen.com) in East and Café Modern

(Meidoornweg 2, 494 0684, http://
modernamsterdam.nl) in North.

The move towards unpretentious
and straightforward cooking is
also seen in the rise of street food.
Sadly due to local bylaws, mobile
stalls selling the food are usually
restricted to operating at festivals,
including the new and hugely
popular Rollende Keukens
('Rolling Kitchens') festival in
Westergasfabriek (see box p128).
Keep your eye out for The Kitchen
of the Unwanted Animal, with such
delicacies as *krokets* made from
swans culled in the name of keeping
Schiphol Airport safe for jets.
Meanwhile there are active efforts
to change bylaws so street food can
return to where it belongs: the street.

Other news is the development of
several 'culinary-boulevards'. One
is located on a stretch of connected
streets in the Jordaan that is home
to the Spanish La Oliva (see p126).
It's become known as 'Little Italy'
because of its highly regarded
restaurants such as Hostaria
(Tweede Egelantiers Dwarsstraat
9, 626 0028); but there are also
other options, such as Japanese
Pancake World (Tweede
Egelantiersdwarsstraat 24, 320
4447, www.japanesepancake
world.com). Another culinary strip
is Amstelveenseweg, bordering
the south end of Vondelpark. It
includes the Indonesian Blauw
(see box p105) and Ron Gastrobar
(see p140). And, more recently, Van
Woustraat in the Pijp transcended
its *shoarma* (shawarma) leanings
to become hub of diverse cuisines.

If you enjoy a stroll that involves
picking out where you're going to
eat dinner, here are a few tips: go
to the Pijp or Amsterdam East if
you crave economical ethnic; cruise
the eateries of Haarlemmerstraat,
Utrechtsestraat, Nieuwmarkt,
the 'Nine Streets' area and
Reguliersdwarsstraat if you

SHORTLIST

Best newcomers
- &Samhoud Places (p120)
- Yokiyo (p76)

Outdoor drinking
- 't Blauwe Theehuis (p136)
- Brouwerij 't IJ (p113)
- 't Smalle (p126)

Best cocktails
- Vesper (p129)
- Hiding in Plain Sight (p114)

A taste of the old school
- Cafe Welling (p136)
- Wynand Fockink (p76)

Beers of distinction
- 't Arendsnest (p93)
- Brouwerij 't IJ (p114)
- Gollem's Proeflokaal (p139)

Lush lunches
- Buffet van Odette (p101)
- Little Collins (p144)
- Small World Catering (p126)

Cheap vegan delights
- De Peper (p139)

Traditional eating
- Bistro bij Ons (p94)
- Moeders (p126)

Posh and proud
- La Rive (p103)

Shipshape
- Pont 13 (p120)
- Barco (p120)

Best burgers
- Getto (p71)
- Butcher (p144)

Fancy picnic pickings
- Caulils (p96)
- Marqt (p141)

DON'T MISS

DON'T MISS

want something more upmarket; and only surrender to Leidseplein if you don't mind being gravely overcharged for a cardboard steak and day-old sushi.

The internet is also a good resource for local culinary knowledge. Check out www.iens.nl and www.specialbite.nl; the latter reliably offers the scoop on all the latest restaurant openings. And don't forget that a snack in Amsterdam can go a long way (see box p74).

Drinking

As the local barfly-cum-columnist Simon Carmiggelt once observed: 'Going for one drink is like jumping off a roof with the plan of falling only one floor.' So knowing some basic rules is a plus. For instance: buy rounds when in a group; do not use German when ordering rounds, and expect a long and drawn out answer if you ask the bartender 'How are you?'

Perhaps the most fundamental rule for Brits is not to whine about

the 'two fingers' of head that comes with a glass of draft pils (lager). You are not being ripped off; it's the 'crown' and the reasoning behind it is sound: by letting a head form during tapping, the beer's hoppy aroma – and hence full flavour – is released, and the drinker's gas intake is minimised (leaving more room for more beer of course).

Another handy tip is to avoid getting completely legless by acquiring a sound knowledge of *borrel hapjes* (booze bites). These tasty bar snacks are formulated to line the stomach during drinking sessions. Inevitably, such menus begin with the strongest of stereotype reinforcers: *kaas* (cheese), which can be ingested either via *tostis* (grilled cheese sandwiches), or pure with dipping mustard. But the most universal and tastiest of *hapjes* are definitely *bitterballen* ('bitter balls'), which are essentially just cocktail versions of the *kroket* (see box p74).

A barfly can also score some major points by giving the Dutch

Worst p18

their rightful credit for inventing gin. In around 1650 a doctor in Leiden came up with the process that allowed juniper berries to be infused into distilled spirits and gin was born – or rather *jenever*, as the local version is called. A few decades later, the Dutch were exporting 10 million gallons of the stuff, as a supposedly innocuous cure for stomach and kidney ailments. They graded the gin by age – *jong*, *oud* and *zeer oud* (young, old and very old) – but also by adding various herbs, spices and flavours. Such liquid elixirs can still be found at *proeflokalen* (tasting houses) like Wynand Fockink (see p76) and Distilleerderij 't Nieuwe Diep (see p114).

The café (or bar – the line between the two is suitably blurred) is central to Dutch social life, serving both as a home from home at all hours of the day and night (most cafés open in the morning and don't shut until 1am; some stay open as late as 3am or 4am at weekends). Whatever the hour, you're as likely to find punters sipping a coffee or coke as the foaming head of a pils – or a shot of local gin.

A cool yet hard-drinking kind of crowd can be found at Café Weber (see p101) and other cafés along Marnixstraat, just off Leidseplein. A short hop in the other direction is Reguliersdwarsstraat, the centre of both the gay scene and an emerging more mixed trendy scene as exemplified by Ludwig (see p104). And one of Amsterdam's best mixed gay bars, Prik (see p84), which serves everyone's favourite bubbly – prosecco – on tap, is but a ten-minute walk away.

Away from the neon, the Jordaan is awash with *bruin* cafés, so called because they've been stained brown by decades of smoking and spilt coffee. Befitting the area's

Il Mattarello p18

newly gentrified status, many, like Café Thijssen (Brouwersgracht 107, 623 8994), are teeming with wealthy nouveau residents; nearby bars, though, are still filled with the last vestiges of the local working-class population. Not far away stands the Westergasfabriek (see box p128), which has several appealing drinking spots, including the WestergasTerras. A similar scene to the Jordaan is to be found in the Pijp, a great place to wander between trendy bars and more salt-of-the-earth watering holes.

Wine buffs will find themselves underwhelmed in Amsterdam's cafés and bars. If you are aghast at the prospect of a beaker of unspecified red or white, head to Nevy (see p120) or La Oliva (see p128), both examples of a recent breed of establishment that specialises in pairing posh food with fine wine.

Cocktails, of course, remain ever popular, be they a do-it-yourself 'craftini' thrown together on a craft night at Nieuwe Anita (see p132), or the ultra-posh secret concoctions made at Vesper (see p129) and Hiding in Plain Sight (see p114).

Beer, though, is resoundingly the local drink of choice: in most places the pils is Heineken or Amstel, but every bar offers a range of Belgian brews and there are several specialist beer bars like In de Wildeman (Kolksteeg 3, 638 2348, www.indewildeman.nl). For a real taste of all the Low Countries' native brews, 't Arendsnest (see p93) has a huge range to choose from.

Smoking

Smoking has been banned from all public spaces, including bars, live music venues, restaurants and clubs, since 2008. However, a few old brown bars still hold out and allow their clientele to puff on their cigarettes and roll-ups.

As for that other kind of smoking – cannabis – things are a little more variable. Many coffeeshops are simply ignoring the smoking ban or offering herbal mixes as an alternative to tobacco. Or they rent out vaporisers: a gizmo that vaporises THC (the active ingredient) at a low temperature so that the leaves stay uncombusted, resulting in a smokeless toke.

In the name of keeping the peace with the EU, some politicians have recently suggested making coffeeshops into private clubs, solely for local use – essentially sending tourists on to the street to score. But as things stand, that won't be happening any time soon. For the time being, Amsterdam's unique selling point remains the fact that you can walk into a café and buy drugs. The power of the anti-coffeeshop movement means that there have been no new openings for years. Meanwhile local weed entrepreneurs are instead investing in countries such as Spain and Portugal, which have moved towards the Netherlands' past lax attitude towards soft drugs. But breeding trends still develop here: you won't get very far without stumbling across organic (bio) highs, which don't pack quite the same punch as genetically modified (and often terrifyingly potent) hydroponic skunk. Dutch weed is known the world over for its unprecedented quality and strength, so if you're a beginner, or used to less powerful dope (Brits, take note), go easy.

Pllek p124

Options: p.25

Shopping

The global financial crisis was slow to affect the Netherlands. Of course, there were plenty of banks that needed bailing out, but the general populace seemed to continue to spend. Hell, even fashion icon Karl Lagerfeld saw fit to open his second flagship shop in Amsterdam in 2013 – and not in the predictable PC Hooftstraat but in the more street Nine Streets shopping district. However that ultimate in lifestyle cars, Tesla, did chose PC Hooftstraat as home for its latest showroom. In sharp contrast, meanwhile, the adorable Uke Boutique (http://www.uke boutique.nl), dedicated to that cutest of stringed instruments, the ukelele, recently opened up – but on the decidedly uncommercial Lijnbaansgracht (no.191). So visitors are still spoiled for choice.

All this spending can make one draw comparisons with the 'tulip mania' of the 17th-century Golden Age, when single bulbs were traded for cash, castles and mountains of cheese, before it all collapsed in an orgy of bankruptcies and suicides.

The buoyancy of the retail sector today could be explained by the simple fact that the Netherlands is a wealthy country (it was listed fifth in the EU's rich list). Yet while the Dutch clearly spend, the population is perhaps less obsessed with shopping than residents of other countries. The influence of Calvinism, that most pared-down of lifestyle choices, is still etched deep into the national psyche, and most people are happy to pack a cheese sandwich for lunch rather than eat out at a stylish café. Contradictions abound, but there

Bloemenmarkt

is clearly a lot to be enjoyed in the world of Amsterdam shopping.

Off to Market

Tulips are perhaps what Amsterdam is best known for exporting, and you can certainly pick up bargains at the floating flower market Bloemenmarkt (see p103). At the more traditional general markets, you'll find people truly enjoying shopping as they bounce between vendors while sniffing out special offers. With food as the great unifier, the market is among the few places at which the multi-ethnic diversity of the city is visible.

People from all walks of life are certainly brought together at the Albert Cuypmarkt (see p146), which claims to be Europe's longest street market, and forms a line all the way through the heart of the Pijp. The daily market offers plenty of snacks, ranging from raw herrings to Surinamese sherbets, along with all manner of household goods. It lies

in close proximity to many pretty cafés, in which you can recharge yourself over a cool drink.

Other neighbourhoods in the city tend to have their own markets: the Ten Katemarkt (Mon-Sat) in Oud West, the Dappermarkt (Mon-Sat) in Oost and the Lindenmark (Sat) in Jordaan are all worth a trip for an authentic shopping experience. Also located in the Jordaan, Saturday's Noordermarkt (see p130) is the place to buy organic farmers' produce amid well-heeled shoppers; the same crowd is back on Monday morning to pick through bric-a-brac and antiques, at a much smaller (yet infinitely superior) variation in Waterlooplein's tourist trap.

Fashion does exist

It's true. The average burgher doesn't think through their attire every time they rush out of the front door. Nevertheless, a fair few designers have achieved success against the odds in Amsterdam, and the country can hold its head high in the catwalk stakes – after all, it's the home city of avant-garde darlings Viktor & Rolf, whose headquarters lie in Museumplein. Meanwhile, Marlies Dekkers (see p141) continues to charm with her feminine lingerie.

Locally produced gentleman's style journal *Fantastic Man* – and its sister publication *The Gentlewoman* – are considered to be two of the hottest new fashion magazines on the planet. It could be said that the biannual Amsterdam Fashion Week is having a rather trendsetting effect.

A couple of Dutch brands have brought street style home: Gsus and G-Star Raw. The latter even has its own branded ferry, which you might see cruising around town. The former, which works alongside the Fair Wear Foundation to protest against sweatshop production, is available at De Bijenkorf (see p76). In fact, Amsterdam can be considered a denim capital of

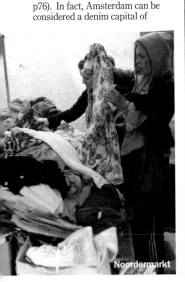

Noordermarkt

SHORTLIST

Best newcomers
- Hutspot (p148)
- The Otherist (p96)
- Options! (p77)

Fancy threads
- 2 (p140)
- Four (p140)

Local fashion
- SPRMRKT (p130)

Spoil yourself
- Rituals (p104)
- Skins Cosmetics (p96)

Kiddy winkels
- Joe's Vliegerwinkel (p77)
- 't Klompenhuisje (p77)

Grown-up pleasures
- Marlies Dekkers (p141)
- Female & Partners (p87)

Unmissable markets
- Albert Cuypmarkt (p146)
- Bloemenmarkt (p103)
- Boerenmarkt (p129)

Blocks of chocs
- Puccini Bomboni (p78)
- Unlimited Delicious (p132)

Cheesy pleasers
- Boerenmarkt (p129)
- De Kaaskamer (p96)

Pre-owned treasures
- Noordermarkt Monday morning (p130)
- Waterlooplein flea market (p115)

Street cred
- Patta (p77)
- Concrete Image Store (p87)

Vintage
- Out of the Closet (p115)

SPRMRKT

sorts since it's also home-base to Blue Blood and Denham.

The fashion map of Amsterdam is divided along clear lines: head to PC Hooftstraat, as star footballers do, for top-end designer clothes; visit the Kalverstraat for high-street stalwarts such as H&M and HEMA. Even though Amsterdam has long lacked an abundance of good boutiques, a wander around the Jordaan, the Nine Streets and Damstraat areas will lead to the discovery of outlets selling quirkier and home-grown labels.

For something hip, try SPRMRKT (see p130) or such 'concept stores' as 290 Square Meters (see p114). And speaking of concepts, here's a new one: a pop-up department store, Hutspot (see p148).

While the populace may be somewhat lacking in fashion sense, in terms of interior design and architecture, the Dutch lead the world (see p48-52 **Living by Design**). To feed your eyes with design of all kind, from seriously high-end homewares to truly swanky jewellery, check out Utrechtsestraat. Overtoom, Rozengracht and Haarlemmerstraat/ Haarlemmerdijk are also much-coveted furnishing destinations.

Open books

The Dutch are freakishly bookish. They enjoy reading, collecting bookends, participating in book weeks – and even book months. So if you're a bookworm, you'll be in good company. Head straight to Spui, bounded at one end by the mighty Waterstone's (see p88) and at the other by the American Book Center (see p84), both of which are multi-storey giants of English literature. Smaller-scale reading pleasures can be found on the shelves of multilingual

Athenaeum Nieuwscentrum

Athenaeum Nieuwscentrum
(see p87), a veritable treasure
trove of journals in all languages.
Another singular browsing
experience awaits if you cross the
Rokin to reach Oudemanhuispoort,
a covered passageway belonging
to the University of Amsterdam –
where books and prints have been
sold since the 18th century.

Incredible edibles

If you're hoping to pick up edible
souvenirs, you'll be truly spoiled
for choice in Amsterdam; head to
De Kaaskamer (see p96) and you'll
see a mountain of cheese – there are
more than 200 varieties, including
plenty of local specialities such as
the popular reypenaer. For fishy
dishes, you can pick up smoked
eel, raw herring or tiny North Sea
shrimps from any number of fish
stalls dotted around town. Head
to Holtkamp (see box p74) for an
array of cakes displayed in a
beautiful interior; you will also be
able to see how this gourmet shop
cooks the humble *kroket*. If you

fancy locally produced, organic
food, visit Marqt (see p141); if it
happens to have lamb from the
North Sea island of Texel, or white
asparagus when it's in season,
make sure you try some.

Talking shop

In general, local shops are open
from 1pm to 6pm on Mondays
(if they open at all on this quiet
day), 10am to 6pm from Tuesday
to Friday (with many open until
9pm on Thursday), and 9am to
5pm on Saturday. Amsterdam
has regular Sunday shopping,
especially along Kalverstraat,
PC Hooftstraat and the Nine
Streets, with stores usually
open between noon and 5pm.
Smaller shops tend to have
more erratic opening hours.
Credit card payment is not quite
universally accepted, so as a rule
of thumb, make sure that you take
enough cash with you when you
go out shopping.

De Kaaskamer

Bags packed, milk cancelled, house raised on stilts.

You've packed the suntan lotion, the snorkel set, the stay-pressed shirts. Just one more thing left to do – your bit for climate change. In some of the world's poorest countries, changing weather patterns are destroying lives.

You can help people to deal with the extreme effects of climate change. Raising houses in flood-prone regions is just one life-saving solution.

**Climate change costs lives.
Give £5 and let's sort it *Here & Now***

www.oxfam.org.uk/climate-change

Be Humankind **Oxfam**

Chicago Social Club p31

WHAT'S BEST
Nightlife

The biggest recent news in Amsterdam's nightlife came in 2013, when this famous party town finally become a 24-hour party town with several locations being given extended licences (see box p86). In the past you might occasionally have got lucky with a decent after-party but, in general, the only option post 4am or 5am at weekends was home; from where you can contact the beer taxi (www.biertaxiamsterdam.nl, 06 2231 0066) to get a late-night delivery – which, incidentally, still remains an option…

This momentous event seems to be a belated antidote to what was perceived as a general trend towards conservatism under the Christian Democrat-led national coalition. Some felt – or still feel – that the city was becoming a victim of overly zealous legislation: smoking had been banned; mushrooms had been banned; coffeeshops were closing. What next? Beer?

But now Amsterdam's nightlife seems set to become yet more diverse. And, really, one has always been able to find everything from minimalist grooves to maximum noise. There are scuzzy venues for students and rockers, meat markets for stags and stalkers, and cutting-edge clubs for hipsters. And when it comes to live music, there has most definitely been a renaissance of late.

It's all live

Ever cruised down the road humming Shocking Blue's 'Venus', or the now classic bass line to

Golden Earring's 'Radar Love'? Or danced a night away to Afrojack? No? Perhaps you've settled down for an evening in with Mahler, performed by the Royal Concertgebouw Orchestra? Whatever your musical bent, these are just a handful of the Netherlands' diverse musical exports. And on any given night in Amsterdam you can be sure to find something to suit your aural taste, from the classy jazz of improv drummer Han Bennink and saxophonist hero Benjamin Herman of the New Cool Collective, to the ex-squatpunks The Ex, who jam with Ethiopian roots musicians. Alternatively, drink and dance to the hip hop orchestra of Kyteman, or enjoy the Eastern European party sounds of the Amsterdam Klezmer Band. Or get goosebumps from poetry-fuelled alternative folksters Spilt Milk. The more musical genres you throw into the mix (think heavy metal, art rock, hip hop and Frisian fado), the longer the list of Dutch musical innovators gets.

Alongside the home-grown talent is a plethora of international acts. With Amsterdam firmly established as one of the world's most important ports of call on the international touring circuit, thanks to such iconic venues as Paradiso (see p106) and Melkweg (see p106), whatever you're seeking, it'll be readily available within close proximity of the canal ring. And with new locations such as North Sea Jazz (see box p128), Westergasfabriek (see box p128), People's Place (see p107) and Tolhuistuin (see box p124), the future looks bright indeed.

The arrival of the new Ziggo Dome (www.ziggodome.nl) by the Arena Stadium in the south-east means there is now a regular selection of monster gigs. With a staggering 17,000 seats, the Ziggo Dome towers over near neighbour Heineken Music Hall (which has a piffling capacity of just 5,500), so it's not surprising it pulls in the biggest international names: Lady Gaga, Madonna and George Michael have all graced the stage.

North Sea Jazz

Additionally, the acoustics are excellent, and the logistical hiccups that often beset such large venues are non-existent.

Fans of alternative music should follow the good work of Subbacultcha (www.subbacultcha.nl), which is booking all the up-and-coming underground guitar and electronica bands. It's also always worth keeping your eyes peeled for what's happening in Haarlem, Utrecht or Rotterdam; you might discover that a performance by your favourite band or DJ is but a short train ride away.

Clubland Amsterdam

The age of massive and extravagant clubs is over, although this torch is being kept somewhat alive by newcomer Air (see p104). More with the times, Trouw (see box p116) seems set to continue its legacy of progressive programming, all in an odd post-industrial setting and complete with a new 24-hour licence. And it's just this kind of grassroots

De Nieuwe Anita

operation, run by a group of like-minded friends, that has taken on the mega-clubs of yesteryear. At the cosiest end of the scale are intimate nooks such as De Nieuwe Anita (see p132), Bitterzoet (see p88) and ClubUp (Korte Leidsedwarsstraat 26, clubup.nl), that go for funky quality over capacity. Similar vibes can be found further afield at Studio K (see p116) and Canvas (see box p116) in the east, or Club 8 (Admiraal de Ruijterweg 56B, www.club-8.nl) in the up-and-coming De Baarsjes neighbourhood.

In general, clubbing in the capital is really no different from clubbing in any large international city. All venues have bouncers, so show up on time and with a mixed crowd to increase your chances of getting in. Storing your coat in the cloakroom might set you back, as might using the toilets (typically between €0.50 and €1), but in many clubs outside the city centre they're free. As a rule, the Dutch aren't great tippers at the bar; if you are feeling generous, however, a 15 per cent tip is considered very generous. Almost no one will actually be

inside a club before midnight: people are either at home or in a bar loosening up.

As for drugs, weed and hash are still fine in the smoking areas, but it's always unwise to solicit for anything stronger – undercover cops have started to appear at the larger techno parties. Plus, what you might think you're buying is not likely to be what you will get.

Gay capital

After a couple of years of serious hand-wringing about whether or not Amsterdam still deserved the Gay Capital title – the doubt largely inspired by a sad spate of incidents, many involving Moroccan youths – the city seems to be getting back on track. Local political parties have made a real effort to make Amsterdam gay-friendly. Meanwhile, Amsterdam Pride (see box p102) has gone the way of many others by embracing corporate sponsorship – some major companies and banks now even have their own floats to make sure the spectators get the message (the main message being that they're keen to emphasise their employee diversity).

Pink Point (www.pinkpoint. org), in a stall just opposite the Homomonument (see p90), serves as a good first port of call for gay or lesbian visitors. Until very recently the scenes for gay men and women were quite separate and they would only get together on occasions such as Queen's Day, Pride, or one-off parties like the mighty Love Dance. Now there are an increasing number of mixed bars and club nights. There's also a shared archive, Homodok (www.ihliq.nl), in the new library Openbare Bibliotheek Amsterdam (see p118). People don't seem to be too worried that Queen's night is now King's night.

Also on the up, gay clubbing has been reinvigorated by a wealth of young talent and plenty of fresh faces, such as cruising club Church (see p104), dance club NYX (see p104), and several new one-off parties are popping up. A word of warning, though: free condoms aren't universal on the scene, and a range of STDs – including HIV – are on the up, with barebacking as popular and controversial here as in any other big city.

Finger on the pulse

The capital's main ticket retailer is the Amsterdam Uitburo (AUB), which operates an elaborate online sales point for events at www.aub.nl, as well as a personal service at the AUB Ticketshop at Leidseplein 26 (open 10am-5pm daily).

Pick up the AUB's free monthly magazine *Uitkrant* (pronounced 'out-krant'), available in theatres, bars, bookshops and the AUB Ticketshop, which is also a great place to collect flyers and other listings leaflets. It is also home to the Last Minute Ticket Shop (www.lastminuteticketshop.nl), which shifts tickets at half their face value from noon (every day of the week), for musical and theatrical events showing that night. The city is now also producing *A-mag*, an English-language quarterly listings magazine, which is available at newsagents.

Club NYX

EYE Film Institute

Arts & Leisure

Welcome to a tiny city that likes to position itself as a huge hub in the cultural universe. The locals give standing ovations to Mahler symphonies and Russian pianist Alexander Melnikov; they lap up the latest operas from Robert Wilson or Peter Sellars. And come King's Day – or any day the Dutch national side are kicking off – it's everyone's duty to dress in orange and join in merry mass hysteria. Just don't call them conformists.

Amsterdam packs a big cultural punch, with its more than fair share of world-class venues. Add to this an active underground scene, and visitors are spoilt for choice. The breadth and quality of the Amsterdam arts experience was long thanks to enlightened funding from government and city alike, resulting in a wealth of arts festivals, along with new buildings such as the Muziekgebouw (see p122). However subsidy cutbacks have resulted in smaller initiatives having to fight for their existence (see box p141) and come up with new business models, or find new sponsors, to survive.

As a sign of the times, the new Nieuwe de La Mar theatre (Marnixstraat, http://delamar.nl) recently reopened near Leidseplein, programming mostly Dutch-language theatre, cabaret and musicals. It was basically a €60 million gift from the VandenEnde Foundation, a cultural fund set up by theatre producer Joop van den Ende to support cultural activities in the Netherlands. The fund also gives support to photography museum Foam (see p98) and the Stedelijk Museum of Modern Art (see p134).

Otherwise, integration and diversity are key words when it comes to the city's cultural scene. Dance clubs like Trouw (see p116) plan to cooperate with the Stedelijk Museum of Modern Art in developing new ways of bringing more culture to the night. Pop venue Melkweg (see p106) is now physically attached to old municipal theatre the Stadsschouwburg (see p107) via a roof complex featuring a flat stage programmed by both institutions. Another pop venue, Paradiso (see p106), is booking shows all over town: from Tolhuistuin (see box p124) in North to the insanely beautiful church De Duif (Utrechtsedwarsstraat 7).

The art scene

While old-fashioned picture painting does still have its place, the art scene is now more about the blur between street art, design, photography and new media. And there's one major industry that is doing very well from the crossover between art and commerce: the local games development industry is showing no downturn during these economically harsh times.

It has often been said that Amsterdam, with its soggy climate and bleak winters, was designed to look as good in black and white as it does in colour, making it especially appealing to amateur photographers. And, as home to Ed van der Elsken (1925-90) and Rineke Dijkstra, the city is a strong supporter of the photographic arts, with Foam providing solid institutional backing. In addition, the studio of Erwin Olaf – who's moving away from the weird towards the emotionally charged – functions as a graduate school of sorts for young photographers.

To locate the pulse of the local scene, check out local style magazine

SHORTLIST

Total sporting experience
- Ajax (p39)

Interdisciplinary agendas
- De Balie (p107)
- Westergasfabriek (p128)

Singular screening experiences
- EYE Film Institute (p124)
- Pathé Tuschinski (p107)

World-class jazz acts
- Bimhuis (p121)
- North Sea Jazz Club (p128)

Best classical
- Concertgebouw (p142)
- Muziekgebouw (p122)

Cutting-edge contemporary
- NDSM (p124)
- Westergasfabriek (p128)

Underground vibes
- W139 (p81)
- NDSM (p124)
- Westergasfabriek (p128)

Cutting edge
- Mediamatic Factory (p116)

Big bands on a small scale
- Melkweg (p106)
- Paradiso (p106)

International belly laughs
- Boom Chicago (p132)
- Comedy Theatre (p79)

World music
- Badcuyp (p148)
- Melkweg (p106)

Best creative festivals
- Over het IJ (p43)
- De Parade (p44)
- Amsterdam Fringe Festival (p44)

DON'T MISS

Blend, the international fashion periodical *Fantastic Man*, the various publications coming from alternative music platform Subbacultcha and even the supplements of some of the daily newspapers. Amsterdam has embraced new media like few other cities. The pioneering Waag Society (www.waag.org) and Mediamatic Factory (see p116) arose from the 'tactical media' scene that perhaps accounts for the city's strong activist streak – which was strengthened after the emergence of the populist politician and one-off film-maker Geert Wilders. Mediamatic received particular acclaim for its El HEMA project, which transformed the iconic Dutch department store HEMA into an Arabic El HEMA, with Middle East-inspired design. Currently Mediamatic is turning its inspired sights to urban farming.

Glamorous new arts centre De Appel (see p122) showcases conceptual work by promising artists such as Allard van Hoorn.

And the Pakhuis de Zwijger (see p122) acts as a hub for a gamut of cutting-edge outfits, complete with a programme of events, conferences and exhibitions. An annual congress in September, the 'cross-media week' PICNIC (www.picnicnetwork.org), was also an immediate success, with talks and seminars on the latest developments in media, technology, art, science and entertainment.

A whole slew of advertising firms such as They, Sid Lee, 180, Wieden+Kennedy and DDB Tribal, provide the city's creatives with their bread and butter. Other communication firms, such as Kesselskramer and Submarine combine working for big-brand clients with more quirky and uncommercial projects. And the front line in the fight between art and commerce can be found at the former shipyards of NDSM (see p124), where an 'art city' of studios butts heads with the European headquarters of MTV.

De Appel

Fuelling Amsterdam's reputation as an international creative melting pot are its art schools; the Rietveld Academy and the Sandberg Institute bring in students from around the globe. This international influence helps to explain why Amsterdam's galleries are more adventurous and welcoming to young artists and curators than those of other art hubs. The Jordaan (see box p131) remains the top spot to wander for art, but De Pijp, the Eastern Docklands and Westerpark are quickly attracting new galleries. Nevertheless, the art scene remains relatively down to earth; witness any event at the Westergasfabriek (see box p128), or one of the monthly previews at W139 (see p81), which could be anything from video installation to performance art.

The silver screen

In 2013, director Alex van Warmerdam's *Borgman* became the first Dutch film to compete for the Golden Palm at Cannes since 1975 (when it was Jos Stelling's *Mariken van Nieumeghen* – since you ask). So no, the Dutch are not exactly big international players when it comes to film. But hopefully Van Warmerdam's dry, absurdist approach will win some more international hearts.

Paul Verhoeven continues to work in the Netherlands after his return from Hollywood, which was marked by the film *Black Book* (2006). As the most expensive film ever to be shot in the Netherlands, it was also the country's most commercially successful. Currently he's working on the filming of the book *De Stille Kracht* by the Dutch writer Louis Couperus (1863-1923). Meanwhile his old friend Rutger Hauer is also back in the country, teaching acting master classes, and lending his skills to smaller independent productions. And *Black Book* star Carice van Houten continues to rise internationally with a recurring role in TV series *Game of Thrones*.

Other internationally recognised film directors who choose to lead more mellow and domestic lives in Amsterdam include Steve McQueen (*Hunger*, *Shame*) and Peter Greenaway, who is in the middle of his Dutch Masters series, which began with *Nightwatching on Rembrandt* (2007). Greenaway is currently busy with *Goltzius and the Pelican Company*, based on the life of a 16th-century engraver of erotic prints. The third entry will be on Hieronymus Bosch and will be released on the 500th anniversary of Bosch's death in 2016.

There is also a new 'town' in town. Cineville (www.cineville.nl) has brought together 13 local arthouse and repertory cinemas, which together screen around 100 films daily; these can now be seen for a mere €18 per month.

There's also a healthy underground film screening scene focused around Cavia (www.filmhuiscavia.nl), De Nieuwe Anita (see p132) and OT301 (see p142), plus local initiatives such as the Klik! Amsterdam Animation Festival are keeping the scene fresh. Meanwhile, the cinema Uitkijk (Prinsengracht 452, 623 7460, www.uitkijk.nl) is so purist that it even refuses to serve popcorn. But it does have a new online platform whereby the public can decide what will be screened in the cinema. Anything's possible – as long as enough people pre-buy tickets.

Theatre & dance

Amsterdam is home to a truly outstanding theatre scene. Ivo van der Hove's Toneelgroep Amsterdam at Stadsschouwburg is just one of many companies, and most of its performances are surtitled in English. International performances have given the company much global acclaim. One fan is playwright Tony Kushner, who came to see its Dutch-language version of his play *Angels in America*. He was so impressed that plans are afoot for him to write a piece specifically for the company. For more cutting-edge theatre, check out the absurdist multimedia works of Pips:lab.

If language is a barrier, then the multi-purpose, multimedia De Balie (see p107) is worth checking out. Alternatively, NDSM (see p124) mounts regular site-specific pieces that transcend linguistic limitations. The Over het IJ (see p43) and De Parade (see p44) fests are worthy of attention, or pack a picnic and head for the Vondelpark's Openluchttheater (see p43. The Amsterdam Fringe Festival (see p44) sees underground companies performing on the main stages of more established theatres and rewriting the rules as they go.

Comedy and cabaret are also very popular. Boom Chicago (see p132) is still going strong after almost a couple of decades and has just moved to a new location. The Comedy Theater (see p79) mixes English- and Dutch-language acts. Dutch cabaret star Hans Teeuwen has crossed over to English but only in the UK – in Holland he now only performs as a very convincing Frank Sinatra-inspired crooner.

Amsterdam is home to countless choreographers and dance companies. The Muziektheater (p108) hosts the internationally renowned De Nederlandse Ballet and often hosts the equally acclaimed Nederlands Dans Theater. Smaller companies who've made a name on the world stage (and who perform regularly inside the capital) include Dansgroep Krisztina de Châtel, Het Internationaal Danstheater and the more street-dance-flavoured ISH (www.thisisish.com), which often performs at the new MC Theater at Westergasfabriek (see box p128).

Classical music

Many of the greatest international orchestras perform in Amsterdam – typically for little more than the price of the biggest rock or pop concerts, and frequently for considerably less.

The city is also home to world-renowned orchestras and soloists, and renditions of the classics are not limited to the grand concert venues, but can also be heard alongside canals, in parks, on the streets or in the halls of the new building of the Conservatory of Amsterdam (see p117) – whose composers-in-training are being brought to the fore thanks to the likes if the Asko Ensemble and Schönberg Ensemble.

Nieuwe de la Mar p34

The Royal Concertgebouw Orchestra, led by chief conductor Mariss Jansons, is one of the world's most famous. It plays at home most weeks during the cultural season – if you get the chance to hear it, even just for a lunchtime concert, don't pass it up. Meanwhile, famed German conductor Marc Albrecht is chief conductor of the Netherlands Opera and Netherlands Philharmonic Orchestra and Chamber Orchestra, and contemporary composer Louis Andriessen is still vying for immortality status; his latest concerto *Tapdance* will premier in Amsterdam in 2014. One of his students, Michel van der Aa, continues to go from strength to strength as he incorporates many visual and theatrical elements in his often site-specific works.

The sporting life

Football remains the city's main game, with fans still pining for Johan Cruijff's and Marco van Basten's '70s and '80s glory days. While plenty of young stars, such as Arjen Robben and Robin van Persie, have made their names and riches internationally, the magic spark is still missing from the national side. The same goes for local team Ajax, who have never really hit their stride beyond a national level since occupying the Amsterdam ArenA (Arena Boulevard 1, Amsterdam Zuidoost, 311 1333, www.amsterdamarena.nl) almost 20 years ago. Fans complain that while the squad is a great training ground, the good players get sold to the big international teams once they've hit their peak. Klaas Jan Huntelaar, Rafael van der Vaart and Wesley Schneider, who have all gone on to find lucrative new homes, rather prove the point. But now with legendary footballers Frank de Boer and Dennis Bergcamp as manager and assistant manager respectively, Ajax will hopefully translate their recent national successes to the international stage once again.

The desire to be the best has, however, payed off elsewhere, and in field hockey, ice skating, swimming, darts and cycling, Dutch stars manage to bag medals on a regular basis. Recently there have been murmurings about Amsterdam hosting the 2028 Olympics. But no-one should book a hotel room quite yet.

Calendar

Amsterdam Light Festival p46

Dates in **bold** are public holidays.

January

1 **Nieuwjaarsdag
(New Year's Day)**

Mid Jan **Hotel Night**
Various locations
www.amsterdamsehotelnacht.nl
The city's hotels open their doors for
special events and deals.

Mid Jan **Amsterdam International
Fashion Week**
Various locations
www.aifw.nl
Putting the city on the fashion map.

Late Jan/early Feb
Chinese New Year
Nieuwmarkt
Celebrations and fireworks.

Late Jan/early Feb **International
Film Festival Rotterdam**
Various locations in Rotterdam
www.filmfestivalrotterdam.com

March

Early Mar **5 Days Off**
Various locations
www.5daysoff.nl
Techno, drum 'n' bass, house and mad
electro mash up.

Early Mar **Amsterdam
Restaurant Week**
Various locations
www.restaurantweek.nl
Special deals on dining out in selected
restaurants across the capital.

Mid Mar **Jenever Festival**
Posthoornkerk
http://jeneverfestival.nl
Dedicated to the Dutch original gin.

Mid Mar **Stille Omgang**
Spui, Red Light District
www.stille-omgang.nl
Silent procession commemorating the
14th-century Miracle of Amsterdam.

Mid Mar **Boekenweek**
www.boekenweek.nl

Various locations
Week of events promoting literature and reading throughout the city.

Mid Mar **Holland Animation Festival**
Utrecht
www.haff.nl
International animation film festival.

Mid Mar **Keukenhof**
Lisse
www.keukenhof.nl
Millions of bulbs bloom until late May.

Mid Mar **Roze Filmdagen**
Various locations
www.rozefilmdagen.nl
International queer film festival.

Mar/Apr **Goede Vrijdag (Good Friday)**

Mar/Apr **Eerste Paasdag (Easter Sunday)**

Mar/Apr **Tweede Paasdag (Easter Monday)**

Mar/Apr **Motel Mozaïque**
Rotterdam
www.motelmozaique.nl
A two-day festival of music, theatre and other arts.

April

Early Apr **Movies that Matter**
Various locations
www.moviesthatmatter.nl
Films about human rights.

Early/mid Apr **CinemAsia**
Various locations
www.cinemasia.nl
Screenings of pan-Asian features and cutting-edge documentaries.

Early Apr
National Museum Weekend
Various locations
www.museumweekend.nl
Free or cheap entry to the city's many museums, plus special events.

Mid Apr **Imagine Film Festival**
EYE (see p124)
www.imaginefilmfestival.nl
More than a week of silver screen schlock, horror, splatter and trash.

29 **King's Night**
All over Amsterdam
The start of the day formerly known as Queen's Day (see box p42).

30 **King's Day**
All over Amsterdam
This epic celebration has become a giant open air disco-cum-flea-market enjoyed by all, republicans included. See box p42.

Late Apr-late June
World Press Photo
Oude Kerk (see p69)
www.worldpressphoto.com
An exhibition of the best of international press photography.

May

4 **Dodenherdenkingsdag (Memorial Day)**
Dam Square
The day culminates in a 7.30pm ceremony, remembering those who lost their lives in World War II.

5 **Bevrijdingsdag (Liberation Day)**
Various locations
www.amsterdamsbevrijdingsfestival.nl
Marking national liberation from Nazi occupation with many concerts.

Mid May **Kunst RAI**
Amsterdam RAI Congress Centre
www.kunstrai.nl
Huge, commercial, five-day exhibition.

Mid May **National Windmill Day**
Around the Netherlands
www.molens.nl
Windmills spin sails and open to the public in this most quaint and quintessentially Dutch of celebrations.

May **Hemelvaartsdag (Ascension Day)**

DON'T MISS

King's Day

Paint the town orange.

In past years, if first-time visitors arrived in Amsterdam on 30 April, they could find themselves overwhelmed – everyone knows that this is a happening town, but on this one day it was pure craziness.

Queen's Day (or Koninginnedag) was rebranded as King's Day (Koningsdag) when Willem-Alexander took over the throne from his mother Beatrix in 2013. And the official date moved from 30 to 27 April so it would fall on his birthday. But since that date is a Sunday in 2014, it will be celebrated on 26 April for that year.

Confused? It doesn't matter. The royal family is soon forgotten amid all the revelry. Party lovers and students of the surreal should make sure that their visit coincides with this date, when up to a million extra people pour into the city, rendering every single street and canal dense with jubilant crowds.

You may happen upon a leather-boy disco party on one side street, or an old-school crooner on the other, or witness a boat bellowing out heavy metal, only to have its amps short-circuited at the next bridge, by a gang of boys – dressed head-to-toe in orange – urinating on them.

If nothing else, you'll come away with a few stories of debauchery to tell the grandchildren. And if you have your own offspring in tow, head to Vondelpark, which is dedicated to children.

Dam Square becomes a fairground; prepare for a mind-boggling overdose of sensations – and for your pockets to empty themselves, as you get tricked into buying just what you always (read never) wanted. How are you going to explain that pair of orange clogs when you get back home?

Meanwhile, the gay and lesbian festivities spread out like ripples from the Homomonument (see p90) and Reguliersdwaarsstraat.

What with all the performances, the markets, the crowds and, of course, the readily flowing alcohol, the streets of Amsterdam offer all anyone could dream of – at least for one day.

Late May-late Sept **ArtZuid**
South neighbourhood
www.artzuid.com
Modern sculpture route through South
neighbourhood.

Late May **London Calling**
Various venues
www.londoncalling.nl
New rock and pop from the UK (and
elsewhere, since they stopped checking
passports).

Late May **Open Studios**
Westelijke Eilanden
www.oawe.nl
Artists open their doors to the public.

June

May/June **Eerste and Tweede
Pinksterdag (first and second
Pentecost)**
The Dutch celebration lasts two days;
Sunday and the subsequent Monday.

Early June-mid Aug
Openluchttheather
Vondelpark
www.openluchttheater.nl
Open-air stage featuring performances
from classical to urban to kids' stuff.

Early June **Holland Festival**
Various locations
www.hollandfestival.nl
Huge, popular and varied arts and contemporary music festival.

Early June
Amsterdam Tattoo Convention
RAI Convention Center
www.tattooexpo.eu.
From bikers to housewives…

Mid June **Oerol Terschelling**
www.oerol.nl
For a fortnight, the Frisian island of
Terschelling, which lies 120km north
of town, stages 200 theatre acts.

Mid June **Open Garden Days**
Various locations
www.opentuinendagen.nl

July

Ongoing
Openluchttheather (see June)

July **Julidans**
Various locations
www.julidans.nl
A month-long international dance festival that draws big names and enthu-
siastic crowds.

Early July **Over het IJ**
NDSM (see p124)
www.overhetij.nl
International festival of large-scale,
avant-garde theatrical projects.

Early July **Pitch Festival**
Westergasfabriek (p128)
http://pitchfestival.nl/
Cutting-edge dance and electronic
music festival.

Mid July **Amsterdam Roots Festival**
Various locations
www.amsterdamroots.nl
World music festival, whose highlight
is the free outdoor Roots Open Air in
Oosterpark.

Mid July
North Sea Jazz
Rotterdam
www.northseajazz.nl
Internationally renowned jazz festival.

Mid July **Amsterdam International
Fashion Weekend (see January)**

Late July **Amsterdam Tournament**
ArenA Stadium
www.amsterdamarena.nl
International footie friendlies.

Late July-mid Aug **Kwaku**
Bijlmerpark
www.kwakuamsterdam.nl
Free festie in the multicultural suburbs.

August

Ongoing **Openluchttheather
(see June); Kwaku (see July)**

Early Aug **Dance Valley**
Spaarnwoude
www.dancevalley.nl
Mega dance music festival

Early Aug **Amsterdam Gay Pride**
Various locations
www.amsterdamgaypride.nl
See box p102. Also look out for the boat parade on Prinsengracht.

Early Aug **De Parade**
Martin Luther Kingpark
www.deparade.nl
Travelling circus-style theatre festival.

Mid Aug **Grachtenfestival**
Various locations
www.grachtenfestival.nl
Canalside classical music concerts.

Mid Aug **Appelsap**
Oosterpark
www.appelsap.net
Outdoor hip hop festival.

Mid Aug **Lowlands**
Walibi World
www.lowlands.nl
Dutch Glastonbury: the latest bands, comedy, global food and fashion.

Mid Aug-mid Sept **Magneetfestival**
Various locations
www.magneetfestival.nl
Anything goes festival (see box right).

Mid Aug 2015 **SAIL**
Waterfront
www.sail-amsterdam.nl
Every five years millions stroll the harbour front to admire dozens of tall ships and thousands of modern boats.

Late Aug **Pluk de Nacht**
Stenen Hoofd
www.plukdenacht.nl
Outdoor film festival with food and singular vibe.

Late Aug **Uitmarkt**
Various locations
www.uitmarkt.nl
Open-air preview of the coming cultural season: theatre, opera and dance.

Late Aug
Amsterdam Restaurant Week
See Mar.

September

Early Sept **Metro 54**
Amsterdam Arenapark
metro54.nl
Urban/mash-up arts festival from pop-up events superstars

Early Sept **Sweelinck Festival**
Oude Kerk (p69)
This biannual, popular organ music festival returns in 2014.

Early Sept **Nederlands Theater Festival**
All over Amsterdam
www.tf.nl
Showcase for Dutch and Belgian theatre, plus Amsterdam Fringe Festival.

Early Sept **Gaudeamus Music Week**
Utrecht
www.muziekcentrumnederland.nl
Contemporary classical music.

Early Sept **Africa in the Picture**
Various locations
www.africainthepicture.nl
Features, docs and shorts from Africa.

Mid Sept **Open Monumentendag**
Various locations
www.openmonumentendag.nl
Free or cheap entry to historic sites.

Mid Sept **Dam tot Damloop**
Amsterdam to Zaandam
www.damloop.nl
Long-running mini-marathon.

Mid Sept **Jordaanfestival**
Marnixstraat/Elandsgracht
www.jordaanfestival.nl
Tears in your beers singalongs.

Late Sept **Picnic**
Westergasfabriek (p128)
www.picnicnetwork.org
Gathering for new media industries.

Curate your own festival

Let us entertain you.

Featuring music, theatre, experimental arts and all means of creative expression, the Magneet Festival (see left) brings a bit of Burning Man to Amsterdam every year. Creative free spirits will find their cultural nirvana in the east of the city on a manmade stretch of sand on Zeeburgereiland in Amsterdam East.

It's a truly collaborative effort – creative ideas can be pitched via an online platform. If the idea is selected by the public, Magneet Festival will then help bring it to life. This makes the festival the first public-voted event of its kind in Europe.

The man behind the concept, Jesse Limmen, began around a decade ago in the hippy village of Ruigoord with €200 worth of beer, a ramshackle bar and a microphone. Later, the mega-alternative Lowlands festival invited him to run a makeshift bar and do-it-yourself event. People would enter their names at a check-in desk, describe their act – whether it be comedy, hip hop, spoken word or whatever – and then grab a beer and a silly costume and wait for their turn on stage. As long as the crowd liked their performance they could continue. Otherwise an MC would intervene. The approach proved insanely popular. Highlights included Dutch rocker Anouk casually coming in for a seven-song set or the Eagles of Death Metal destroying the drum kit.

Today, Magneet has evolved into a month-long festival. The festival grounds are filled with experimental constructions, tents and podiums – settings for music, theatre, fine arts, children's activities and more. While the offerings are diverse, the philosophy remains the same: 'No spectators, only participators.'

Magneet's other motto is 'Leave no trace'. Everyone, whether spectator or participant, is expected to leave the grounds in a better state than they found them. Which may prove tricky for those behind the 'Colour Blind' concept set to be put into action in 2013: hosing colourful dyes into the air and letting them fall where they may… You have been warned.

October

Early Oct **International Buddhist Film Festival Europe**
EYE (see p124)
www.bffe.org
Movies inspired by the Buddhist faith.

Mid Oct **ING Amsterdam Marathon**
Various locations
www.amsterdammarathon.nl

Mid/late Oct **Cinekid Festival**
Various locations
www.cinekid.nl
Child-centred film and media festival.

Mid/late Oct **Amsterdam Dance Event**
Various locations
www.amsterdam-dance-event.nl
Dance music festival and conference.

End Oct **Bock Beer Festival**
Beurs van Berlage (p63)
www.pint.nl
Festival of seasonal beer.

End Oct **Gay Leather Pride**
Various locations
www.amsterdamleatherpride.eu
Leather boys and their hangers-on and strap-ons.

November

Nov **Klik Amsterdam**
EYE
http://klikamsterdam.nl
An animation festival with heart.

Early Nov **Affordable Art Fair**
Amsterdam North
http://affordableartfair.com/Amsterdam
Name says it all.

Early Nov **Amsterdam Film Week**
Various locations
amsterdamfilmweek.com
Intimate event with star power

Early Nov **Museum Night**
Various locations

www.museumnachtamsterdam.nl
Late-night opening and special events.

Mid Nov **London Calling**
Various locations
www.londoncalling.nl (see Apr).

Mid Nov **Sinterklaas Intocht**
Prins Hendrikkade, Dam to Leidseplein
www.sintinamsterdam.nl
Children's Christmas parade.

Mid Nov **Crossing Border**
The Hague
www.crossingborder.nl
International literature and music fest.

Mid/late Nov **International Documentary Film Festival (IDFA)**
Various locations
www.idfa.nl
Big documentary festival.

Mid Nov to mid Jan **Amsterdam Light Festival**
www.amsterdamlightfestival.com
Light artists light up town.

Late Nov **High Times Cannabis Cup**
Various locations
www.cannabiscup.com
Contest promoting cannabis.

December

1 **Lovedance**
Paradiso (p106)
www.lovedance.nl
World AIDS Day charity gala.

5-6 **Sinterklaas (St Nicolas)**
Various locations
Traditional gift-giving parties, which are popular with children.

25 **Eerste Kerstdag (Christmas)**

26 **Tweede Kerstdag (Boxing Day)**

31 **Oudejaarsavond (New Year's Eve)**

Itineraries

Silodam

Living by Design

The Dutch love of design comes into view as you descend towards **Schiphol Airport** and glide over a Mondrian-like grid pattern of landscape. A dedication to arrangement is apparent in the ballet-like elegance of Dutch football players, who open space to score and close lines to defend. And an eye for detail underpins a multitude of creative spheres, from art to architecture, whether on paper, canvas or computer.

The history of Dutch design has been influenced by the orderliness of Calvinism and the 20th-century modernist movement De Stijl. Drawing upon that part of the Dutch psyche that craves order, abstraction artists such as Theo van Doesburg, Piet Mondrian and Gerrit Rietveld sought rules of equilibrium, which can be applied to everyday design as much as art. Just surf the web or leaf through *Wallpaper** magazine to see the legacy of the style today. And

yet a counterpoint has always existed in the Dutch people's strong desire for personal expression (perhaps an echo of the stubbornness required to battle the sea).

This eclectic mix of functionality and wit has resulted in worldwide acclaim – just consider the playful, Lego-like residential building Silodam by MVRDV Architects or the sharp angles exhibited on the new Palace of Justice, both in the western Docklands area.

Furthermore, there's an active sense of 'city design' at work: urban planners carefully quote from the work of sociologist Richard Florida, who argues that the 'creative class' can play a beneficial role in urban development. Creative types are starting work in deprived neighbourhoods, ranging from the Red Light District to De Baarsjes district west of the Jordaan, and the former shipyards **NDSM** (see box p124).

Start this local design tour in the **Red Light District** (see box p85). As you begin to wander around, you may notice yourself endlessly looping in towards its geographical centre; there's poetry in this: Albert Camus in *The Fall* described the radiating canal girdle as resembling the circles of hell. But it can also be interpreted as a form of social control: it has traditionally kept visiting sailors (and later packs of stag-partying Brits) centralised, while leaving the rest of the city for residents to live their daily lives.

To witness how design has infiltrated every level of Dutch life, cross the Damrak from the Red Light District to visit a major outlet of the ubiquitous department store **HEMA** (Nieuwendijk 174-176, www. hema.nl). A quarter of the Dutch population wakes to the ring of a HEMA alarm clock, one in three men wear HEMA underwear and one in four women a HEMA bra. The department store sells 506,000 kilogrammes of liquorice every year, 14 million units of *tompouce* (a pink-glazed custard cake) annually, and one smoked sausage per second. New, smaller outlets are now appearing at train stations and a larger outlet recently opened in the *banlieues* of Paris. Currently there's even an improbably successful *HEMA the Musical* touring the country. Even though HEMA remains the economical place to shop for basics, it's made a name for itself as a source of affordable design objects – even its sales flyers are graphics classics. It has featured products designed by big names such as Piet Hein Eek, Gijs Bakker and Hella Jongerius, and had a hit with its Le Lapin whistle kettle, selling more than 250,000 units. If you like to shop, you might also want to check out supermarket **Marqt** (see p141), which has taken branding to the next level.

For a stroll deep into the heart of local design, visit that most higgledy-piggledy neighbourhood, the Jordaan. From Nieuwendijk, take the Mandenmakerssteeg, Dirk van Hasseltssteeg, Lijnbaansteeg, Herenstraat and Prinsenstraat (all in a straight line), to a former

Red Light District

Bread coffee & canals

Taste the real
flavour of bread
at our cosy basement
with a view
over the famous
Amsterdam canals.

Sandwiches, bread,
pastries, coffee,
tea & juices.

Ⓑ **BROOD**

Zeedijk 66 (Chinatown)

WWW.BBROOD.NL

Moooi

school at Westerstraat 187, now the studio of design star and inventor of the Knotted Chair, **Marcel Wanders** (www.marcelwanders.com). On the ground floor, step into his stylish store, **Moooi** (www.moooi.com), the showroom for his work and the portfolios of other creatives such as Studio Job, Piet Boon and Jurgen Bey. But don't come here expecting to shop for bargains. Another disciple of Richard Florida, Wanders is now actively 'designing' other creative hubs elsewhere in the city, as well as the newly opened stellar hotel **Andaz Amsterdam** (see box p168).

Since the 1980s, there has been a backlash against Conceptual art's anti-functional rhetoric, which would have pleased adherents of De Stijl, who hoped the future would bring a frenzy of cross-disciplinary activity. Photographers (Anton Corbijn, Rineke Dijkstra), cartoonists (Joost Swarte) and architects (Rem Koolhaas) are considered to be 'artists'. The free-thinking artist and architect John Körmeling

received much acclaim for his Dutch pavilion, Happy Street, at the World Expo 2010 in Shanghai. It's probably not a coincidence he's based in Eindhoven, renowned for not only being home to Philips but also the remarkable Dutch Design Week (www.ddw.nl). Meanwhile the whimsical and bright inventions of the Atelier van Lieshout in Rotterdam are to be found in museum collections across the world. The nation's colleges have been a catalyst for this process by encouraging artists and designers to study together, while welcoming a large number of foreign students, who have forged universal visual languages.

After taking in the bustling design scene, backtrack into town via Rozengracht, which hosts a wide range of different design and furniture stores, including the upmarket but funky **SPRMRKT** (see p130). Then take a right down the north side of Prinsengracht, past the previously mentioned Andaz Amsterdam, to one of the city's most-famed Valhallas,

ITINERARIES

Frozen Fountain (see p96). This is a paradise for lovers of contemporary furniture and homewares. While staying abreast of innovative young Dutch designers, such as furniture maestro Piet Hein Eek, the 'Froz' exhibits and sells international ranges of products, by the likes of Marc Newson, modern classics and even photography.

The surrounding **Nine Streets** area (see p89) is a great place in which to wander at leisure. On reaching Spui square, browse in the **Athenaeum Nieuwscentrum** (see p87), a great place to buy Amsterdam-centric design books and magazines, before continuing further north-east, down Lange Brugsteeg and Grimburgwal, to take a left into Oudezijds Achterburgwal. At the corner of Rusland, stop at **WonderWood** (p78), which sells wonderfully

sculpted original woodworks, re-editions of global classics and plywood items from the 1940s and '50s. At the end of Rusland, take a right down Kloveniersburgwal and a left down the picturesque Staalstraat, where you'll reach the newly expanded complex of Amsterdam's famed design collective: **Droog Hotel** (see p77). Droog can rightfully lay claim to having the wittiest selection of products around, thanks to the likes of Marcel Wanders, Hella Jongerius, Richard Hutten and Jurgen Bey. Droog's international clout remains apparent with the continued success of its shop in New York City. But, if the prices seem a little high, visit the HEMA around the corner, at Kalverstraat 212, to hunt for some more friendly-priced Dutch products. There's design for every budget in this creative city.

NDSM

Down by the Water

Amsterdam's eastern dockland area is one of city's premier eating and entertainment hotspots. But, perhaps more interestingly, it's also a fantastic showcase for the Netherlands' rather daring experiments in housing. If you want to explore the future of Amsterdam, hop on a bike, pick up a map and get moving.

First, head north-west of Centraal Station, past the startling modern architecture of the new Palace of Justice and IJdock development (www.ijdock.nl) along Westerdok, to the **Westelijke Eilanden** (Western Islands) near the Jordaan, to get a taste of life during the Golden Age, when Amsterdam was the richest port in the world. These artificial islands were originally created in the 17th century to sustain maritime activity. Although there are now trendy warehouse flats and a yacht basin on Realeneiland, Prinseneiland and Bickerseiland –

where one-time shipyards, tar distillers and salters and smokers of fish were based – the area still remains the city's best setting for a scenic stroll evoking seafaring times, a fact aided in no small measure by the sizeable community of local artists.

Since 1876, the route to the open sea has been the North Sea Canal. Because the working docks also lie to the west, there's little activity on the IJ behind Centraal Station, aside from a handful of passenger ships and free **ferries** sailing across the water to Amsterdam Noord – one of which will take you to the vibrant cultural breeding ground that is the former shipping yard **NDSM** (see box p124). Here, vivid apocalyptic splendour, artistic endeavours and old-school squat aesthetics can be found alongside funky student container housing and the state-of-the-art MTV headquarters – the epitome of old-meets-new.

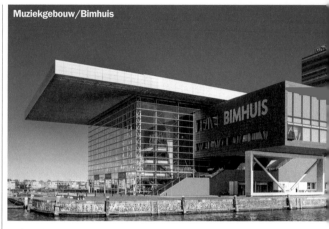

If you keep to the south side, follow the water eastwards from Centraal Station before joining up with and following **Oostelijke Handelskade** and its parallel boardwalk. Initially, you pass the **Muziekgebouw** (see p122), an epicentre of new music, which is also home to the **Bimhuis** (see p121), and incorporates studios, rehearsal spaces, exhibition galleries, and a grand café and restaurant, complete with a terrace overlooking the scenic waters of the IJ. Its close neighbour is the spectacular, wave-shaped, glass passenger terminal for luxury cruise ships. Visit the website www.ptamsterdam.nl for lists of all docking times, should you wish to admire the ships in situ.

Before proceeding to clubs **Café Pakhuis Wilhelmina** and **Panama** (for both, see p121), former shipping canteen **Koffiehuis KHL** (see p120) and the youth prison-turned-designer accommodation **Lloyd Hotel** (see p174), take a walk down the airy **Jan Schaeferbrug** to the left – starting off by going through the

Pakhuis de Zwijger (see p122), an old cocoa storage warehouse that has been reinvented as a new media centre. If you are more culturally curious, pop in for a drink at its charming café.

The bridge will take you to the tip of **Java-eiland**, which at first glance, may look like a dense, designer confinement, but it's not hard to be charmed by the island's dividing pedestrian street, which will have you crossing canals on

ITINERARIES

funky bridges and walking past a startling variety of architecture. At Azartplein, the island suddenly changes its name to **KNSM-eiland**, in honour of the Royal Dutch Steam Company (KNSM), once based here. Here you can opt to visit the excellent local bookshop **Van Pampus** (KNSM-laan 303, 419 3023, www.boekhandelvan pampus.nl) or **De Kompaszaal** (KNSM-laan 311, 419 9596, www.kompaszaal.nl), a café and restaurant in the former arrivals and departures hall of KNSM, which has the feel of a 1950s cruise ship, complete with watery views from the terrace. Otherwise, veer north and follow **Surinamekade**, with houseboats on one side and the visible interiors of artists' studios on the other. Pass 'Black Widow' tower and loop around the island's tip and back along KNSM-laan, turning left into **Barcelonaplein**, and then right when you pass through the abstract sculpted steel archway. You may also want to make some time for refreshment at one of the waterside bars and restaurants, or invest in an art coffin at the alternative burial store De Ode; either way, linger and look at the imposing residential Piraeus building by German architect Hans Kollhoff, if only for its eye-twisting inner court.

The two peninsulas to the south are Borneo and Sporenburg, the work of urban planning and landscape architecture firm West 8. The plots are all differently sized, to encourage the many architects involved – a veritable *Who's Who* of international stars – to come up with creative low-rise living. Cross over to **Sporenburg** via the

Scheepstimmermanstraat p56

Roest

Verbindingsdam to the building that has probably already caught your eye: the mighty silver Whale residential complex, designed by architect Frits van Dongen, over on Baron GA Tindalplein. In folky contrast, a floating Styrofoam park produced by erstwhile Provo Robert Jasper Grootveld has been set in front of it on Panamakade.

From here, cross over to **Borneo** on the swooping red bridge. Turn left up **Stuurmankade** – past a still more violently undulating pedestrian bridge – and pause to enjoy the view at the end (and imagine an even better one, enjoyed by the residents of the blue and green glass cubes that jut out of the buildings). Then return west along **Scheepstimmermanstraat**, easily Amsterdam's most eccentric street, where every single façade on show – from twisting steel to haphazard plywood – manages to be more bizarre than the next.

Where Panamalaan meets Piet Heinkade, you may opt to take the IJtram from CS to IJburg (the stop is right by the huge public artwork

Folly for the Bees, the stack of giant tables with beehives below), or return to Oostelijk Handelskade and to the singular Lloyd Hotel and its neighbouring café **De Kantine** (Rietlandpark 375, 419 4433). Another option is to head up Czar Peterstraat, a once dangerous street, but now pleasant area, with quirky shops and cafés, and hit urban beach **Roest** (see p122) or go for a home-brewed beer at **Brouwerij 't IJ** (see p113).

More energetic types might prefer to take a 20-minute bike ride to **IJburg**, heading south via C van Eesterenlaan and Veelaan, then left down Zeeburgerdijk. This in turn connects up with Zuiderzeeweg, which then merges into a bridge that ends at a set of traffic lights. Here, follow the cycle path to the right, which takes you to IJburg.

Originally set for completion in 2012, seven artificial islands were to be home to 45,000 people inhabiting more than 18,000 units, many of which will float on the water. Unfortunately, due to economic problems, there are only currently three islands and 16,000 residents. It's a somewhat subdued version of what had been hyped as a future showcase of sorts for Dutch landscape and residential architecture. There's still plenty to look at, though funky beach **Blijburg** (see box p121) remains a clear highlight.

On the way back to town, make sure that you stop at the chip stand, **Eiburgh Snacks** (Zuiderzeeweg, beside no.2), which you may have already spotted on the corner between the two bridges. The snack store serves some of the best fries in town, along with a hearty, homemade pea soup.

For more detailed information on architectural tours of all these areas and more, contact ARCAM (www.arcam.nl).

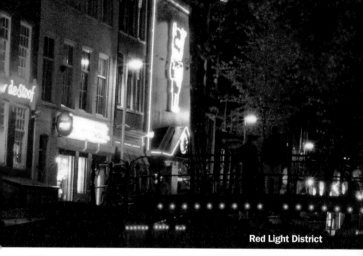

Red Light District

True Grit

With all of Amsterdam's building, rebuilding and rebranding going on it's sometimes easy to forget that the city was such a draw for hippies, squatters and clubbers back in the days when the holy trinity of sex, drugs and rock 'n' roll held sway. Is there still some gritification to be found among the gentrification? Short answer: yes. And we are not even speaking about the dodgier alleys of the Red Light District. There's still much to be discovered as you take this alternative tour of the city, taking in the favourite haunts of hippies of the 1970s, artistic squatters of the '80s and hedonistic clubbers of the '90s.

The city's first inhabitants, squatters all of them, settled what was to become Amsterdam sometime before 1000 AD. With the building of the first city walls in 1342, the impoverished founders had to squat outside the wall's perimeter, setting the trend for the poor to move further outwards as

the city expands, which continues to this day. Squatting had become so accepted as a way of life by the late 1960s that a 'how to' guide, *The Handbook for Squatters,* became a national bestseller in 1969.

Amsterdam is famous the world over for being a place where 'anything goes' but most people who spend more than a couple of days here start to notice fairly quickly that the local population itself isn't exactly freewheeling. Those Red Light District attractions that lure millions of visitors to the city are largely designed for tourists, not locals. It's rare that you'll find a Dutch person hanging out in a coffeeshop, unless they're hosting foreign visitors. 'Tolerance' is a word that gets bandied about a lot in Amsterdam, but the word doesn't necessarily mean 'acceptance' of all kinds of behaviour, and it also doesn't mean encouragement of experimentation and vice. It means, 'We don't mind if you do your thing, as long as it doesn't interfere with the otherwise normal operation of business here… and as long as it doesn't hurt anyone else.' The city's famed tolerance made it a safe haven for Spanish and Portuguese Jews in the 16th century, Huguenots in the 1700s, Belgians during World War I and Hungarians after the 1956 revolution. Its atmosphere of intellectual and artistic freedom has made it a destination for thinkers and creative types from René Descartes in the 17th century to UK filmmaker and artist Steve McQueen today.

However, it could be argued that the same tolerance that allowed Amsterdam to become known as a Jewish capital of Europe before World War II (engendering the nickname Mokum or 'home') was counteracted by the Dutch 'tolerance' of the deportation and extermination of the same Jewish community under Nazi occupation. There may have been a resistance movement here, but in the end, 90 per cent of the Netherlands' Jews were killed during the war – the highest proportion of any western European country, and the second highest in all of Europe after Poland.

Start your what's-left-of-tolerance tour in front of the **Athenaeum Nieuwscentrum** (see p87) on Spui square, which is home to the University of Amsterdam. Many freethinkers have congregated here since the 1960s. The *Lieverdje* ('Little Darling') statue, a spindly and pigeon dropping-covered statue of a boy wearing knee socks, was the site for Provo 'happenings' in the '60s. Alternatively called the flashiest of street scene-makers or proto-Yippies, the Provos played absurdist mind games with the unsuspecting powers of their day. They took on tobacco companies by chain smoking; they testified to

the benefits of trepanation – the act of drilling a hole in one's head to release pressure, open the third eye and induce a pleasant high; they promoted the White Constable Plan, which envisaged cops dressed in white, distributing sparks for joints, chickens to the hungry and oranges to the thirsty; and they even disrupted the wedding of Queen Beatrix of Orange with rumours of LSD in the water supply and horse feed, to craze the animals that drew the royal carriage. To cut a long story short, it was classy hippy fun. The Provos' main jester was 'anti-smoke magician' Robert Jasper Grootveld, who went on to make Styrofoam garden arks that can be spotted docked or even motoring around town. He died in 2009, but his legacy lives on at www. drijvendetuinen.nl, which has a map of ark locations and workshop times.

After the movement ended, many ex-Provos squatted outside the city limits at **Ruigoord** (www. ruigoord.nl), which remains an artists' village of eco-hippies who hold solstice festivals on their grounds and concerts in their church. If you take a bike ride in that direction you might want to drop in on 'community farm' **Ons Genoegen** (www.buurtboerderij.nl), just beyond Westergasfabriek, for some hippie-inspired pancakes, before heading further to **ADM** (www.admleeft.nl), a former shipping yard and squat that is one of the last great 'free spaces' populated by 120 artists and weirdos.

Meanwhile, **Spui Square** itself is less absurdist these days, but the Friday book market still retains a certain contra vibe from the time of the Provos, thanks in part to the resident harpist.

Head north down Spuistraat to discover a squatting landmark – a squat called the **Vrankrijk**

(Spuistraat 216, www.vrankrijk. org). Today, many nostalgic residents weep for the salad days of the 1980s and '90s, when less political and more cultural squats such as Silo and Vrieshuis Amerika provided the coolest cheap studio space around and threw the best parties. Over the following years, the powers that be shut down these squats, until they realised that such cultural beehives could enhance the city's creative image, and coined the brand name of Iamsterdam. So, in an effort to claw back some of their lost prestige and emigrating artists, the authorities created less affordable non-squat 'squats' called *broedplaatsen* (breeding grounds).

The world of Amsterdam's squats used to be divided into umpteen categories. As well as *broedplaatsen*, there were proper squats, re-appropriated buildings that had been left empty for more than a year; 'anti-squats', with temporary residents paying low rent so squatters couldn't move in; and 'bought squats', sold cheaply by the city to their inhabitants to relieve themselves of a headache. The Vrankrijk is the most famous example of this latter type, mainly thanks to its colourful exterior. However, this great variety of low- or no-rent accommodation came to an end in 2010 when squatting became illegal in the Netherlands. But that doesn't mean that squats have vanished from the cityscape – some have disbanded, while a few remain, with no one seeming to be concerned by their presence.

Across the street from the Vrankrijk, you can enjoy a similarly greasy – and smoky – ambience at punk rock night bar **The Minds** (Spuistraat 245, www.theminds.nl).

Next, backtrack to Spui square and head eastwards, along the Singel canal to arrive opposite the floating flower market, the **Bloemenmarkt** (see p103), where you can pay homage to the legendary nightclub RoXY, opened in 1987 at Singel 465 by, among others, the DJ Eddy de Clercq and the artist Peter Giele.

Not all squatters partied constantly in those days. Some worked hard as artists, and were ready to reap the benefits by selling their work for inflated prices during the global art boom of the late 1980s. With money in pocket, they could then party continuously; and the RoXY came to represent that era. While de Clercq and DJ Joost van Bellen brought house music to the city, Peter Giele helped to provide the club with different thematic decors, which happily embraced a certain hedonistic attitude that filtered through to those that danced. Ecstasy not only helped them to have a good time, but also played a part in building a sense of community. The party ended on 21 June 1999, when, during Giele's wake, the club burned down after fireworks were let off in tribute to his life's motto: 'from one flame comes many'.

From here, you can follow the Amstel river to Amstelstraat 24 (now **Club Air**, see p104), where Manfred Langer opened another legendary nightclub, iT, in 1989. It was intended to be the ultimate gay disco, and indeed became a magnet for two-metre-tall transvestites wearing acres of leather. Soon straights and international names were clamouring to get in, but the club started to fade when Langer died in 1994 (he was taken to his final resting place in a pink Chevrolet convertible). There was a huge drugs raid in 1999, after which the club did reopen a couple of times, but never really took off again. Its disappearance pre-empted the clean-up of nightclubs today. Gone are the days of being

ITINERARIES

Vondelpark

able to test your pill at every party. The result is that more than half of so-called ecstasy pills sold in the city lack the active ingredient MDMA.

If that fact brings out the activist in you, then head via Blauwbrug (the 'blue bridge') to **Waterlooplein** (see p108), where you can research the old-school anarcho-squat movement at the book and magazine store **Fort van Sjakoo** (Jodenbreestraat 24, www.sjakoo.nl), which was named after a local criminal who stole from the rich, but probably didn't pass on his takings to the poor. For further research on what's left of the squat scene, visit the website www.squat.net.

Otherwise, you can take the Metro from Waterlooplein to Weesperplein station, then catch tram 7 or 10 to **Vondelpark**. Here, you can reflect on how the 1970s were much simpler times: to entice people to visit Amsterdam, all you had to do was borrow KLM's advertising strategy. The airline published posters cajoling a long-haired American audience to 'Sleep in Hippie Park' – word of mouth did the rest. Even today, Vondelpark remains a magnet for the bongo-lovers among us.

However, the surrounding streets witnessed the turbulent events of 1980, the most violent year in the Netherlands since World War II. In February that year, an organised group of squatters reclaimed a building from which they had previously been evicted at Vondelstraat 72 by constructing barricades to a punk rock soundtrack. They drew supporters and disrupted local traffic until army tanks came in to disperse the crowds. On 30 April 1980, the date of Queen Beatrix's inauguration, huge riots broke out, which were quashed by tear gas. As a result, squatting became more highly politicised, with factions emerging and infighting taking place in groups. By the mid 1980s, the protest movement was in decline.

If you want to end your tour on a more upbeat note, indulge in the low-tech aesthetic and approach still exhibited by relatively new locations such as the urban beaches **Roest** (see p122) and **Hanneke's Boom** (see p120). Then there are such cosy and funky clubs as **De Nieuwe Anita** (see p132). Although it may be the 21st century, and generations of hippies, squatters and clubbers have moved out or grown up, there are still plenty of opportunities to relax – and reminisce – in Amsterdam.

Amsterdam by Area

Dam Square

The Old Centre

The compelling Old Centre (aka Oud Centrum) surfs on a wave of contradiction. On one side, the surface delights of shops jostle with the fine pursuits of the mind, whereas on the other the trappings of sex jar with the icons of religion. Marked off by Centraal Station, Singel and Zwanenburgwal, the area is bisected by Damrak, which turns into Rokin south of Dam Square. The ancient Old Side (Oude Zijde) lies on the east, and the misleadingly titled New Side (Nieuwe Zijde) stretches along a gentle area to the west – the landmarks have actually been around for years, the most notable being Spui Square.

The Old Side

Straight up from Centraal Station, just beyond touristy Damrak and the Beurs van Berlage, lies **Dam Square**, the heart of the city since

the first dam was built across the Amstel here in 1270. Once a hub of social and political activities, today it's a convenient meeting point for tourists, the majority of whom convene under the erect **National Monument**, a 22 metre (70 foot) white obelisk dedicated to the Dutch servicemen who died in World War II. The west side of the square is flanked by the **Koninklijk Paleis** (Royal Palace), and next to it the 600-year-old **Nieuwe Kerk** stands proudly.

The root of Amsterdam's infamy is the nearby **Red Light District**, which is currently undergoing a clean-up. The city authorities are seeking to halve the number of prostitutes and coffeeshops in the hopes of attracting a classier line-up of cafés, shops and restaurants – and tourists. But while sex remains the main hook upon which the area hangs its reputation, it's actually secondary to window shopping.

Free for all

Have fun without spending.

Cheapskates, take note: you don't have to spend a fortune to have fun in Amsterdam. This list of activities shows just how easily budget visitors can have fun for free across the capital.

View from Openbare Bibliotheek Amsterdam

- The view from **NEMO** (see p118).
- Complimentary coffee at various branches of **Albert Heijn** (see p84).
- The **Rijksmuseum**'s gardens (see p134).
- Open-air concerts and the great outdoors of **Vondelpark** (see p133).
- The Civic Guard Gallery at the **Amsterdam Museum** (see p81), plus the neighbouring atmospheric inner courtyard **Begijnhof** (see p81).
- **Noordermarkt** flea market on Monday mornings (see p130).
- Tuesday lunchtime concerts at the **Muziektheater** (see p108).
- Wednesday lunchtime concerts at the **Concertgebouw** (see p142).
- Exploring the *hofjes* – courtyard almshouses – of the Jordaan.
- Tasting free samples of organic foodstuffs at the Saturday farmers' market on **Noordermarkt** (see p130).
- Smelling the flowers on sale at the **Bloemenmarkt** (see p103).
- Checking the biggest barometer in the Netherlands; the neon light on the **Hotel Okura Amsterdam** (see p177) tells you what tomorrow's weather will be like: blue for good; green for bad; white for changeable.
- Watching horseriding in the epic **Holland's Manege** (Vondelstraat 140, 618 0942).

- Lounging at one of the city beaches (see box p120).
- Reading through the international papers and glossies at the relatively new public library **Openbare Bibliotheek Amsterdam** (see p118). And then proceeding to the top floor café to take in the view (pictured).
- Visiting the **City Archives** (see p101 **Stadsarchief Amsterdam**).
- Free ferry rides from behind Centraal Station to North (see box p124).
- Interactive Dutch films at **EYE Film Institute** in North (see box p124).
- Free guided tours (www.new amsterdamtours.com) – but they do appreciate tips.
- Free jazz jams at the **Bimhuis** (see p121) every Tuesday at 10pm from September to June.
- Noord/Zuidlijn viewpoint: across from Rokin 96 in the middle of the street, descend the stairs to see the current state of Amsterdam's new subway (see box p68).
- Free diamond factory tour at **Gassan Diamonds** (see p110).

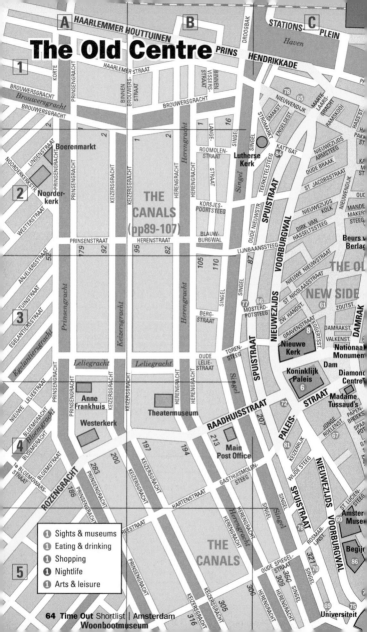

The Old Centre

HAARLEMMER HOUTTUINEN

PRINS HENDRIKKADE

STATIONS PLEIN

Haven

DROOGBAK

THE CANALS (pp89-107)

Boerenmarkt

Noorderkerk

Lutherse Kerk

Beurs Berlag

THE OLD

NEW SIDE

Nieuwe Kerk

Nationaal Monument

Koninklijk Paleis

Dam

Diamond Centre

Madame Tussaud's

Anne Frankhuis

Westerkerk

Theatermuseum

Main Post Office

Amster Muse

Begij

THE CANALS

Universiteit

- ❶ Sights & museums
- ❶ Eating & drinking
- ❶ Shopping
- ❶ Nightlife
- ❶ Arts & leisure

Woonbootmuseum

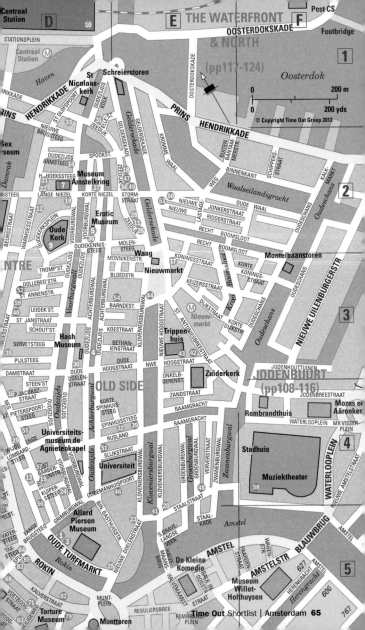

Even though people do buy an incredible amount here – sales are estimated to be worth around €500 million per year – most wander around, gazing at the live exhibits and taking in the history of the area at the **Erotic Museum** or **Hash Marihuana Hemp Museum Oudezijds** (Achterburgwal 148, 624 8926, http://hashmuseum.com). And yet, in the centre of this illicit activity rises up the **Oude Kerk** (Old Church), Amsterdam's oldest building, while the equally pious **Museum Ons' Lieve Heer op Solder** lies nearby.

At the bottom of Zeedijk, the castle-like **De Waag** (Weigh House) stands in the centre of terrace-rich Nieuwmarkt. Dating from 1488, it was built as a gatehouse and later contained an Anatomical Theatre (where Rembrandt painted his *Anatomy Lesson of Dr Nicolaes Tulp*). Yet more relative tranquillity exists on the Nes, home to many of the city's theatres and several charming cafés. When you reach the end of Nes, turn left and cross over a bridge to hunt down the **Oudemanhuis Book Market**. People have traded books, prints and sheet music here since the 18th century and it holds an enduring appeal for artists: Van Gogh chose to buy prints from the market to decorate his room.

Sights & museums

Allard Pierson Museum
Oude Turfmarkt 127 (525 2556, www.allardpiersonmuseum.nl). Tram 4, 9, 14, 16, 24, 25. **Open** 10am-5pm Tue-Fri; 1-5pm Sat, Sun. **Admission** €6.50; free-€5 reductions; MK. **No credit cards. Map** p65 D5 ❶
Established in Amsterdam in 1934, the Allard Pierson claims to hold one of the world's richest university collections of archaeological finds, gathered from ancient Egypt, Greece, Rome and the Near East. However, only those with a specific interest in such matters are likely not to be bored; many of the displays are dry, and will appeal just to scholars. With the exception of a few accessible items, such as the full-size sarcophagi and the model of a Greek chariot, it's a dull experience.

Beurs van Berlage
Damrak 243, entrance at Beursplein 1 (530 4141, www.beursvanberlage.nl). Tram 4, 9, 16, 24, 25. **Open** *Exhibitions* 10am-6pm daily. *Café* 10am-6pm Mon-Sat; 11am-6pm Sun. **Admission** varies. **No credit cards. Map** p65 D2 ❷
Designed in 1896 by Hendrik Berlage as the city's stock exchange, the palatial Beurs paved the way for the Amsterdam School. Although some jaded critics thought it 'a big block with a cigar box on top', it is now considered one of the country's most important architectural achievements. Built as a socialist statement, each of its nine million bricks was intended by Berlage to represent the individual, while much of the interior artwork warns against capitalism. It is now a classical concert hall, exhibition space and media centre, with its own café. Tours of the building take place every Saturday at 10.30am (€14.50).

Bijzondere Collecties
Oude Turfmarkt 129 (525 7333, www.bijzonderecollecties.uva.nl). Tram 4, 9, 14, 16, 24, 25. **Open** 9.30am-5pm Mon-Fri; 1-5pm Sat, Sun. Library closed at weekends. **Admission** €7.50; €3.75-€6.50 reductions; MK. **Map** p65 D5 ❸
They like their paper products at the University of Amsterdam's Special Collections: documents, prints, maps, atlases, photos and endless rows of books. The invaluable pre-1850 collection is especially strong on the history of printing, Hebrew and Judaica studies, Protestantism and medicine; the post-1850 collection focuses more on

meritorious design, with exhibitions ranging from the likes of 1001 Women to book advertising from the 18th century. The shop has an excellent selection of design-related books.

Cannabis College

Oudezijds Achterburgwal 124 I (423 4420, www.cannabiscollege.com). Tram 4, 9, 14, 16, 24, 25/Metro Nieuwmarkt. **Open** 11am-7pm daily. **Admission** free. **Map** p65 D3 **④**

The college, occupying two floors in a 17th-century listed monument in the Red Light District, provides the public with an array of information about the cannabis plant (including its medicinal uses). The place is run by volunteers and admission is free. However, staff request a small donation if you wish to wander around the indoor garden.

Erotic Museum

Oudezijds Achterburgwal 54 (627 8954, www.erotisch-museum.nl). Tram 4, 9, 16, 24, 25/Metro Nieuwmarkt. **Open** 11am-1am Mon-Thur; 11am-2am Fri-Sun. **Admission** €7. **No credit cards**. **Map** p65 D2 **⑤**

The Erotic Museum resides in the heart of the Red Light District, trying its best to attract the punters, but it's not really sexy. Prize exhibits include an odd bicycle-powered dildo and a few of John Lennon's erotic drawings. Lovers of Bettie Page will enjoy the original photos of the pin-up queen on display.

Koninklijk Paleis (Royal Palace)

Dam (information 620 4060, tours 624 8698, www.paleisamsterdam.nl). Tram 1, 2, 4, 5, 9, 13, 14, 16, 17, 24, 25. **Open** *June-Aug* 11am-5pm daily. *Sept-May* noon-5pm Tue-Sun. **Admission** €7.50; free reductions; MK. **No credit cards. Map** p64 C3/4 **⑥**

Originally erected in the 17th century as the city hall, this classic building is a symbol of the confidence that Amsterdam felt at the beginning of its Golden Age as the richest port in the world. Famously built on a foundation of 13,659 wooden piles sunk deep into the sand, the Koninklijk Paleis was rated as the eighth wonder of the world. It was transformed into a royal palace during harder times, after Napoleon had made his brother, Louis, King of the Netherlands in 1808; this era can be traced through the fine collection of furniture on display inside. Except for the statue of Atlas bearing his worldly load, which can be seen at the back of the building, the light-infused interior is far more impressive

Nieuwe Kerk p69

Old station, new hub

Refurbishment and a new Metro link.

Centraal Station.

Amsterdam is being ripped apart. The redevelopment activity is an attempt to right a wrong: the building of Centraal Station during 1882-89. Although it's impossible to imagine Amsterdam without its 'Old Holland'-style masterpiece (or its mirror-image, the Rijksmuseum), the building acted as a cultural marker, separating the city from its harbour and Amsterdam North across the IJ – as well as its history as the world's richest city port during its 17th-century Golden Age.

With the scheduled completion of the Noord-Zuidlijn metro link in 2017, the north will be connected to the outlying south via Centraal Station, which is also undergoing total refurbishment, due to be completed in 2015. The station will finally become truly central, with two front sides: one will face across the waters towards a gentrifying north, and the other, traditional front side will look out towards the Old Centre and the radiating horseshoe of canals with their gabled houses. It's hoped that the metro line will give a

boost to the rising business centre, Zuidas, in the south, where many new office blocks are largely empty.

Work on the 9.5-kilometre line started in 2003 and has always been mired in controversy. Most of the aldermen who initiated the project have now moved on, leaving the city with a legacy that's at best merely too expensive, and at worst out of control. The Noord-Zuidlijn has run over its original budget – a staggering €1.65 billion – paid for by the council and the government. The whole project will cost the council over €900 million, not the estimated €317 million; and if it stays on the current schedule it will still be completed six years later than originally projected. Part of the problem lies in the difficulties of digging beneath a city built on poles; time-consuming processes had to be invented to construct tunnels 40 metres deep. While leaking walls and sinking old buildings stopped work in 2009, everything now seems set for Amsterdam to get itself a proper A-train.

than the dark and forbidding exterior. The Citizens' Hall, with its Baroque decoration in grand marble and bronze depicting a miniature universe (with Amsterdam at its centre), is meant to make you feel about as worthy as the rats carved into the stone over the door of the Bankruptcy Chamber. Gentler displays of creativity can be observed in the chimney pieces, painted by the likes of Ferdinand Bol and Govert Flinck, pupils of Rembrandt (who had his own sketches rejected). The building became state property in 1936 and the Dutch Royal family still use it for dinner parties when they feel the need to impress international guests.

Museum Ons' Lieve Heer op Solder

Oudezijds Voorburgwal 40 (624 6604, www.opsolder.nl). Tram 4, 9, 16, 24, 25. **Open** 10am-5pm Mon-Sat; 1-5pm Sun. **Admission** €8; free-€4 reductions; MK. **No credit cards.** **Map** p65 D2 ❼

Originally known as the Museum Amstelkring, this place is a well-kept secret. The main attraction is upstairs, and goes by the name Our Sweet Lord in the Attic. Built in 1663, this attic church was used by Catholics during the 17th century, when they were banned from worshipping after the Alteration. The altarpiece features a painting by the noted 18th-century artist Jacob de Wit. Meanwhile, the beautifully preserved rooms on the lower floor offer a realistic glimpse of what life was like during the 17th century. The museum will remain open during ongoing renovations, but there may be disruptions for visitors.

Nieuwe Kerk (New Church)

Dam (626 8168, recorded information 638 6909, www.nieuwekerk.nl). Tram 1, 2, 4, 5, 9, 13, 14, 16, 17, 24, 25. **Open** 10am-5pm daily. **Admission** varies. **No credit cards.** **Map** p64 C3 ❽

The sprightly Nieuwe Kerk dates from 1408, but due to a series of fires much has been renewed since. It is thought that the ornate oak pulpit and great organ were constructed some time after 1645, when the building was gutted by the Great Fire. Behind the black marble tomb of naval hero Admiral de Ruyter (1607-76) – who helped to win the second Anglo-Dutch war by daringly sailing up the Medway in 1667 – is a white marble relief depicting the sea battle in which he died. Poets and Amsterdam natives including PC Hooft and Joost van den Vondel are also buried here. Bonus fact: the sundial on the tower was used to set all of the city's clocks until as recently as 1890. Today, the church hosts the occasional concert and regular, generally excellent, archaeological and modern art exhibitions.

Oude Kerk (Old Church)

Oudekerksplein 23 (625 8284, www. oudekerk.nl). Tram 4, 9, 16, 24, 25. **Open** 11am-5pm Mon-Sat; 1-5.30pm Sun. **Admission** €5; free-€4 reductions; MK. **No credit cards.** **Map** p65 D2 ❾

The Oude Kerk began life as a simple wooden chapel in 1306, but today rates as Amsterdam's most interesting church. It's easy to imagine the Sunday Mass chaos during its heyday in the mid-1500s, when it had 38 altars, each with its own guild-appointed priest. Now it serves more as a radical contrast to the surrounding Red Light District, but still holds lessons: the inscription over the bridal chamber states 'marry in haste, mourn in leisure'. Look out for the floor grave of Rembrandt's wife, Saskia, who died in 1642. Also note the Gothic and Renaissance façade above the northern portal, and the stained-glass windows, parts of which date from the 16th and 17th centuries. For shock value, check out the carvings in the choir benches of men evacuating their bowels – they tell a moralistic tale. Occasional art shows cover a range of fascinating subjects, from contemporary local art to the World Press Photo Exhibition.

Eating & drinking

1e Klas

Line 2B, Centraal Station (625 0131, www.restaurant1eklas.nl). Tram 1, 2, 4, 5, 9, 13, 16, 17, 24, 25, 26. **Open** 8.30am-11pm daily. €€€. **Brasserie.** **Map** p65 D1 ⑩

This former brasserie for first-class commuters is now open to anyone who wants to kill some time in style, while waiting for their train – with a full meal or just a snack. The delightful art nouveau interior will whisk visitors straight back to the 1890s. Other great eating options can be found in the west tunnel: try Julia's (www.julia sophetstation.nl) for healthy pasta or Shakies (www.shakies.nl) for organic juices, coffees and bagels.

A Fusion

Zeedijk 130 (330 4068, www.a-fusion.nl). Tram 4, 9, 16, 24, 25/ Metro Nieuwmarkt. **Open** noon-11pm daily. €€€. **Chinese.** **Map** p65 E2 ⑪

This laid-back, loungey affair looks as though it's been taking notes from the hipper, more happening side of New York's Chinatown. The dark and inviting interior harbours big screens playing Hong Kong music videos and the place serves bubble teas (lychee!), and some of the tastiest pan-Asian dishes in town.

De Bakkerswinkel

Warmoesstraat 69 (489 8000, www.bakkerswinkel.nl). Tram 1, 2, 4, 5, 9, 13, 16, 17, 24, 25, 26. **Open** 8am-6pm Tue-Fri; 8am-5pm Sat; 10am-5pm Sun. **Café.** **Map** p65 D2 ⑫

The freshly renovated Bakkerswinkel is a fantastic bakery and tearoom, where you can indulge lunchtime hunger pangs with lovingly prepared sandwiches, hearty soups and the most divine slabs of quiche you've ever tasted. Get takeaway from the branch at nearby Warmoesstraat 133; check the website for other branches around town.

Bierfabriek

Rokin 75/Nes 92 (528 9910, www.bierfabriek.com). Tram 4, 9, 14, 16, 24, 25. **Open** 4pm-1am Mon-Thur; 4pm-3am Fri; 2pm-3am Sat; 2pm-1am Sun. **Map** p65D4 ⑬

See box p73.

Brouwerij de Prael

Oudezijds Armsteeg 26/Oudezijds Voorburgwal 30 (408 4470, www.deprael.nl). Centraal Station. **Open** *Brewery* noon-midnight Tue-Sat; noon-11pm Sun. *Store* noon-7pm Tue-Fri, noon-5pm Sat; noon-6pm Sun. **Map** p65 D2 ⑭

See box p73.

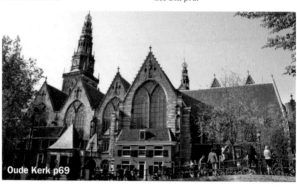

Oude Kerk p69

Brasserie Harkema

Nes 67 (428 2222, www.brasserie harkema.nl). Tram 4, 9, 14, 16, 24, 25. **Open** 11am-midnight daily.
€€€. French. Map p65 D4 ⑮
This former tobacco factory has titillated the local scene with its sense of designer space, excellent wines and a kitchen that stays open late, serving reasonably priced European classics.

Bubbles and Wines

Nes 37 (422 3318, www.bubbles andwines.com). Tram 4, 9, 14, 16, 24, 25. **Open** 3.30pm-1am Mon-Sat; 2-9pm Sun. **€€€. Wine bar. Map** p65 D4 ⑯
A long, low-ceilinged room with the feel of a wine cellar, one with mood lighting, banquettes and champagnes on offer. There are more than 50 wines by the glass and 180 by the bottle; posh nosh includes Osetra caviar, truffle cheese and foie gras. The final bill is unlikely to suit the faint-hearted or light of wallet.

Café Bern

Nieuwmarkt 9 (622 0034, www.cafe bern.com). Tram 4, 9, 16, 24, 25/ Metro Nieuwmarkt. **Open** 4pm-1am daily. **€€. No credit cards. Dutch. Map** p65 E3 ⑰
Despite its Swiss origins, the cheese fondue was adopted by the Dutch as a noted national dish long ago. Sample its culinary conviviality at this suitably cosy bar that was allegedly established – oddly enough – by a nuclear physicist.

Café 't Mandje

Zeedijk 63 (622 5375, www.cafet mandje.nl). 4, 9, 16, 24, 25/Metro Nieuwmarkt. **Open** 4pm-1am Mon-Wed; 3pm-1am Thur; 2pm-3am Fri, Sat; 2pm-1am Sun. **No credit cards. Café. Map** p65 E2 ⑱
This historic café, open for more than 80 years, was the city's first (moderately) openly gay and lesbian bar. The proprietor Bet van Beeren, who died over 40 years ago, was legendary for her role as (probably) the world's first lesbian biker chick. It was closed for years but reopened a while back to suggest that, yes, time can stand still. A replica of the café can be seen at the Amsterdam Museum (see p81).

Centra

Lange Niezel 29 (622 3050, www. restaurantcentra.nl). Tram 4, 9, 14, 16, 24, 25. **Open** 1.30-10.30pm daily. **€€. Spanish. Map** p65 D2 ⑲
Good, wholesome, homely Spanish cooking with a suitably unpretentious atmosphere to match. The tapas, lamb and fish dishes are all great, and the place gets justifiably busy as a result.

De Doelen

Kloveniersburgwal 125 (624 9023). Tram 4, 9, 14, 16, 24, 25/Metro Waterlooplein. **Open** 10am-1am Mon-Thur, Sun; 9am-3am Fri, Sat. **No credit cards. Bar. Map** p65 E5 ⑳
An old-fashioned drinking hole – complete with gritted floors – on one of the main tourist drags. Rough edges are smoothed by sophisticated breakfasts (fruit smoothies, muesli), international snacks (houmous, tapenade) and frosty jugs of sangria in summer, along with bands on Sundays.

Getto

Warmoesstraat 51 (421 5151, www.getto.nl). Tram 1, 2, 4, 5, 9, 13, 16, 17, 24, 25, 26. **Open** 4pm-1am Tue-Thur; 4pm-2am Fri, Sat; 4pm-midnight Sun. **€€. Global. Map** p65 D2 ㉑
Cheap and cheerful food is served at Getto in surprisingly plush surroundings, catering to a mostly gay and lesbian crowd. On Wednesdays all burger dinners cost €10. Combined with the popular weekday cocktail happy hours, this makes it the ideal place for an inexpensive date.

Greenhouse Effect

Warmoesstraat 53-55 (624 4974, www.greenhouse-effect.nl). Tram 4, 9, 16, 24, 25. **Open** *Coffeeshop* 9am-1am daily. **Bar** 9am-1am Mon-Thur, Sun; 9am-3am Fri, Sat. **No credit cards**. **Bar/coffeeshop**. Map p65 D2 ㉒

This snug shop is shaped like a long, sleek train carriage, and features a polished interior and reliably high-quality ganja. It tends to fill up fast, but there's a separate space with the same name next door, where you'll discover a full bar as well as regular DJs. If the drink and dope combination renders you immobile, make a beeline for the hotel (see p165) upstairs.

De Jaren

Nieuwe Doelenstraat 20-22 (625 5771, www.cafedejaren.nl). Tram 4, 9, 14, 16, 24, 25. **Open** 9.30am-1am Mon-Thur, Sun; 9.30am-2am Fri, Sat (kitchen closes 10.30pm). **Bar**. Map p65 E5 ㉓

An entire cross-section of Amsterdam – students, tourists, lesbigays, trendy mums and the fashion pack – come here for lunch, coffee or something stronger throughout the day, which can make it difficult to get a seat. Be prepared to fight for a spot on the popular Amstel-side outdoor terrace on sunny summer afternoons.

Kapitein Zeppos

Gebed Zonder End 5 (624 2057, www.zeppos.nl). Tram 4, 9, 14, 16, 24, 25. **Open** noon-1am Mon-Thur, Sun; noon-3am Fri, Sat. **Bar/Belgian**. Map p65 D4 ㉔

A hidey-hole down the poetically named 'Prayer Without End' alley – a reference to the Santa Clara convent that stood here in the 17th century. Now it's a light-drenched, multifaceted café and restaurant with an understated Belgian theme: it's named after a 1960s Flemish TV detective, there's Belgian beer on tap, Belgian-inspired food coming from the kitchen and the most frequently heard soundtrack of choice is *chanson*.

Katoen

Oude Turfmarkt 153 (626 2635, www.cafekatoen.nl). Tram 4, 9, 14, 16,

24, 25. **Open** 9am-1am Mon-Thur; 9am-3am Fri, Sat; noon-1am Sun. **No credit cards**. **Café**. Map p65 D5 ㉕

If shopping on Kalverstraat gets too much, run screaming across Rokin to this oasis of calm on the edge of the Old Centre. It has the stripped-down good looks of the 1950s (Formica tables, polished wood) and a satisfying but inventive menu of salads, rolls and stone oven pizzas.

Latei

Zeedijk 143 (625 7485, www.latei. net). Tram 4, 9, 16, 24, 25/Metro Nieuwmarkt. **Open** 8am-6pm Mon-Wed; 8am-10pm Thur, Fri; 9am-10pm Sat; 11am-6pm Sun. **No credit cards**. **Café**. Map p65 E2 ㉖

Packed with kitsch bric-a-brac and funky Finnish wallpaper – all of which, wallpaper included, is for sale – this little café serves up healthy juices and snacks all day, plus fish, vegetarian and vegan dinners from Thursday to Saturday, based around Japanese and Korean cuisine.

Mata Hari

NEW *Oudezijds Achterburgwal 22 (205 0919, http://matahari-amsterdam.nl). Tram 4, 9, 16, 24, 25/Metro Nieuwmarkt.* **Open** noon-1am Mon-Thur, Sun; noon-3am Fri, Sat. €€€€. **Mediterranean/ Dutch**. Map p65 D2 ㉗

Named after the exotic but tricksy Dutch courtesan, it's appropriate that this new bar, restaurant and lounge has brought a touch of comfort and class to the Red Light District. Sympathetic lighting, retro furniture and an exquisite open kitchen serving dishes such as 'chocolate salami with forget-me-not liqueur' make the seduction complete.

Nam Kee

Zeedijk 111-113 (624 3470, www.namkee.net). Tram 4, 9, 16, 24, 25/Metro Nieuwmarkt. **Open** noon-11pm daily. €€. **No credit cards**. **Chinese**. Map p65 E2 ㉘

What's brewing?

Craft beer and social enterprise.

Brouwerij de Prael

For decades, **Brouwerij 't IJ** (see p113) ruled the roost when it came to locally brewed golden elixirs. Now **Bierfabriek** (see p70) offers not only homebrewed beers, but some of the finest roast chicken in town. Just be wary on Friday nights when the joint gets taken over by the after-work crowd attracted to the table-top taps for serving your own beer.

And who says that psychiatric patients and alcohol shouldn't mix? The brewery and shop **Brouwerij de Prael** (see p70) in the heart of the Red Light District is proving all the critics wrong. Originating 15 years ago in an industrial estate on the outskirts of town, De Prael was set up on the basis of its owners' background in mental healthcare and love of brewing to the sound of quirky local songs. By establishing De Prael as a 'social firm', with commercial objectives, they were able to invest all the earnings back into the foundation. Currently they employ 70 staff, all of whom have a psychiatric condition: 80 per cent are schizophrenic and the others suffer from borderline personality disorders. Yes, there are plenty of jokes, but the rules are simple: no drinking on the job and be on time.

All the beers from the De Prael brewery share their names with tears-in-your-beers singers. For instance, Mary is called after Mary Servaes (aka the Zangeres Zonder Naam) and as a triple, its strong alcohol content makes it as robust as the lady herself. Johnny, a blonde beer, was named after the fair-haired Johnny Jordaan; Heintje is as fresh and fruity as Hendrik (Hein) Nicolaas Theodoor Simons was reputed to be.

Afterwards, perhaps you can keep up the theme by dining at the Freud (Spaarndammerstraat 424, 688 5548, www.restaurant freud.nl), a restaurant run by former psychiatric patients.

Snack attack

Give grease a chance.

Yokiyo

Street food is very popular in Amsterdam. As proof, note the success of Korean restaurant **Yokiyo** (see p76). But there are cheaper options: the rolled 'pizzas' from Turkish bakeries, Dutch *broodjes* (sandwiches) from bakers and butchers, and the more spicy Surinamese *broodjes* from 'Chin-Indo-Suri' snack bars (see box p105).

Fast food can tell you a lot about the tastes of a nation. You simply must try a raw herring: the best time is between May and July when the *nieuw* (new) catch hits the stands, as it's then that their flesh is at its sweetest, since the high fat content has not yet been burned off by the arduous business of breeding. You don't need extras like onions or pickles, and they're cheap as chips.

Speaking of chips, the best are the chunky Belgian ones (*Vlaamse*), double-fried to ensure a crispy exterior and creamy interior. Enjoy them along with your pick of toppings, such as *oorlog* (war):

mayo, spicy peanut sauce and onions. **Vleminckx** (see p85) and **Manneken Pis** (Damrak 41) are two of the best places to eat them.

The local term for a greasy snack – *vette hap* – is translated literally as 'fat bite', which says a lot for the honesty of the Dutch. At the ubiquitous Febo, you can put your change into a glowing *automaat* and, in return, get a hot hamburger, *bamibal* (a deep-fried noodle ball of vaguely Indonesian descent), or a *kaas soufflé* (a cheese treat). The most popular choice is the *kroket*, a melange of meat and potato with a deep-fried skin, best served on a bun with hot mustard. The best place to try these is **Van Dobben** (see p103), just off Rembrandtplein. While this 1945-vintage late-night venue is the uncontested champion when it comes to the *kroket*, you can also find a more refined shrimp variation at nearby bakery **Holtkamp** (Vijzelgracht 15, 624 8757). That's right folks, just give grease a chance.

Cheap, terrific food has earned this Chinese joint a devoted following – the oysters in black bean sauce have achieved cult status. If it's busy, try the equally excellent neighbours New King (Zeedijk 115-117, 625 2180), Wing Kee (Zeedijk 76, 623 5683) or Si Chuan (Warmoesstraat 17, 420 7833).

NRC Restaurant-Café

NEW *Rokin 65 (755 3553, www.nrc restaurantcafe.nl). Tram 4, 9, 14, 16, 24, 25.* **Open** 8am-1am Mon-Fri; 9.30am-1am Sat, Sun. **€€**. **International**. Map p65 D4 ㉙
The Netherlands' premier quality newspaper recently moved from Rotterdam to the big city of Amsterdam and wanted to make a splash. So it appended its new offices with a café-restaurant to which it hopes to attract the local intelligentsia. You can order fish and chips wrapped in yesterday's paper, opt for a full-fledged meal or just linger over a coffee and sandwich. Don't miss the excellent small bookshop.

Oriental City

Oudezijds Voorburgwal 177-179 (626 8352, www.oriental-city.nl). Tram 4, 9, 14, 16, 24, 25. **Open** 11.30am-11.30pm daily. **€€€**. **Chinese**. Map p65 D3 ㉚
The views from Oriental City are truly spectacular, overlooking Damstraat, the Royal Palace and the canals, plus, the dim sum is among the best you'll find in Amsterdam.

Queen's Head

Zeedijk 20 (420 2475, www.queens head.nl). Tram 1, 2, 4, 5, 9, 13, 16, 17, 24, 25, 26. **Open** 4pm-1am Mon-Thur, Sun; 4pm-3am Fri, Sat. **No credit cards**. **Bar**. Map p65 D1 ㉛
The Queen's is a fun and attitude-free gay bar with a similarly minded clientele, plus a great view over a canal at the back. It holds regular special nights, with drag acts and DJs and parties on Queen's Day (now King's Day, 30 April), plus bear nights, football

nights (during the season), Eurovision Song Contest nights and so on.

Rusland

Rusland 16 (627 9468, http:// coffeeshop-rusland-amsterdam.com). Tram 4, 9, 14, 16, 24, 25/Metro Nieuwmarkt or Waterlooplein. **Open** 7am-1am daily. **No credit cards**. **Coffeeshop**. Map p65 E4 ㉜
Well known as the oldest coffeeshop in the city, this 'Russian' den has hardwood floors and colourful cushions that complement an efficient multi-level design. The top floor has a bar that serves over 40 different loose teas and healthy fruit shakes; below is a decent pipe display. It's off the well-trodden tourist path, which means lower prices and smaller crowds for the punter.

Skek

Zeedijk 4-8 (427 0551, www.skek.nl). Tram 1, 2, 4, 5, 9, 13, 16, 17, 24, 25, 26. **Open** 4pm-1am Mon; noon-1am Tue-Thur, Sun; noon-3am Fri, Sat. **Café**. Map p65 D1 ㉝
This café-cum-music joint is run by the student organisation that heads up the Filmtheater Kriterion, and it focuses on value and quality. While student visitors lap up the great discounts, other music lovers will probably get more out of the regular singer/songwriter and jazz shows on offer. It also serves nice, affordable lunches and dinners.

Thaise Snackbar Bird

Zeedijk 77 (snack bar 420 6289, restaurant 620 1442, www.thai-bird.nl). Tram 1, 2, 4, 5, 9, 13, 16, 17, 24, 25, 26. **Open** *Snack bar* 1-10pm daily. *Restaurant* 5-11pm daily. **€€€**. **Thai**. Map p65 E2 ㉞
Easily the most authentic Thai place in town. No doubt because of this, it's also the most crowded. But it's worth the wait, whether you drop by for *tom yum* soup or go for a full-blown meal. If you plan to linger, settle down in the restaurant (Zeedijk 72-74) across the street rather than the snack bar itself.

Wynand Fockink

Pijlsteeg 31 (639 2695, www.wynand-fockink.nl). Tram 4, 9, 14, 16, 24, 25. **Open** 3-9pm daily. **No credit cards.** **Bar. Map** p65 D3 ⑳

Tucked away in a side alley behind the Krasnapolsky and largely unchanged since 1679, this tasting house has been a meeting place for Freemasons since the year dot, with past visitors including Churchill and Chagall. The menu of liqueurs and jenevers reads like a list of surrealist artworks: Parrot Soup; The Longer the Better; Rose Without Thorns.

Yokiyo

NEW *Oudezijds Voorburgwal 67 (331 4562, http://yokiyo.nl). Centraal Station.* **Open** 6.30pm-midnight Tue-Wed; noon-3pm, 6.30pm-midnight Thur, Sun; noon-3pm, 6.30pm-1am Fri, Sat. **€€€. Korean. Map** p65 D2 ㊱

Influential Korean-American chef David Chang has some worthy disciples in this new 'Korean Social Food Experience', with BBQ, kimchi and other bold-flavoured foodstuffs. Join the fun at the bar, on the long dining table or upstairs on one of the round tables with built-in Korean BBQs. Late opening hours are another plus.

Shopping

Betsy Palmer

Rokin 9-15 (422 1040, www.betsy palmer.com). Tram 4, 9, 14, 16, 24, 25. **Open** noon-6.30pm Mon; 10.30am-6.30pm Tue, Wed, Fri; 10.30am-9pm Thur; 10am-6pm Sat; 1-6pm Sun. **Map** p65 D4 ㊲

Tired of seeing the same shoes in every store, Dutch fashion buyer Gertie Gerards put her money where her mouth was and set up shop. Betsy Palmer is her in-house label, which sits alongside a huge variety of other labels that change regularly as they sell out.

De Bijenkorf

Dam 1 (0900 0919 premium rate, www.bijenkorf.nl). Tram 1, 2, 4, 5, 9, 13, 14, 16, 17, 24, 25. **Open** 11am-8pm Mon; 10am-8pm Tue, Wed; 10am-9pm Thur, Fri; 9.30am-8pm Sat; 11am-8pm Sun. **Map** p64 C3 ㊳

Amsterdam's most notable department store has a great household goods section and a good mix of clothing (designer and own-label), kids' wear, jewellery, cosmetics, shoes and accessories.

Book Exchange

Kloveniersburgwal 58 (626 6266, www.bookexchange.nl). Tram 4, 9,

NRC Restaurant-Café p75

14, 16, 24, 25/Metro Nieuwmarkt.
Open 10am-6pm Mon-Sat; 11.30am-
4pm Sun. **No credit cards**. **Map**
p65 E4 ③⑨

The owner of this bibliophiles' treasure
trove is a shrewd buyer who is willing
to do trade deals. Choose from a range
of second-hand English and American
titles (mainly paperbacks).

Condomerie

*Warmoesstraat 141 (627 4174,
www.condomerie.com). Tram 4, 9,
14, 16, 25.* **Open** 11am-6pm Mon-Sat;
1-5pm Sun. **Map** p65 D3 ④⓪

An astounding variety of innovative
and imaginative rubbers of the non-
erasing kind, designed to wrap up
trouser snakes of all shapes and sizes.

Droog Hotel

NEW *Staalstraat 7A/B (523 5059,
www.droogdesign.nl). Tram 4, 9, 14,
16, 24, 25.* **Open** noon-6pm Tue-Sat.
Map p65 E5 ④①

Dutch dynamo Droog has expanded its
HQ into a flagship 'hotel' – a city-centre
design mall where you can attend a lec-
ture series or an exhibition, get beauty
advice at Cosmania and, yes, even
spend the night in the single suite. The
historic building's rag trade origins are
continued at ice-cool boutique Kabinet.
The Droog shop still sells some of the
wittiest ranges around: Jurgen Bey,
Richard Hutten, Hella Jongerius and
Marcel Wanders. See also p52.

Joe's Vliegerwinkel

*Nieuwe Hoogstraat 19 (625 0139,
www.joesvliegerwinkel.nl). Tram 4, 9,
14, 16, 24, 25/Metro Nieuwmarkt.*
Open noon-6pm Tue-Fri; noon-5pm
Sat. **Map** p65 E3 ④②

Kites, kites and yet more kites. Also a
quirky array of boomerangs, yo-yos
and kaleidoscopes at this wonderfully
colourful shop.

't Klompenhuisje

*Nieuwe Hoogstraat 9A (622 8100,
www.klompenhuisje.nl). Tram 4, 9,*
14/Metro Nieuwmarkt. **Open** 10am-
6pm Mon-Sat. **Map** p65 E3 ④③

Delightfully crafted and reasonably
priced children's shoes, traditional
clogs and handmade leather and
woollen slippers are available here.

Nieuwmarkt Antique Market

*Nieuwmarkt (no phone). Tram 4, 9, 14,
16, 24, 25/Metro Nieuwmarkt.* **Open**
May-Oct 9am-5pm Sun. **Map** p65 E3 ④④

A few streets away from the ladies in
the windows, this antiques and bric-a-
brac market attracts browsers looking
for other kinds of pleasures. Old books,
furniture and objets d'art.

Options!

NEW *Damrak 49 (620 1400, www.
optionsamsterdam.com). Tram 1,
2, 5, 16, 24, 25.* **Open** 11am-7pm
Mon, Sun; 10am-7pm Tue, Wed, Sat;
10am-9pm Thur, Fri. **Map** p64 C2 ④⑤

Part of fashion hotel the Exchange (see
p165), this design department store can
provide one-stop shopping for anyone
looking for – yes – tasteful souvenirs.
The mostly handmade products have
been sourced from both local and international designers around the world
and includes stationary, ceramics, furniture and one-offs. For fans of the
Japanese MUJI stores.

Oudemanhuis Book Market

*Oudemanhuispoort (no phone).
Tram 4, 9, 14, 16, 24, 25.* **Open**
9am-5pm Mon-Sat. **No credit cards**.
Map p65 E4 ④⑥

People have been buying and selling
books, prints and sheet music from this
shop since the 18th century.

Patta

NEW *Zeedijk 67 (331 8571, www.
patta.nl). Tram 4, 9.* **Open** noon-7pm
Mon-Wed, Fri, Sat; noon-9pm Thur;
1-6pm Sun. **Map** p65 E2 ④⑦

Named after the Surinamese slang for
shoes, this store is where trainer

AMSTERDAM BY AREA

fetishists come to commune: all the expected brands, from Adidas to New Balance, are here. Plus clothing by Stussy and Rockwell.

Puccini Bomboni

Staalstraat 17 (626 5474, www. puccinibomboni.com). Tram 4, 9, 14/Metro Waterlooplein. **Open** noon-6pm Mon, Sun; 9am-6pm Tue-Sat. **Map** p65 E4 ㊽

Tamarind, thyme, lemongrass, pepper and gin are just some of the flavours of these delicious and imaginative hand-made chocolates, all lacking in artificial ingredients. There's a second location at Singel 184 (427 8341).

Toko Dun Yong

Stormsteeg 9 (622 1763, www.dun yong.com). Tram 4, 9, 14, 16, 24, 25/Metro Nieuwmarkt. **Open** 9am-6pm Mon-Sat; noon-5pm Sun. **Map** p65 E3 ㊾

Visit Amsterdam's largest Chinese food emporium for the full spectrum of Asian foods and ingredients, ranging from shrimp- and scallop-flavoured egg noodles to fried tofu balls and fresh veg. You can also seek out a fine range of traditional Chinese cooking appliances and utensils, as well as indulge in Japanese ramen soups at Le Fou Fow (open 12.30-5pm Mon-Wed, Sun) on the second floor.

De Wijnerij

NEW *Binnen Bantammerstraat 8 (625 6433, www.dewijnerij.com). Tram 4, 9, 14, 16, 24, 25/Metro Nieuwmarkt.* **Open** 11am-6.30pm Tue-Fri; 10am-6.30pm Sat. **Map** p65 E2 ㊿

This friendly and passionate wine shop specialises in French wines and unique distillates. The owners usually work with smaller wine producers, many of whom use organic ingredients. De Wijnerij also sells jenevers – Dutch gin – from local producers Van Wees. With another wine and liquor shop De Twee Engelen (no.19) and the relaxed café/terrace Cafe

Captein en Co (no.27), this street is a delight for all thirsty people.

WonderWood

Rusland 3 (625 3738, www. wonderwood.nl). Tram 4, 9, 16, 24, 25. **Open** noon-6pm Wed-Sat. **Map** p65 D4 ㈱

The name says it all: wonderfully sculpted wood in the form of shop-made originals, re-editions of global classics and original plywood from the 1940s and '50s. Wonderful.

Nightlife

Winston Kingdom

Warmoesstraat 131 (623 1380, www.winston.nl). Tram 4, 9, 16, 24, 25. **Open** 9pm-3am Mon-Thur; Sun; 9pm-4am Fri, Sat. **No credit cards**. **Map** p65 D3 ㈲

An intimate venue that attracts a mixed crowd with its alternative rock and independent dance. Winston's yearly Popprijs (pop prize) gives hope to many student rock bands; Cheeky Mondays brings relief at the beginning of the working week with jungle and drum 'n' bass; and other nights see everything in live music from garage to folk to funky ska.

Arts & leisure

Amsterdam Marionetten Theater

Nieuwe Jonkerstraat 8 (620 8027, www.marionettentheater.nl). Tram 1, 2, 4, 5, 9, 13, 16, 17, 24, 25, 26. **Map** p65 E2 ㈳

Opera as you've never seen it before. Picture a scene with puppets wearing rich velvet costumes, expert puppeteers and classic works by Mozart and Offenbach, and you'll have an idea of what the marionette theatre is all about. One of the last remaining outposts of an old European tradition, the theatre also offers private lunches, dinners or high teas, to be taken while the puppets perform. Delightful.

Options! p77

Bethaniënklooster

Barndesteeg 6B (625 0078,
www.bethanienklooster.nl). Tram 4,
9, 14, 16, 24, 25/Metro Nieuwmarkt.
No credit cards. Map p65 E3 54
Hidden down a small alley between
Damstraat and the Nieuwmarkt, this
former monastery is a wonderful stage
for new classical and jazz talent to
cut its musical teeth. In between enjoying free public performances by
Amsterdam's top music students, you'll
also have the chance to tune into some
reputable ensembles and quartets.

De Brakke Grond

Nes 45 (622 6866, www.brakke
grond.nl). Tram 4, 9, 14, 16, 24, 25.
No credit cards. Map p65 D4 55
Belgian culture does stretch beyond
beer, and De Brakke Grond is here to
prove it. Mind you, some good Belgian
beer will go down a treat after visiting
the gallery or checking out a band. If
you're lucky you might find a stray
Belgian joining you at the bar of the
adjoining café/restaurant.

Comedy Theatre

Nes 110 (422 2777, www.comedy
theater.nl). Tram 4, 9, 14, 16, 24,
25. **Map** p65 D4 56
This old tobacco hall is now a comedy
theatre on the city's most venerable
theatre street. Hyping itself as the 'club
house' for comedians, its programming combines politically hard-hitting
performers with straightforward
stand-up. Expect to see local legends
like Javier Guzman, as well as international ones such as Tom Rhodes or
Lewis Black. It also books bigger acts
such as Eddie Izzard in larger venues.
To make sure that at least some of the
acts are English-speaking on the
night of your visit, it's best to phone
the venue in advance.

Frascati

Nes 63 (751 6400, tickets 626 6866,
www.theaterfrascati.nl). Tram 4, 9,
14, 16, 24, 25. **No credit cards.**
Map p65 D4 57
A cornerstone of progressive Dutch
theatre since the 1960s, Frascati gives
promising artists the chance to put
their productions on one of its three
stages. Its mission: to challenge the
bounds of traditional theatre by team-
ing up professionally trained artists
with those from the street, resulting in
a variety of theatre and dance shows
featuring MCs and DJs, such as the
youthful Breakin' Walls festival.

AMSTERDAM BY AREA

Canal cruising

Take to the water.

During a sojourn in the city, Hans Christian Andersen wrote, 'The view from my window, through the elms to the canal outside, is like a fairy tale.' Canals are what people imagine when they think of 'Amsterdam', and they continue to enchant visitors today. Like any other city built on water, Amsterdam is best seen from a boat. It has 75 kilometres (47 miles) of waterways and a total of 165 canals spanned by 1,400 bridges (more than Venice): look at the bottom right-hand corner of a bridge to see its number.

The tourist boats provide a doughty service, but they can't squeeze into the narrower waterways. Self-piloted hire boats are few and far between: in fact, there are only two such outfits, **Canal Motorboats** (Zandhoek 10A, 422 7007, www.canalmotor boats.com) on Realeneiland, and **Boaty** (Jozef Israëlkade, between Ferdinand Bolstraat & 2e Van der Helststraat, 06 2714 9493, www.boaty.nl) on a dock outside Hotel Okura (p177) in the Pijp, which rents only silent electric motor boats. The boats of both firms have a capacity of six. If these don't suit, just befriend a boating local or charter a tour.

Amsterdam also has its own gondola service, **Stichting Battello** (686 9868, mobile 06 4746 4545, www.gondel.nl), and it's suitably unique. Not only will you glide silently and comfortably along at an angle that reveals this city at its more picturesque, you'll also be chauffeured by one of two one-time Guinness World Record holders: Hans, 'the tallest gondolier in the world', and Tirza, 'the only woman gondolier in the world'.

Best suited to lovey-dovey couples, a ride will cost a group of up to six people around €100 an hour. You can also bring along your own food or drink, or get them to arrange refreshments for a reasonable price. The standard course is around the Jordaan, but you are welcome to stipulate your own route should you desire.

Muziektheater

Amstel 3 (625 5455, www.het-
muziektheater.nl). Tram 9, 14/Metro
Waterlooplein. **Map** p65 F4 **58**

The Muziektheater is Amsterdam at its
most ambitious. This plush, crescent-
shaped building, which opened in 1986,
has room for 1,596 people and is home
to both the Dutch National Ballet and De
Nederlandse Opera, although the stage
is also used by visiting companies such
as Nederlands Dans Theater and the latest Peter Sellars or Robert Wilson opera.
On top of that, the lobby's panoramic
glass walls offer impressive views out
over the River Amstel.

W139

Warmoesstraat 139 (622 9434,
www.w139.nl). Tram 4, 9, 16, 24, 25.
Open noon-6pm Mon-Wed, Fri, Sat;
noon-10pm Thur. **No credit cards**.
Map p65 D3 **59**

In its two decades of existence, W139
has never lost its squat aesthetics and
sometimes overly conceptual edge,
while a recent renovation has brought
even more light and fresh inspiration.
Legendary openings.

The New Side

The Spui is the square that caps
the area's three main arteries,
which start down near the west
end of Centraal Station: middle-
of-the-road walking and shopping
street Kalverstraat (called
Nieuwendijk before it crosses the
Dam), Nieuwezijds Voorburgwal
and the Spuistraat.

The nearby **Begijnhof** is a
group of houses built around a
secluded courtyard and garden.
Established in the 14th century,
it provided modest homes for the
Beguines, a religious sisterhood.
Nowadays its residents are still
female and it's the best known of
the city's many *hofjes* (almshouses).
In the centre is the **Engelse Kerk**
(English Reformed Church), built

in around 1400 and given over to
Scottish Presbyterians living in the
city in 1607. Also in the courtyard
is a Catholic church, secretly
converted from two houses in 1665
after the banning of open Catholic
worship after the Reformation. And
nearby is one of several entrances
to the **Amsterdam Museum**.

The Spui plays host to many
markets – the most notable being
the book market on Fridays. You
can leave Spui by going up
Kalverstraat, Amsterdam's main
shopping street, or Singel past
Leidsestraat: both routes lead
directly to the **Munttoren** (Mint
Tower) at Muntplein. Right across
from the floating flower market,
this medieval tower was once the
western corner of Regulierspoort,
a gate in the city wall in the 1480s.
The Munttoren is prettiest when
it's floodlit at night, but daytime
visitors may enjoy hearing its
carillon ringing out at noon.

From here, walk down Nieuwe
Doelenstraat past the newly
revamped Hôtel de l'Europe
(a mock-up of which featured
in Hitchcock's *Foreign*
Correspondent). This street also
connects with scenic Staalstraat,
which is the city's most popular
film location, having appeared
in The Diary of Anne Frank and
Amsterdamned. Walk up here and
you'll end up in Waterlooplein.

Sights & museums

Amsterdam Museum

Kalverstraat 92/Sint Luciensteeg
27 (523 1822, www.amsterdam
museum.nl). Tram 1, 2, 4, 5, 9, 14,
16, 24, 25. **Open** 10am-5pm daily.
Admission €10; free-€7.50 reductions;
MK. **No credit cards. Map** p64 C5 **60**
Recently rebranded from its previous
incarnation as the Amsterdam Historical
Museum, the city's municipal museum
really does Amsterdam's rich history

justice, with both artefacts and high-tech flourishes. Built on the site of a 1414 convent, the museum's current home dates from the 17th century, and is itself a delight. The exhibits meanders through Amsterdam's past, charting the city's rise from a fishing village to Ecstasy capital. Expect archaeological artefacts (including recent finds from the dig of the NZ-lijn underground, see box p68), works of art (by the likes of Ferdinand Bol and Jacob Corneliszoon) and plenty of quirkier displays: bike enthusiasts might want to cruise the city streets, while lesbian barflies will want to pay homage to Bet van Beeren, late owner of the infamous Café 't Mandje (see p71). Upon exiting, don't miss the Civic Guard Gallery (free admission) that leads to the peaceful Begijnhof and Spui square.

Eating & drinking

Belgique

Gravenstraat 2 (625 1974/ www.cafe-belgique.nl). Tram 1, 2, 4, 5, 9, 14, 16, 24, 25. **Open** 2pm-1am daily. **No credit cards. Bar. Map** p64 C3 ⑥①

One of the city's smallest bars packs in eight beers on tap, plus another 50 bottled brews – mainly from neighbouring Belgium. It sometimes even manages to squeeze in an eight-piece bluegrass band. A gem of a pub, complete with dripping candles and hearty cheer.

Café de Dokter

Rozenboomsteeg 4 (626 4427, www.cafe-de-dokter.nl). Tram 1, 2, 4, 5, 9, 14, 16, 24, 25. **Open** 4pm-1am Tue-Sat. **No credit cards. Bar. Map** p65 D5 ⑥②

Officially the smallest bar in all of Amsterdam, Café de Dokter is also one of the oldest, dishing out the cure for whatever ails you since 1798. Centuries of character and all kinds of charming gewgaws are packed into the compact space, giving it a unique old-world ambience. Whisky figures large (there's a monthly special) and the range of old-

school bar snacks includes the likes of smoked *osseworst* with gherkins.

Dampkring

Handboogstraat 29 (638 0705, www. dampkring-coffeeshop-amsterdam.nl). Tram 1, 2, 4, 5, 9, 14, 16, 24, 25. **Open** 10am-1am daily. **No credit cards. Coffeeshop. Map** p65 D5 ⑥③

Known for its unforgettable (even bearing in mind temporary memory loss) interior, the visual experience of Dampkring's decor makes even a mushroom trip look grey. Moulded walls and sculpted ceilings are covered in deep auburns laced with caramel-coloured wooden panelling, making a perfect location for watching the movie *Ocean's Twelve*. Monitors show the same George Clooney and Brad Pitt scene all day long.

Gartine

Taksteeg 7 (320 4132, www.gartine.nl). Tram 1, 2, 4, 5, 9, 14, 16, 24, 25. **Open** 10am-6pm Wed-Sun. **€€. No credit cards. Slow food. Map** p65 D5 ⑥④

Open only for breakfast, lunch and a full-blown high tea, Gartine is a temple to slow food, served by a friendly couple who grow the veg and herbs just outside of town on days when the place is closed.

Gebroeders Niemeijer

NEW *Nieuwendijk 35 (707 6752, www.gebroedersniemeijer.nl). Tram 1, 2, 5, 13, 17.* **Open** 8.15am-6.30pm Tue-Fri; 8.30am-5pm Sat; 9am-5pm Sun. **Bakery/tearoom. Map** p84 D1 ⑥⑤

In stark contrast to the rest of the dingy shopping street it's found on – very near Centraal Station – Gebr Niemeijer is an artisanal French bakery and bright and light tearoom that serves full lunches and breakfasts. All breads and pastries are made by hand and baked in a stone oven. Sausages come from local producers Brandt en Levie and the cheeses from the city's best French cheese purveyors, Kef (Marnixstraat 192, www.kaasvankef.nl).

The brown stuff

Amsterdam loves coffee.

A new kind of coffeeshop is bubbling up: ones that are serious about the bean and not the weed. Countless independent coffee houses run by caffeinated obsessives have been popping up like stalks in recent years.

The Dutch actually played a fundamental role in establishing the world's coffee market. In 1690 a cheeky Dutchman plucked away the coffee monopoly from the Arabs by smuggling a coffee plant out of Mocha, Yemen. It ended up in Amsterdam's **Hortus Botanicus** (see p110), where descendants of the original Arabica plant still survive. Some clones went off to Dutch colonies in Sumatra, Java, Ceylon (now Sri Lanka) and Suriname where they flourished.

Now, over three centuries later, Amsterdam is regaining its status as a coffee hub. The city is home to the European headquarters of Starbucks. But so far the company's local ambitions have been held in check by the ubiquitous local franchise Coffee Company.

Screaming Beans (www. screamingbeans.nl) was one of the first companies to roast its own beans at its **Original Coffeebar** (Hartenstraat 12). A second location (1e Constantijn Huygensstraat 35) broadened its repertoire to include highly rated French wines and cuisine.

With a relaxed and international vibe, the two locations of **Two For Joy** (Frederiksplein 29/ Haarlemmerdijk 182, www.two forjoy.nl) are more reminiscent of London coffee houses, with their vast array of techniques (filter, drip, AeroPress) and beans.

With its monthly Friday Night Bean Battle, **Espresso Fabriek** (Gosschalklaan 7, www.espressofabriek.nl) forms the focal point of the local barista scene. Folks come together to talk shop and admire the 3-group Kees van der Westen lever machine at the main location at the Westergasfabriek (see box p128).

Located in the heart of the Red Light District, **KOKO Coffee & Design** (Oudezijds Achterburgwal 145) combines coffee with art, design, retro furniture and quality browsing mags. Coffeeheads are also known to head to the Jordaan for the Arabica Yellow Bourbon coffee served at Brazilian lunch café **Cafezinho** (Tweede Laurierdwarsstraat 50, www. cafezinho.moonfruit.com). Indeed, those beans have travelled far – but now they're coming home.

Prik

Spuistraat 109 (320 0002, www.prik amsterdam.nl). Tram 1, 2, 5, 13, 17.
Open 4pm-1am Tue-Thur, Sun; 4pm-3am Fri, Sat. **No credit cards. Bar.**
Map p64 C3 🟦

'Queer or not, Prik is hot!' – so runs the strap line of Prik, a well-known and popular gay haunt that attracts a diverse crowd to enjoy its delicious snacks and groovy sounds.

Supperclub

Jonge Roelensteeg 21 (344 6400, www.supperclub.nl). Tram 1, 2, 5, 13, 16, 17. **Open** 7.30pm-1am Mon-Thur, Sun; 7.30pm-3am Fri, Sat. €€€€.
Global. Map p64 C4 🟦

With its white decor, beds for seating, irreverent food combos and wacky acts, this is an arty joint. At the very least, you'll remember your visit; the owners even have their own cruise ship that trawls the local waters offering diners a more dramatic backdrop.

Tokyo Café

Spui 15 (489 7918, www.tokyocafe.nl). Tram 1, 2, 4, 5, 9, 14, 16, 24, 25.
Open noon-11pm daily. €€€.
Japanese. Map p65 D5 🟦

Thought to be haunted, this Jugendstil monument now hosts its umpteenth eaterie in the form of a Japanese café complete with a lovely terrace, teppanyaki pyrotechnics and a sushi and sashimi bar. High-quality dishes may offer little protection against local ghosts, but will certainly keep hunger at bay.

Tweede Kamer

Heisteeg 6 (422 2236). Tram 1, 2, 5.
Open 10am-1am daily. **No credit cards. Coffeeshop. Map** p64 C5 🟦

Small and intimate, this shop embodies the refined look and feel of vintage jazz sophistication – which makes it an extremely pleasant place to get stoned. Aided by a bakery just around the corner, its spacecakes are delicious and hugely effective. The house hash is

highly regarded, but seating inside is limited; if there's no room, walk over to nearby Dutch Flowers (Singel 387).

D'Vijff Vlieghen

Spuistraat 294-302 (530 4060, www.vijffvlieghen.nl). Tram 1, 2, 5, 13, 17.
Open 6-10pm daily. €€€€. **Dutch.**
Map p64 C5 🟦

The Five Flies achieves a rich Golden Age vibe – it even has a Rembrandt room, with etchings – but also works as a purveyor of kitsch. The food is best described as posh Dutch. Unique, and appropriately pricey.

Vleminckx

Voetboogsteeg 33 (no phone). Tram 1, 2, 5. **Open** 11am-6pm Mon-Sat; noon-5.30pm Sun. €. **No credit cards.**
Chips. Map p65 D5 🟦

Chunky Belgian chips served with your choice of toppings. Opt for the *oorlog* (war) variety: chips with mayo, spicy peanut sauce and onions.

Shopping

Albert Heijn

Nieuwezijds Voorburgwal 226 (421 8344, www.ah.nl). Tram 1, 2, 4, 5, 9, 13, 14, 16, 17, 24, 25. **Open** 8am-10pm daily. **Map** p64 C4 🟦

This massive shop, just behind Dam Square, is one of countless branches of Albert Heijn in Amsterdam. It contains virtually all the household goods you could ever need, though some of the range is unnecessarily expensive.

American Book Center

Spui 12 (625 5537, www.abc.nl). Tram 1, 2, 4, 5, 9, 14, 16, 24, 25. **Open** noon-8pm Mon; 10am-8pm Tue, Wed, Fri, Sat; 10am-9pm Thur; 11am-6.30pm Sun. **Map** p64 C5 🟦

An Amsterdam institution since 1972, the American Book Center stocks a truly enormous selection of English-language books and magazines from the US and UK. Check out the nearby ABC Treehouse (423 0967,

Red light revamp

The big clean-up.

Mata Hari

Are you a loud, obnoxious tourist, prone to trawling through the Red Light District in a drunken pack? If so, your time is running out.

In 2008, a plan was launched to clean up the infamous district. When he presented Project 1012, deputy mayor Lodewijk Asscher cited his inspiration as the clean-up of New York City by mayor Rudy Giuliani.

New legislation has allowed the city to withdraw property rights from those suspected of criminal activities – but then it bought the properties from these owners at what turned out to be hugely inflated prices. In the end, the city's goal is to close 200 of the nearly 500 window brothels and 26 of the 76 coffeeshops. Some windows became 'fashion booths' as part of the 2009 initiative Red Light Fashion (www.redlightfashion amsterdam.nl), in which designers were offered former bordello rooms as affordable studios for a year.

More high-end restaurants such as **Anna** (www.restaurantanna.nl) and bars such as **Mata Hari** (see p72) have already opened. And there are also many smaller businesses being – perhaps grudgingly – accepted into the mix. These include: art and design bookshop **San Serriffe** (Sint Annenstraat 30, www.san-serriffe.com), the kick-ass potter **JC Herman Pottery** (Sint Jansstraat 15, www.jcherman.org) and the cookie, cake and cupcake artistry of **CAKE Amsterdam** (Sint Jansstraat 51, www.cakeamsterdam.com, open by appointment only).

Red Light Radio (Oudekerksplein 22, www.redlightradio.net) is one of the more inspired new uses of old red-light spaces. As local DJs spin live – everything from black metal to dubstep – in a former bordello window, music hounds come from afar to browse the two record shops or simply hang out.

Although most Amsterdammers support the idea of stamping out the criminal elements that run the people- and drug-trafficking associated with the prostitution industry, many say the plans will deter tourism. Others argue the area is already the closest thing to a happy safe-sex Disneyland. The one thing that is certain is that the area is changing.

24-hour party town

You can sleep when you're dead.

Paradiso

For years, locals complained that Amsterdam's nightlife was dead. Local law forced clubs and pubs to close early; underground parties were vigorously monitored and shut down; even finding food in the wee hours proved difficult. It was a crime against all that is cosmopolitan. As a result, many agreed that if you sought bona fide nightlife, Rotterdam was the place to head to. But not everyone was ready to give up and leave.

In 2003, the position of 'night mayor' (*nachtburgemeester*) was introduced – a concept swiped from, yes, Rotterdam. Though not an official government post, successive mayors used it to rebuild bridges of communication between the nocturnal souls and the daytime politicians. One message was clear: people were looking for a late-night scene that was low-key and laid-back, rather than big, bold and trendy. People also wanted longer opening hours.

Finally, in 2013, five drinking and dining zones, with more to follow, were given extended licences. They included the various bars and clubs located on the arts complex

Westergasfabriek (see box p128), the club **Trouw Amsterdam** (see box 116) and three locations in up-and-coming Amsterdam North directly across from Centraal Station. **De Overkant** (www.de overkant.com) is an old industrial complex turned events hall. **Tolhuistuin** (see box p124), which will have bands booked by legendary venue **Paradiso** (see p106), is in the former gardens and pavilion of the abandoned Shell Tower. And the Shell Tower itself will undoubtedly become the true focal point as it is renovated into **Twenty4Amsterdam** (http://twenty4amsterdam.com). When completed in 2016, it will feature a hotel, artist and recording studios, panoramic dining in a rotating restaurant and the highest dancefloor in the city.

These 24-hour licences won't mean these venues will stay open constantly, selling alcohol 24-7. Some may opt for serving breakfast to unwinding clubbers or launching a new exhibition at dawn. But at least the city can finally experiment with the possibilities. So fasten your seatbelts.

Voetboogstraat 11), which regularly hosts various workshops, open-mic nights and author readings.

Artplein Spui

Spui (www.artplein-spui.nl). Tram 1, 2, 4, 5, 9, 14, 16, 24, 25. Open Mar-Dec 10am-6pm Sun. No credit cards. Map p64 C5 ⓴
Oil paintings, acrylics, watercolours, graphic arts, sculpture, ceramics and jewellery are found at this small open-air (and therefore weather-dependent) Sunday arts and crafts market. There's a rotating system for the 60 or so artists, and buskers are usually on hand to lend a little atmosphere. The perfect place to take a Sunday stroll.

Athenaeum Nieuwscentrum

Spui 14-16 (bookshop 514 1460, news centre 514 1470, www.athenaeum.nl). Tram 1, 2, 4, 5, 9, 14, 16, 24, 25. Open Bookshop 11am-6pm Mon; 9.30am-6pm Tue, Wed, Fri, Sat; 9.30am-9pm Thur; noon-5.30pm Sun. News centre 8am-8pm Mon-Wed, Fri, Sat; 8am-9pm Thur; 10am-6pm Sun. Map p64 C5 ⓵
This is where Amsterdam's highbrow literary browsers usually choose to hang out and chew the cultural fat. The Athenaeum Nieuwscentrum, as its name might suggest, also stocks newspapers from around the world, as well as a wide choice of magazines and periodicals in many languages. Continue your browsing at the Friday Book Market on Spui square.

Concrete Image Store

Spuistraat 250 (625 2225, www. concrete.nl). Tram 1, 2, 5. Open noon-7pm Mon-Wed, Fri, Sat; noon-9pm Thur; 1-6pm Sun. Map p64 C5 ⓶
This shop/gallery's concept is more loose and humorous than rigidly concrete: a cross-fertilisation of street fashion, artist-made dolls, limited-edition shoes, and exhibitions of photography and graphic design.

Female & Partners

Spuistraat 100 (620 9152, www. femaleandpartners.nl). Tram 1, 2, 5, 13, 17. Open 1-6.30pm Mon; 11am-6.30pm Tue, Wed, Fri; 11am-9pm Thur; 11am-6pm Sat; 1-6pm Sun. Map p64 B3 ⓷
The opposite of most enterprises here, Female & Partners welcomes women (and, yes, their partners) with an array of erotic clothes, videos and toys.

Hemp Works

Nieuwendijk 13 (421 1762, www. hempworks.nl). Tram 1, 2, 5, 13, 17. Open 11am-7pm daily. Map p64 C1 ⓸
One of the first shops in Amsterdam to sell hemp clothes and products, and now one of the last, Hemp Works has had to diversify into seed sales and fresh truffles (since mushroom sales were banned in 2009) to keep its trade ticking over, and it's also been a notable Cannabis Cup winner for its homegrown strain of the stinky weed.

Marks & Spencer

NEW *Kalverstraat 226 (330 0080, www.marksandspencer.nl). Tram 4, 9, 14, 16, 24, 25. Open 9am-7pm Mon-Wed, Fri, Sat; 9am-9pm Thur; noon-6pm Sun. Map p65 D5* ⓹
After over a decade's absence, the British food and clothing chain returned to Amsterdam in 2013 to a glowing response: the aisles were packed and within hours the sausages and crumpets sold out. It was the talk of the expat town for weeks. So if you have an urge for an Indian ready-meal or just feel it's time for some fresh underwear, look no further!

PGC Hajenius

Rokin 92-96 (623 7494, www. hajenius.com). Tram 4, 9, 14, 16, 24, 25. Open noon-6pm Mon; 9.30am-6pm Tue-Sat; noon-5pm Sun. Map p65 D4 ⓺
With its quaint art deco interior, Hajenius has been a smoker's paradise

(tobacco, that is, not dope) for over 250 years, offering cigarabilia from Dutch pipes to cigars.

Vrolijk

Paleisstraat 135 (623 5142, www. vrolijk.nl). Tram 1, 2, 5, 13, 14, 17. **Open** 11am-6pm Mon; 10am-6pm Tue-Fri; 10am-5pm Sat; 1-5pm Sun. **Map** p64 C4 ⬤

The best selection of rose-tinted international reading – whether fiction or fact – that you'll find in all of Amsterdam, in addition to a wide variety of CDs, DVDs and guides. It has a second-hand section upstairs, and also offers a range of novelty T-shirts, condoms and gifts that are always a big hit with tourists.

Vroom & Dreesmann

Kalverstraat 203 (0900 235 8363 premium rate, www.vroomen dreesmann.nl). Tram 1, 2, 4, 5, 9, 14, 16, 24, 25. **Open** noon-7.30pm Mon; 10am-7.30pm Tue, Wed, Sat; 10am-9pm Thur; 10am-8pm Friday; noon-7pm Sun. **Map** p65 D5 ⬤

V&D means good quality products at prices that are just a small step up from those at the more ubiquitous HEMA. It stocks a staggering array of toiletries, cosmetics, leather goods and watches, clothing and underwear for all the family, kitchen items and travel gear and suitcases.

Waterstones

Kalverstraat 152 (638 3821, www.waterstones.com). Tram 1, 2, 5, 9, 14, 16, 24, 25. **Open** 10am-6pm Mon; 9.30am-6.30pm Tue-Wed, Fri; 9.30am-9pm Thur; 10am-6.30pm Sat; 11am-6pm Sun. **Map** p65 D5 ⬤

A mighty, if familiar, temple to literature in an area that's already bursting with bookshops. Thousands of books, magazines and videos, all of them in English, are on sale in this reputable store, and the children's section is especially delightful.

Nightlife

Bitterzoet

Spuistraat 2 (421 2318, www. bitterzoet.com). Tram 1, 2, 5, 13, 17. **Open** 8pm-3am Mon-Thur, Sun; 8pm-4am Fri, Sat. **No credit cards.** **Map** p64 C2 ⬤

This busy, comfy and casual bar doubles as a venue for theatre and music. Bands and DJs embrace alternative rock, jazz, world and urban sounds, as demonstrated by once-a-monther Blue Note Trip: jazz for hipper literates. Next door, you can indulge in your tastebuds with street foods of the world at sister establishment De Goudvis Club (Spuistraat 4, 737 2121, www.degoudvisclub.nl).

Arts & leisure

Arti et Amicitiae

Rokin 112 (623 3508, www.arti.nl). Tram 4, 9, 14, 16, 24, 25. **Open** noon-6pm Tue-Sun. **No credit cards.** **Map** p65 D5 ⬤

This marvellous old building houses a private artists' society, whose initiates regularly gather in the first-floor bar. Members of the public can climb a Berlage-designed staircase to a large exhibition space, home to some great temporary shows.

Engelse Kerk

Begijnhof 48 (624 9665, www. ercadam.nl). Tram 1, 2, 4, 5, 9, 14, 16, 24, 25. **No credit cards.** **Map** p64 C6 ⬤

Nestled tightly within the idyllic courtyard of Begijnhof, the English Reformed Church has been hosting weekly concerts of baroque and classical music here since the early 1970s. The church's acoustics are genuinely haunting when combined with the sound of the authentic period instruments used in performances. The church's healthy evening schedule also raises funds to help secure the building's future.

The Canals

Singel was the medieval city moat; other canals such as Herengracht, Keizersgracht and Prinsengracht, which follow its line outwards, were part of a Golden Age renewal scheme for the rich. The connecting canals and streets, originally home to workers and artisans, have a number of cafés and shops. Smaller canals worth seeking out include Leliegracht, Bloemgracht, Egelantiersgracht, Spiegelgracht and Brouwersgracht.

We've split venues on the canals into two: the Western Canal Belt (between Singel and Prinsengracht, south of Brouwersgracht, north and west of Leidsegracht); and the Southern Canal Belt (between Singel and Prinsengracht, running from Leidsegracht in a south-easterly direction towards the Amstel).

Western Canal Belt

Prinsengracht is easily the most charming of the canals in this area. Pompous façades have mellowed as shady trees, cosy cafés and some of Amsterdam's more funkadelic houseboats have grown in number here. There's some good shopping to be had; further north, the smart **Nine Streets** linking Prinsengracht, Keizersgracht and Herengracht all offer a diverse mix of speciality shops for browsing.

On your way up Prinsengracht, the tall spire of the 375-year-old **Westerkerk** rears into view. Its tower is the tallest structure in this part of town, and climbing up it affords a good view of the **Anne Frank Huis**, now a museum of remembrance to the life of the aspiring diarist and other victims of the Holocaust. Fans of René Descartes – if you think, you therefore probably are – can pay tribute at his house around the corner at Westermarkt 6; and art-lovers can admire the interiors of the **Bijbels Museum** (Bible Museum) and the photography foundation, **Huis Marseille**.

Anne Frank Huis

Sights & museums

Anne Frank Huis

Prinsengracht 263 (556 7105, 556 7100, www.annefrank.org). Tram 13, 14, 17. **Open** *mid Sept-mid Mar* 9am-7pm Mon-Fri, Sun; 9am-9pm Sat. *Mid Mar-June, early-mid Sept* 9am-9pm Mon-Fri, Sun; 9am-10pm Sat. *July, Aug* 9am-10pm daily. **Admission** €9; free-€4.50 reductions; MK. **Map** p91 A3 ❶

During World War II, the young Jewish diarist Anne Frank and her family hid for two years in rooms behind a bookcase in the back annexe of this 17th-century canal house. On 4 August 1944, they were arrested and transported to concentration camps, where Anne died with sister Margot and their mother. Her father, Otto, survived, and decided that Anne's diary should be published. The rest is history: Anne fulfilled her dream of becoming a bestselling author with tens of millions of copies having since been printed in 70 languages. Today, more than a million visitors a year come to witness these sober unfurnished rooms. A new wing not only tells the story of Anne's family and the persecution of Jews, but also presents the difficulties of fighting discrimination of all types. You can book ahead online to avoid the queues.

Bijbels Museum

Herengracht 366-368 (624 2436, www.bijbelsmuseum.nl). Tram 1, 2, 5. **Open** 10am-5pm Tue-Sat; 11am-5pm Sun. **Admission** €8; free-€4 reductions; MK. **No credit cards.** **Map** p91 C5 ❷

Housed in two handsome Vingboons canal houses, Amsterdam's own Bible Museum aims to illustrate life and worship in biblical times with archaeological finds from Egypt and the Middle East, including a remarkable mummy of an Israeli woman, models of ancient temples and a slideshow. There's also a splendid collection of Bibles, covering several centuries – look out for the rhyming Bible from 1271. A little dry in places, the museum attracts folk who seek to admire the restored houses, splendid Jacob de Wit paintings and the sprawling gardens.

Het Grachtenhuis

Herengracht 386, (421 1656, http://hetgrachtenhuis.nl) Tram 1, 2, 5. **Open** 10am-5pm Tue-Sun. **Admission** €12, free-€6 concessions; MK. **Map** p91 C5 ❸

See box p97.

Homomonument

Westermarkt (www.homomonument.nl). Tram 13, 14, 17. **Map** p91 A3 ❹

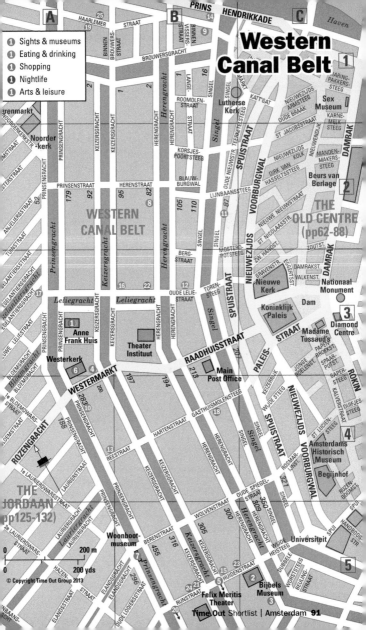

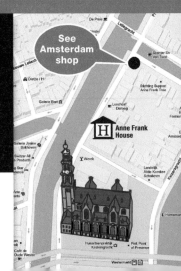

Unveiled in 1987, Karin Daan's three-sectioned pink triangular monument to the memory of persecuted gays and lesbians was a world first. Flowers are often left on it for personal remembrance, especially during gatherings such as World AIDS Day. More information on gay and lesbian life is available from COC Amsterdam (see p183).

Huis Marseille

Keizersgracht 401 (531 8989, www. huismarseille.nl). Tram 1, 2, 5. **Open** 11am-6pm Tue-Sun. **Admission** €5; free-€3 reductions. **No credit cards.** **Map** p91 B5 ⑤
Located in a monumental 17th-century house, this photography foundation hosts the latest from hotshot snappers such as David Goldblatt, Valerie Belin and Jacqueline Hassink – along with legends such as Walker Evans.

Westerkerk

Prinsengracht 277-279 (624 7766, tower 689 2565, www.westerkerk.nl). Tram 13, 14, 17. **Open** 11am-3pm Mon-Sat. *Tower* Apr-June, Sept 10am-5.30pm Mon-Fri; 10am-7.30pm Sat. July, Aug 10am-7.30pm Mon-Sat. Oct 11am-3.30pm Mon-Fri; 10am-5.30pm Sat. **Admission** Free. Tower €7.50. **No credit cards.** **Map** p91 A3 ⑥
Before noise pollution, it was said that if you heard the bells of Westerkerk's tower, dating from 1631, you were in the Jordaan. The tower also offers a great view of this neighbourhood, provided you don't suffer from vertigo: the 85m (278ft) tower sways by 3cm (1.2in) in a good wind. It's thought that Rembrandt is buried in the church itself, although no one is quite sure where: Rembrandt died a pauper, and as a result, he is commemorated inside the building with a simple plaque. If queues for the tower are long, you can also enjoy expansive views at the Zuidertoren or the Ouderkerkstoren, which are both handled by the same office (689 2565). You can also check their concert listings.

Huis Marseille

Woonbootmuseum

Prinsengracht, opposite no. 296 (427 0750, www.houseboatmuseum.nl). Tram 13, 14, 17. **Open** *Jan, Feb, Nov, Dec* 11am-5pm Fri-Sun. *Mar-Oct* 11am-5pm Tue-Sun. Closed last 3wks Jan. **Admission** €3.75; €3 children under 152cm (5ft). **No credit cards.** **Map** p91 B5 ⑦
The Houseboat Museum is not just a museum about houseboats: it's actually located on one. Aside from a few explanatory panels, the *Hendrika Maria* is laid out exactly as a houseboat would be so as to help visitors imagine what it's like to live on the water. It's more spacious than you might expect and does a good job of selling the lifestyle afforded by its unique comforts.

Eating & drinking

't Arendsnest

Herengracht 90 (421 2057, www. arendsnest.nl). Tram 1, 2, 5, 13, 17. **Open** 2pm-midnight Mon-Thur, Sun; 2pm-2am Fri, Sat. **Bar.** **Map** p91 B2 ⑧
A temple to the humble hop, the 'Eagle's Nest', in a lovely old canal house, sells

mainly Dutch beer. Many of the customers are real ale types, but even amateurs will have a ball sampling the wares: 30 beers on draft and more than 120 bottled, from house ale Herengracht 90 to Texelse Skuumkoppe. Also available are 100-plus Dutch jenevers and liquors, and several Dutch whiskies.

Bistrot Neuf
NEW *Haarlemmerstraat 9 (400 3210, http://bistrotneuf.nl).* Tram 1, 2, 4, 5, 9, 13, 17, 24, 25, 26. **Open** noon-11pm daily. **€€€**. **French**. **Map** p91 B1 **❾**
This elegantly designed bistro serves French cuisine alongside an extensive and well thought out wine list, which includes almost 30 reasonably priced by-the-glass options for reds alone. The carte offers classics like *escargots* seeped in parsley and garlic butter, and other European classics with a twist such as a duck in an elderberry sauce. Finish with chocolate fondant or crème brûlée.

Bistro Bij Ons
NEW *Prinsengracht 287 (627 9016, http://bistrobijons.nl).* Tram 13, 14, 17. **Open** 5-10.30pm Wed-Sun. **€€€**. **Dutch**. **Map** p91 A4 **❿**

In the shadow of the Westerkerk, two archetypal Amsterdam hostesses serve typical Dutch fare (think vegetable soup with meatballs, grandma's traditional *stamppot* mash and warm apple pie) in a canal house restaurant with a living room vibe and watery views. A fun night out at a friendly price.

Greenwoods
Singel 103 (623 7071, http://greenwoods.eu). Tram 1, 2, 5, 13, 14, 17. **Open** 9.30am-6pm Mon-Thur; 9.30am-7pm Fri-Sun. **Tearoom**. **Map** p91 B2 **⓫**
Service at this teashop is friendly but can be on the slow side. Everything is freshly made, though, so forgive the staff: cakes, scones and muffins are baked daily on the premises. From 'quick' breakfast (two scrambled eggs with chives served with toast) and organic yoghurt and muesli to eggs florentine and full English, Greenwoods covers all bases.

Grey Area
Oude Leliestraat 2 (420 4301, www.greyarea.nl). Tram 1, 2, 5, 13, 14, 17. **Open** noon-8pm daily. **No credit cards**. **Coffeeshop**. **Map** p91 B3 **⓬**

Greenwoods

Run by two blokes living the modern American dream: running a stellar Amsterdam coffee shop, which offers some of the best weed and hash on the planet (try the Bubble Gum or Grey Mist Crystals). Also on offer are large glass bongs, a vapouriser and free refills of organic coffee. The owners are highly affable and often more baked than the patrons: sometimes they stay in bed and miss the noon opening time.

Hartenkaas

Reestraat 19 (626 5271, www. hartenkaas.nl). Tram 1, 2, 5. **Open** 9am-4pm daily. **No credit cards. Takeaway sandwiches. Map** p91 A4 ⑬
This takeaway shop rates its sandwiches as the best in the city and, putting cockiness aside, the claim is close to the truth. A mere €4.80 and an ability to make a choice from dozens of different toppings and tasty combinations is all that you need for a hearty lunch in between patrolling the Nine Streets shopping area.

Kobalt

Singel 2a (320 1559, www.cafekobalt.nl). Tram 1, 2, 4, 5, 9, 13, 17, 24, 25, 26. **Open** 8am-1am Mon-Thur, Sun; 8am-3am Fri, Sat. **Bar. Map** p91 B1 ⑭
This rather sophisticated bar near Centraal Station is a great way to beat the train delay blues. It has free Wi-Fi, round-the-clock food from breakfast to tapas to dinner, and any drink that you can name, from ristretto to champagne. DJs spin Friday nights, while Sunday afternoons are dedicated to slinky live jazz shows.

De Pels

Huidenstraat 25 (622 9037). Tram 1, 2, 5. **Open** 10am-1am Mon-Thur, Sun; 10am-3am Fri, Sat. **No credit cards. Bar. Map** p91 B5 ⑮
The Nine Streets are littered with characterful bars, and this one is a lovely old-style, tobacco-stained example that has an intellectual bent. In fact, De Pels

can justifiably claim a prime spot in Amsterdam's literary and political legacy: writers, journalists and social activists often meet at this erstwhile Provo hangout to chew the fat (the Provos were a 1960s counterculture movement). It's a nice spot in which to relax, even if you aren't feeling in a cerebral mood.

Da Portare Via

Leliegracht 34 (no phone, www.da portarevia.nl). Tram 1, 2, 5, 13, 14, 17. **Open** 5-10pm daily. **No credit cards. €. Italian. Map** p91 B3 ⑯
This restaurant ties with Yam-Yam (see p129) for the best pizza in town contest. That's thanks to a very hot wood-fuelled oven, which pumps out crusty thin crusts in the best Italian style. You can only buy takeaway pizza, but there are plenty of canal-side benches nearby. Or ask politely at the neighbouring old bar Brandon (Keizersgracht 157) if it's OK to eat there. Check the website for the three other locations.

Twee Zwaantjes

Prinsengracht 114 (625 2729, www.detweezwaantjes.nl). Tram 1, 2, 3, 5, 10, 13, 14, 17. **Open** 3pm-1am Mon-Thur, Sun; 3pm-3am Fri, Sat. **No credit cards. Bar. Map** p91 A3 ⑰
Oom-pah-pah, oom-pah-pah – that's how it goes at this salt-of-the-earth bar when the locals are out in force and the air is filled with song. It's relatively quiet during the week, but weekends are real singalong, swingalong affairs, with revellers booming out tear-jerking tunes on such subjects as love, sweat and the Westerkerk.

Shopping

Brilmuseum/Brillenwinkel

Gasthuismolensteeg 7 (421 2414, www.brilmuseumamsterdam.nl). Tram 1, 2, 5, 13, 14, 17. **Open** 11.30am-5.30pm Wed-Fri; 11.30am-5pm Sat. **No credit cards. Map** p91 B4 ⑬

Officially, this 'shop' is an opticians' museum, but don't let that put you off. The fascinating exhibition features glasses throughout the ages, and if you like what you see then most of the pairs on display are also for sale.

Caulils

NEW *Haarlemmerstraat 115 (412 0027, www.caulils.com). Tram 1, 2, 4, 5, 9, 13, 17, 24, 25, 26.* **Open** 11am-7pm Mon-Fri; 9am-6pm Sat. **Map** p91 A1 ⑲

Fervent Amsterdam foodies rate this delicatessen as the best shop in the country. The selection is impeccably honest and refined and specialises in raw milk cheeses, exotic cold cuts and singular wines. Stock your picnic basket with class.

Frozen Fountain

Prinsengracht 645 (622 9375, www.frozenfountain.nl). Tram 1, 2, 5, 7, 10. **Open** 1-6pm Mon; 10am-6pm Tue-Fri; 10am-5pm Sat; 1-5pm Sun. **Map** p91 B5 ⑳

The 'Froz' is a paradise for lovers of contemporary furniture. It stays abreast of innovative Dutch designers like Piet Hein Eek, the maestro of furniture made from recycled wood; it also sells stuff by the non-Dutch likes of Marc Newsom, plus modern classics and photography.

De Kaaskamer

Runstraat 7 (623 3483, www. kaaskamer.nl). Tram 1, 2, 5. **Open** noon-6pm Mon; 9am-6pm Tue-Fri; 9am-5pm Sat; noon-5pm Sun. **No credit cards.** **Map** p91 B5 ㉑

De Kaaskamer offers more than 200 varieties of domestic and imported cheeses, plus pâtés, olives, pastas and wines. Have fun quizzing shop staff on the cheese varieties and related trivia: they seriously know their stuff.

The Otherist

NEW *Leliegracht 6 (320 0420, www.otherist.com). Tram 7, 13, 14,*

17. **Open** noon-5pm Mon, Sun; 11am-6.30pm Wed-Sat. **Map** p91 B3 ㉒

Out to stock your own cabinet of curiosities or looking for the ultimately unique gift? The Otherist is one-stop-shopping heaven: glass eyeballs, 'vegan mini-skulls', butterfly specimens, amulets, hip flasks, medical posters and an ever-changing selection of other curiosa and handmade design items. Indeed, very 'other'.

Pâtisserie Pompadour

Huidenstraat 12 (623 9554). Tram 1, 2, 5. **Open** 10am-6pm Mon-Fri; 9am-5pm Sat; noon-6pm Sun. **Map** p91 B5 ㉓

This fabulous *bonbonnerie* and tearoom with a delightful 18th-century interior imported all the way from Antwerp is likely to satisfy your sweet tooth, regardless of your age.

Skins Cosmetics

Runstraat 11 (528 6922, www. skins.nl). Tram 1, 2, 5. **Open** 11am-7pm Mon; 10am-7pm Tue-Wed, Fri; 10am-8pm Thur; 10am-6pm Sat; noon-5pm Sun. **Map** p91 B5 ㉔

The flagship store for Amsterdam's own skincare and fragrance empire has expanded its stock, and now includes cosmetics by REN, Dr Brandt, Leonor Greyl, Aveda and Le Labo. There's plenty of room in which to try the stock and enjoy beauty services. Drop in to sample some of the skincare line RéviVe, or perfumes from some of today's greatest noses.

Vlaamsch Broodhuis

Haarlemmerstraat 108 (528 6430, www.vlaamschbroodhuys.nl). Tram 3/bus 18, 21, 22. **Open** 8am-6.30pm Mon-Fri; 8am-6pm Sat; 9.30am-6pm Sun.* **No credit cards.** **Map** p91 A1 ㉕

The name might be a bit of a mouthful, but it's worth a visit to wrap your gums around the tasty sourdough breads, fine French pastries and fresh salads, among other treats.

Canal city

Amsterdam's waterways are the city's hallmark.

Het Grachtenhuis

God may have made the water, but you can thank man for the canals… Keeping the sea and surrounding bog at bay are Amsterdam's 165 *grachten* (canals). Crossed by 1,400 bridges, they stretch for 75.5 kilometres (47 miles) around the city, and are, on average, three metres deep. Some 10,000 bicycles, 100 million litres (22 million gallons) of sludge and 50 corpses (usually of drunk tramps) are dredged from their murky depths every year.

The major canals and their radial streets are where the real city exists. What they lack in sights, they make up for with places for scenic coffee slurping, quirky shopping, aimless walks and meditative gable-gazing.

From 1600 to 1650, during Amsterdam's Golden Age, the city's population ballooned fourfold, and it was obliged to expand once again. Construction began on the most elegant of the major canals, the *grachtengordel* (girdle of canals or canal ring) circling the city centre. Herengracht (Lords' Canal) was where many of the ruling

assembly had their homes. So that there would be no misunderstanding about status, Herengracht was followed further out by Keizersgracht (Emperors' Canal) and Prinsengracht (Princes' Canal). Immigrants, meanwhile, were housed outside the Canal Ring, in the Jordaan. An excellent new museum, **Het Grachtenhuis** (see p90), presents the history of this urban engineering wonder.

The Canal Ring's waterways provide an attractive border between the tourist-laden centre and the gentler, artier, more 'local' outskirts. When the Canal Ring was declared a UNESCO World Heritage Site in 2010, some worried that Amsterdam would become like Venice, where tourism seems to dominate any local character. However, the vibe remains the same – whether it's during Gay Pride (see box p102), the classical Canal Festival or the perhaps ill-advised annual Amsterdam City Swim. Indeed: while the waters look pretty, you're best advised to wash in your hotel room. Otherwise, just enjoy the views…

Southern Canal Belt

The Southern Canal Belt boasts two main squares: **Rembrandtplein** and **Leidseplein**. Rembrandtplein is unashamedly tacky and home to an array of tasteless (and worse) establishments, ranging from traditional striptease parlours to even seedier modern peepshow joints and nondescript cafés. Fortunately, there are a few exceptions to the prevailing tawdriness – new designer grand café Van Rijn (no.17), its upstairs neighbour De Kroon (no.17-I), the art deco building Schiller (no.26), and HL de Jong's eclectic masterpiece, the **Pathé Tuschinski** on Reguliersbreestraat.

Also nearby is the floating flower market at the southern tip of Singel (the **Bloemenmarkt**). From the square, walk south along shopping and eating street Utrechtsestraat, or explore the picturesque Reguliersgracht and Amstelveld. Whichever you choose, you'll cross **Herengracht** on your journey. As the first canal to be dug in the glory days, Herengracht attracted the richest of merchants and is still home to the most overblown houses on any of Amsterdam's canals.

The stretch built between Leidsestraat and Vijzelstraat is known as the **Golden Bend**. Around the corner on Vijzelstraat is the highly imposing city archive, the **Stadsarchief**. Nearby on Keizersgracht is the cutting-edge photography museum **Foam**.

Leidseplein, reached via the chaotic Leidsestraat or the gallery-filled strip of Nieuwe Spiegelstraat, is the tourist centre of Amsterdam. It's packed with merrymakers drinking at cafés and is dominated by the **Stadsschouwburg**, along with many cinemas, theatres and restaurants. Max Euweplein offers a route to the greener pastures of **Vondelpark**.

Sights & museums

Foam (Photography Museum Amsterdam)

Keizersgracht 609 (551 6500, www.foam.org). Tram 16, 24, 25. **Open** 10am-6pm Mon-Wed, Sat, Sun; 10am-9pm Thur, Fri. **Admission** €8.75; free-€6 reductions; MK. **Map** p99 C2 ㉙

Located in a tightly renovated canal house, this excellent museum displays a comprehensive array of talent, from rising stars (Ryan McGinley, Viviane Sassen) to big names (Weegee, Diane Arbus, Malick Sidibé and Richard Avedon). The café's food is a feast for the eyes as well as the stomach. Also check the website for exhibitions and pop-ups in other locations.

Museum Geelvinck

Keizersgracht 633 (715 5900, www.geelvinck.nl). Tram 16, 24, 25. **Open** 11am-5pm Mon, Wed-Sun. **Admission** €6; free-€4 reductions; MK. **Map** p99 C2 ㉗

This 17th-century canal house has four 'style rooms', including a library and a 'Red Room' from the Louis XV period, along with paintings by Pieter de Ring (1615-60). Despite such grandeur, the highlight is the back garden, which hosts regular concerts of chamber music.

Museum Willet-Holthuysen

Herengracht 605 (523 1822, www. willetholthuysen.nl). Tram 4, 9, 14. **Open** 10am-5pm Mon-Fri; 11am-5pm Sat, Sun. **Admission** €8; free-€6 reductions; MK. **Map** p99 D1 ㉘

Upon the death in 1889 of Abraham Willet-Holthuysen, remembered as 'the Oscar Wilde of Amsterdam', his wife Sandrina Louisa, a hermaphrodite, left this 17th-century house and contents to the city on the condition that it was preserved and opened as a museum. The family found inspiration for the sumptuous decor in the neoclassical Louis XVI style. The French-style

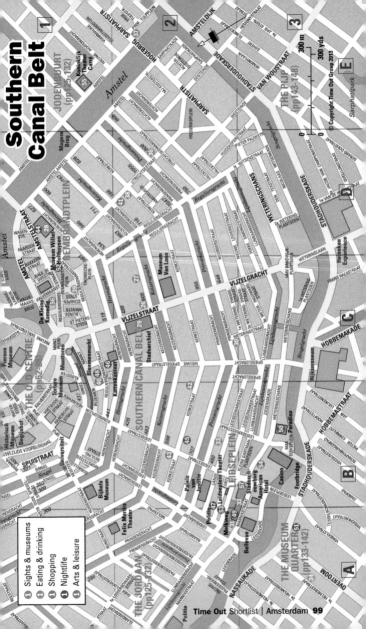

Southern Canal Belt

Legend
- 1 Sights & museums
- 1 Eating & drinking
- 1 Shopping
- 1 Nightlife
- 1 Arts & leisure

THE OLD CENTRE

JODENBUURT (pp125-132)

THE PIJP (pp143-148)

THE JORDAAN (pp125-132)

THE MUSEUM QUARTER (pp133-142)

© Copyright Time Out Group 2013

hop on hop off
canal cruise amsterdam

garden has a sundial, while the house contains an impressive collection of rare objets d'art, glassware, silver, china and paintings – including one of a shocked-looking Abraham (painted on his honeymoon perhaps?).

Stadsarchief Amsterdam

Vijzelstraat 32 (251 1511, www. stadsarchief.amsterdam.nl). Tram 16, 24, 25. **Open** 10am-5pm Tue-Fri; noon-5pm Sat, Sun. **Admission** free. **Map** p99 C2 ㉙

The city archives are located in an epic and decorative 1926 building that's shrouded in esoteric mists. The highly ornate structure was designed by architect KPC de Bazel, a practitioner of theosophy – a spiritualist movement founded by the chain-smoking Madame Blavatsky. The grand centrepiece is the Treasure Room. As embellished as Tutankhamun's tomb, it displays the prizes of the collection. The archives also host exhibitions and film screenings. There is an excellent bookstore for browsing and a café.

Eating & drinking

Buffet van Odette

NEW *Prinsengracht 598 (423 6034, http://buffet-amsterdam.nl). Tram 16, 24, 25.* **Open** 10am-9pm Mon, Wed-Sun. **€€**. **Café**. **Map** p99 C2 ㉚

A café that's so healthy it's sinful. Service is slow, but the wait is worth it once you receive your hearty sandwiches, made with bread from local bakery Hartog, salads and a range of home-made cakes. For breakfast, opt for a croissant with butter or jam, an omelette or both when ordering a 'complete' breakfast – coffee or tea and juice included.

Cafe Weber

Marnixstraat 397 (622 99 10, http:// weberlux.nl). Tram 1, 2, 5, 6, 7. **Open** 7pm-3am Mon-Thur, Sun; 7pm-4am Fri, Sat. **No credit cards**. **Bar**. **Map** p99 A2 ㉛

Along with neighbour Café Lux (Marnixstraat 403), Café Weber offer a similar formula to art students and the terminally hip who gather at these temples to pre-clubbing pleasure. There is no food or frippery, just booze, DJ-spun music and a party vibe.

Eat at Jo's

Marnixstraat 409 (638 3336). Tram 1, 2, 5, 7, 10. **Open** noon-9pm Wed-Sun. **€€**. **No credit cards**. **Global**. **Map** p99 B3 ㉜

Each day brings a new menu to this cheap and eminently cheerful international kitchen, where fish, meat and vegetarian dishes are all lovingly prepared. Star spotters take note: whichever act is booked to play at the Melkweg may well eat here beforehand.

Everything on a Stick

NEW *Prinsengracht 478 (626 1874, www.eoas.nl). Tram 1, 2, 5, 7, 10.* **Open** 6-11pm Tue, Wed, Sun; 6pm-midnight Thur-Sat. **€€€**. **International**. **Map** p99 B2 ㉝

This surprisingly chic and streamlined restaurant channelling a *Snakes on a Plane* kind of literalism – everything is, indeed, skewered – offers two hours of unlimited eating for a set price of around €25. Think juicy chicken teriyaki, tempura vegetables and crunchy sesame-encrusted tuna, all washed down with inventive cocktails.

Hap Hmm

1e Helmerstraat 33 (618 1884, www. hap-hmm.nl). Tram 1, 3, 12. **Open** 4.30-8pm Mon-Fri. **€**. **No credit cards**. **Dutch**. **Map** p99 A3 ㉞

Hungry but hard up? You need some of the Dutch grandma cooking served in this living room-style canteen, which packs famished punters with meat and potatoes for around €6.

Lion Noir

NEW *Reguliersdwarsstraat 28 (627 6603, www.lionnoir.nl). Tram 1, 2, 5.* **Open** 11.30am-1am Mon-Thur;

Canal Pride

Celebrations take to the water.

Amsterdam Pride is one of the lesbian and gay community's most anticipated events, and the extended weekend of crowded street parties, parades, vibrant drinking and noise draws thousands of spectators – straight and gay – all eager to join in the fun.

The festival offers thousands of distractions, running through the A to Z of camp: androgyny, barely clad boys, flirtation, leather, lesbians, Muscle Marys, PVC poseurs, and, of course, theatrics.

Then there's the dizzying array of affiliated events: street parties, more street parties, singalongs, performances and Pride's apex, the awesome Saturday afternoon Canal Parade – the world's only floating Pride parade – which winds along the Prinsengracht and Amstel canals between 2pm and 6pm. Canals spill over with topless mermaids, half-naked firefighters, Marilyn Monroe lookalikes, pole dancers, Spartans, beauty queens, angels and wrestlers, all waving from a hundred different boats. The Canal Parade draws thousands of onlookers – estimates put them at 350,000, and no one's clocking who's gay and who ain't. Then there are the politicians who hitch rides on these boats in the name of scoring canal-cred points.

As time goes on, everyone puts in overtime on drinking, cultivating the following day's hangover – although they've probably drunk their way through the first one, as the partying technically starts on Friday. Or Thursday, depending on who you ask. Either way, the closing party takes place during the late Sunday afternoon on Rembrandtplein, with a huge number of Dutch artists, DJs and those with enough energy left to sign off the celebration.

Like Queen's Day (or King's Day as it's now called, see box p42), when the city's population doubles and crams into the centre for the event, Pride is terribly Amsterdam. It's relaxed, tolerant, positive, outrageous and definitely worth celebrating.

11.30am-3am Fri; 6pm-3am Sat; 6pm-1am Sun. €€€. **French**. Map p99 C1 ⑤
The emphasis at Lion Noir is firmly on meat, with hearty but not overwhelming mains including top-notch foie gras and duck breast medallions. Inside, the velvet and artfully aged leather furnishings, stuffed birds and (yes) ornamental dog skeletons, combined with the genetically perfect staff, give the impression of an Abercrombie & Fitch shoot curated by Tim Burton.

Onder de Ooievaar

Utrechtsestraat 119 (624 6836, www. onderdeooievaar.nl). Tram 4. **Open** 10am-1am Mon-Thur, Sun; 10am-3am Fri, Sat. **Bar**. Map p99 D2 ㊱
Here you have a highly uncomplicated venue for an evening's carousing among a mixed bunch of trendsetters, locals and a few visitors. Highlights include 't IJ beer on tap, the downstairs pool table and the rather lovely Prinsengracht-side terrace.

La Rive

InterContinental, Prof Tulpplein 1 (520 3264, www.restaurantlarive.com). Tram 7, 10/Metro Weesperplein. **Open** 6.30-10pm Tue-Sat; 5-9pm Sun. €€€€. **French**. Map p99 E2 ㊲
While Hôtel de l'Europe has Excelsior, it's La Rive at the InterContinental that overshadows the rest of the high-end competition, and it does so by serving chef Roger Rassin's superb French cuisine without excessive formality. Perfect for stylish dining, if money is no object. The kitchen also supplies treats to the hotel's new cocktail bar.

Tempo Doeloe

Utrechtsestraat 75 (625 6718, www.tempodoeloerestaurant.nl). Tram 4. **Open** 6-11.30pm daily. €€€€. **Indonesian**. Map p99 D2 ㊳
This cosy and rather classy Indonesian restaurant is widely thought to be one of the city's best and spiciest purveyors of rice table. Phone ahead, because reservations are required.

Lion Noir

Van Dobben

Korte Reguliersdwarsstraat 5-9 (624 4200, www.eetsalonvandobben.com). Tram 4, 9, 14, 16, 24, 25. **Open** 10am-9pm Mon-Wed; 10am-1am Thur; 10am-2am Fri, Sat; 11.30am-8pm Sun. €. **No credit cards**. **Dutch**. Map p99 C1 ㊴
A *kroket* is the national version of a croquette: a mélange of meat and potato with a crusty, deep-fried skin best served on a bun with lots of hot mustard – and this 1945-vintage latenighter is the uncontested champion.

Shopping

Bloemenmarkt (Flower Market)

Singel, between Muntplein & Koningsplein (no phone). Tram 1, 2, 4, 5, 9, 14, 16, 24, 25. **Open**

AMSTERDAM BY AREA

9am-6pm Mon-Sat; 11am-5.30pm Sun.
No credit cards. Map p99 B1/C1 ⓴

This fascinating collage of colour is the world's only floating flower market, with 15 florists and garden shops (although many also hawk rather cheesy souvenirs these days), all permanently ensconced on barges along the southern side of Singel. Plants and flowers usually last well.

Concerto

Utrechtsestraat 52-60 (623 5228, www.concerto.nl). Tram 4, 9, 14. **Open** 10am-6pm Mon-Wed, Fri, Sat; 10am-9pm Thur; noon-6pm Sun. **Map** p99 D2 ⓴

Head here for classic Bach recordings, obscure Beatles items or that beloved old Diana Ross album that got nicked at your party. Anything really. There are also second-hand 45s and new releases at very reasonable prices.

Lambiek

Kerkstraat 132 (626 7543, www.lambiek.net). Tram 1, 2, 5, 16, 24, 25. **Open** 11am-6pm Mon-Fri; 11am-5pm Sat; 1-5pm Sun. **Map** p99 B2 ⓴

Lambiek, founded in 1968, claims to be the world's oldest comic shop. It stocks thousands of books from all around the world; its on-site cartoonists' gallery hosts exhibitions every two months.

Rituals

Leidsestraat 62 (625 2311, www.rituals.com). Tram 1, 2, 4, 5, 9, 14, 16, 24, 25. **Open** noon-6pm Mon; 10am-6pm Tue, Wed, Fri, Sat; 10am-9pm Thur; noon-6pm Sun. **Map** p99 B2 ⓴

We all have to brush our teeth and do the washing up, and this franchise has a host of gizmos to ritualise those daily grinds. And just as it cleverly mixes products for body and home, this outlet ingeniously integrates with the minimal space it occupies. The original flagship store is nearby: Kalverstraat 73.

Nightlife

Air

Amstelstraat 16 (820 0670, www.air.nl). Tram 4, 9, 14. **Open** 11pm-4am Thur; 11pm-5am Fri, Sat. Varies Wed, Sun. **Admission** €10-€20. **No credit cards. Map** p99 D1 ⓴

Like a phoenix from the ashes, a new large club has risen in the same location as now-defunct Club It. Musically, the offerings at Air are varied. Thursdays have tended to be creative, arty, interactive nights where house prevails, whereas Fridays usually have a more techno feel. On Saturday things tend to be a bit more commercial, and on Sunday the evening kicks off early. For a yet more mammoth clubbing experience check out the opportunities at Escape (Rembrandtplein 11, www.escape.nl).

Church

Kerkstraat 52 (no phone, www.clubchurch.nl). Tram 1, 2, 5. **Open** 8pm-1am Tue, Wed; 10pm-4am Thur; 10pm-5am Fri, Sat; 4pm-4am Sun. **No credit cards. Map** p99 B2 ⓴

The more extrovert side of the gay spectrum is well represented by cruising club Church. It has it all plus more: a bar with Greek-style columns, a stage perfect for drag-queen acts, a great sound and light system and various dark, dark chambers… Cheeky theme nights abound.

Club NYX

NEW *Reguliersdwarsstraat 42 (www.clubnyx.nl). Tram 1, 2, 5.* **Open** 11pm-5am Fri-Sat (open until 9am 1st Sat of mth). **No credit cards. Map** p99 C1 ⓴

Gay Street stalwart Club Exit has been reborn as mixed Club NYX, named for the Greek goddess of the night. Three floors offer distinct vibes – making liberal use of graffiti, glitter and concrete – and a toilet DJ keeps the party going while you wash your hands at a giant pink phallus.

Seriously hot stuff

Indonesian food is an Amsterdam staple.

Blue Pepper

In 1949, with Indonesian Independence, 180,000 residents of the 'Spice Islands' came to the Netherlands to become Dutch citizens. As a result, even the ubiquitous snack bar serves bastardised versions of the islands' cuisine. A reflection of its origins – an archipelago of more than 1,000 islands, with historical influences from Chinese and Arabian to Portuguese and Dutch – Indonesian food actually mingles many cuisines, with an almost infinite range of dishes.

To add to the confusion are the many Chin-Indo-Suri eateries, serving cheap dishes that have incorporated the tastes of the many immigrants from China (often via Indonesia) and Surinam, another former colony whose Caribbean style is usually represented by the pancake-like roti. The usual dishes at these places are satay, *gado-gado* (steamed veg and boiled egg served with rice and satay sauce), *nasi goreng* (onion fried rice with meat, veg and egg) and *bami goreng* (the same but with noodles).

While they're particularly great for the budget-challenged, all visitors should go to an authentic purveyor of *rijsttafel* (rice-table), a Dutch construct that nobly tries to include as many dishes as possible.

In days gone by, you had to go to the Hague for the most authentic Indonesian restaurants, but Amsterdam now offers ample choices of its own. There's **Tempo Doeloe** (p103), quirky **Coffee & Jazz** (Utrechtsestraat 113, 624 58 51) and the haute **Blue Pepper** (Nassaukade 366, 489 7039, www.restaurantbluepepper.com). Then there are the stellar cheap takeaways, such as **Toko Joyce** (Nieuwmarkt 38, 427 9091, www.tokojoyce.nl) and **Sari Citra** (Ferdinand Bolstraat 52, 675 4102) in De Pijp.

Top of the pile, however, is the relatively expensive **Blauw** (Amstelveenseweg 158-160, 675 5000, www.restaurantblauw.nl). The restaurant serves authentic dishes, but with a twist. Its rice-table is a feast for the well-walleted gods.

Club NYX p104

Jimmy Woo's

Korte Leidsedwarsstraat 18 (626 3150, www.jimmywoo.com). Tram 1, 2, 5, 7, 10. **Open** 11pm-3am Thur, Sun; 11pm-4am Fri, Sat. **Map** p101 B2 ㊼

Amsterdam has never seen anything quite so luxuriously cosmopolitan as club Jimmy Woo's. Now you too can marvel at the lounge area filled with a mixture of modern and antique furniture, and confirm for yourself the merits of its bootylicious light design and sound system. If you should have problems getting past the doormen, try the equally hip and happening **Chicago Social Club** (Leidseplein 12, 530 7303, www.chicagosocialclub.nl) next door.

Ludwig

Reguliersdwarsstraat 37 (625 3661, www.barludwig.com). Tram 1, 2, 5. **Open** 6pm-1am Wed-Thur, Sun; 6pm-3am Fri-Sat. **Map** p99 C1 ㊸

Insanely hip at times, Ludwig is named for the bi-curious Bavarian 'fairytale king' famed for his wild parties. It serves his legacy well, from the industrial kitsch interior to the gay-friendly (but not exclusive) party programme. Design bells and whistles come courtesy of illustrator Parra and his crew.

Melkweg

Lijnbaansgracht 234A (531 8181, www.melkweg.nl). Tram 1, 2, 5, 7, 10. **Open** hours vary. **No credit cards.** **Map** p101 A2 ㊾

A former dairy (the name translates as 'Milky Way'), Melkweg has become world renowned as an always innovative home to live music in a host of different styles. The complex also hosts a theatre, cinema, art gallery and café, and holds weekend club nights to boot, so it's no surprise it's a key cultural beacon in the centre of the city. Membership is compulsory for anyone wanting in.

Paradiso

Weteringschans 6-8 (626 4521, www.paradiso.nl). Tram 1, 2, 5, 7, 10. **Open** hours vary. **No credit cards.** **Map** p101 B3 ㊿

A cornerstone of the live music and clubbing scene and a name synonymous with quality shows across the city, this former church is in such demand that it often hosts several events in one day. The main hall has a rare sense of grandeur, with multiple balconies and stained-glass windows peering down upon performers and DJs. The smaller hall upstairs is a fantastic place to catch new talent. Membership is compulsory.

People's Place

NEW *Stadhouderskade 5 (589 5467, peoplesplaceamsterdam.nl). Tram 1, 2, 5, 7, 10.* **Open** hours vary. **Map** p99 A3 ❺❶

Named after Tommy Hilfiger's first store, above whose European headquarters it's located, People's Place is a hotspot for the coolest music – programmed by the legendary Paradiso – for audiences of 20 to 650, in a flexible space with a superlative sound system.

Studio 80

Rembrandtplein 17 (521 8333, www.studio-80.nl). Tram 4, 9, 14, 16, 24, 25. **Open** 10pm-4am Wed, Thur, Sun; 11pm-5am Fri, Sat. **Map** p99 C1 ❺❷

In the midst of Rembrandt Square lurks this former radio studio, a black pearl waiting to be discovered. Dirty disco, deep electronic acid and hip hop are shown off at very reasonable prices. The city's progressive techno and minimal crowds find their home here and bring their record bag- and synthesiser-wielding friends from across Europe.

Sugar Factory

Lijnbaansgracht 238 (626 5006, www.sugarfactory.nl). Tram 1, 2, 5, 7, 10. **Open** hours vary. **No credit cards. Map** p99 A2/B2 ❺❸

This 'night theatre' club has found its niche as a place where performance meets clubbing, catering to both beat freaks and more traditional music fans at the same time. Resident DJs and club nights liven up the week, while WickedJazzSounds livens up Sunday evenings with musicians and even bona fide big bands. Occasional alternative rock bands are booked here by the Melkweg.

Arts & leisure

De Balie

Kleine Gartmanplantsoen 10 (553 5151, www.debalie.nl). Tram 1, 2, 5, 7, 10. **No credit cards. Map** p99 B3 ❺❹

Theatre, new media, photography, cinema and literary events sit alongside lectures, debates and discussions about social and political issues at this influential centre for the local intelligentsia. Throw in a café and you've got healthy food for both mind and body.

Koninklijk Theater Carré

Amstel 115-125 (0900 252 5255 premium rate, www.theatercarre.nl). Tram 7, 10/Metro Weesperplein. **Map** p99 E1 ❺❺

It's the dream of many to perform in this glamorous space, formerly home to a circus and recently refurbished in a very grand style. The Carré hosts some of the best Dutch cabaret artists and touring operas, as well as the odd big music name. If mainstream musical theatre is more your thing, this is the place to come to see and hear Dutch versions of popular blockbusters like *Grease* and *Cats*.

Pathé Tuschinski

Reguliersbreestraat 26-34 (http://www.pathe.nl). Tram 4, 9, 16, 24, 25. **Map** p99 C1 ❺❻

This exuberant cinema is named after Abraham Tuschinski, the city's most illustrious cinematic entrepreneur, who built the structure in 1921 as a 'world theatre palace'. The interior and exterior are a striking combination of rococo, art deco and Jugendstil.

Stadsschouwburg

Leidseplein 26 (624 2311, www.ssba.nl). Tram 1, 2, 5, 7, 10. **Map** p99 B3 ❺❼

The Stadsschouwburg (or Municipal Theatre) is an impressive 19th-century building. The original stage is a traditional horseshoe shape, it seats 950 and is known for its progressive theatre and opera productions – occasional contemporary music performances are also held. The new 'black box' Rabozaal connects with the Melkweg and occasionally the doors are thrown open for indoor festivals.

AMSTERDAM BY AREA

Dappermarkt p115

Jodenbuurt, the Plantage & the Oost

Located south-east of the Red Light District, Amsterdam's Jewish quarter is a mix of old and new architectural styles. Enter the skull-adorned gateway between Sint Antoniesbreestraat 130 and 132 to discover the **Zuiderkerk** (South Church); for the more energetic, its tower affords a great view of the whole neighbourhood.

Crossing the bridge at the end of Sint Antoniesbreestraat leads you to the **Rembrandthuis**. Immediately before this, however, are steps to the Waterlooplein flea market, dominated by the **Stadhuis-Muziektheater** (the City Hall-Music Theatre). Also close at hand are the **Joods Historisch Museum** (Jewish Historical Museum) and **Hermitage Amsterdam** (see box p112).

Stroll down Muiderstraat to discover the largely residential Plantage area that lies south-east of Mr Visserplein. The attractive Plantage Middenlaan winds past the **Hortus Botanicus**, near the **Verzetsmuseum** (Museum of Dutch Resistance), and along the edge of **Artis**, the city zoo, towards the **Tropenmuseum**.

Jews began to settle here more than 200 years ago, and the area soon grew with the investment of 19th-century diamond money. The Plantage is still wealthy, with graceful buildings and tree-lined streets, although its charm has sadly faded somewhat.

Further south of Mauritskade is **Amsterdam Oost** (East), with its green heart Oosterpark and multicultural vibe.

Sights & museums

Artis
Plantage Kerklaan 38-40 (0900 278 4796, www.artis.nl). Tram 9, 10, 14.

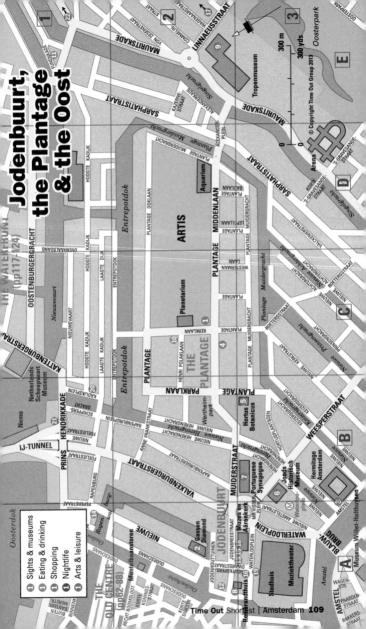

Jodenbuurt, the Plantage & the Oost

THE WATERFRONT (pp117-124)

Legend
- ① Sights & museums
- ① Eating & drinking
- ① Shopping
- ① Nightlife
- ① Arts & leisure

Oosterpark

Tropenmuseum

Arena

ARTIS

- Aquarium
- Planetarium

THE PLANTAGE

Wertheim-park

- Hortus Botanicus ⑤

Netherlands Scheepvaart Museum

Nemo

IJ-TUNNEL

Montelbaanstoren

THE OLD CENTRE (pp62-88)

JODENBUURT

- Gassan Diamonds ②
- Portuguese Synagogue ⑦
- Joods Historisch Museum ⑥
- Mozes en Aäronkerk

Hermitage Amsterdam

Stadhuis

Muziektheater

Museum Willet-Holthuysen

WATERLOOPLEIN

BLAUW BRUG

© Copyright Time Out Group 2013

300 m
300 yds

Open *Summer* 9am-6pm daily. *Winter* 9am-5pm daily. **Admission** €17.95; free-€16.95 reductions. **No credit cards**. Map p109 C2 ❶

The first zoo in mainland Europe (and the third oldest in the world) provides a relaxing day out for children and adults. It's so chilled here that if the weather is nice, staff allow you to stay beyond closing time. On special occasions they even give gay animal tours – those pink flamingos are outlandish! Along with the usual animals of all sexual orientations, Artis has an indoor 'rainforest' for nocturnal creatures and a 120-year-old aquarium with a simulated canal, complete with eels and bike wrecks. Further attractions include a planetarium, a savannah landscape, a geological museum and, for kids, a petting zoo and playgrounds. During the summer months, Saturday opening hours are extended until sunset and the zoo hosts special concerts, performances and tours.

Gassan Diamond

Nieuwe Uilenburgerstraat 173-175, (622 5333, www.gassan.com). Tram 9, 14/Metro Waterlooplein. **Open** 9am-5pm daily. **Admission** free. **Map** p109 A2 ❷

Amsterdam is famous for its diamond trade, something it owes largely to the Jewish population in and around the Jodenbuurt area. Of the many sparkler shops, Gassan Diamond comes out on top, with an epic building that once housed 357 polishing machines, at a time when it was the biggest diamond processing plant in the world. Get in the mood by upgrading from the free tour to one that includes champagne. But remember: falling in love with a piece of compressed carbon is the easy part – working out how you're going to pay for it may prove to be a little more tricky.

Hermitage Amsterdam

Nieuwe Herengracht 14 (530 8755, www.hermitage.nl). Tram 4, 9/

Metro Waterlooplein. **Open** 10am-5pm daily. **Admission** €15; free-€12 reductions; MK. **No credit cards**. Map p109 B3 ❸

See box p112.

Hollandsche Schouwburg

Plantage Middenlaan 24 (531 0340, www.hollandscheschouwburg.nl). Tram 9, 10, 14. **Open** 11am-5pm daily. **Admission** (includes Joods Historisch Museum & Portugese Synagoge) €12; free-€6 reductions; MK. **Map** p109 C2 ❹

In 1942, this grand theatre became a main point of assembly for some 70,000 of the city's Jews, before they were taken to the transit camp at Westerbork. It's now a monument with a small but poignant exhibition, and a memorial hall displaying 6,700 surnames by way of tribute to the 104,000 Dutch Jews who were exterminated. The façade is intact, with most of the inner structure removed to make way for a memorial.

Hortus Botanicus

Plantage Middenlaan 2A (625 9021, www.dehortus.nl). Tram 9, 14/Metro Waterlooplein. **Open** 10am-5pm daily. **Admission** €8.50; free-€4.50 reductions. **No credit cards**. Map p109 B3 ❺

The Hortus has formed a peaceful oasis here since 1682, although it was originally set up more than 50 years earlier when East India Company ships brought back tropical plants and seeds to supply doctors with medicinal herbs (as well as coffee plant cuttings, one specimen of which continued to Brazil to kickstart the South American coffee industry). Other highlights include a massive water lily, the Victoria Amazonica, which blooms only once a year, and the oldest potted plant in the world, a 300-year-old cycad – on display in the 1912 palm greenhouse. Other conservatories maintain desert, tropical and subtropical climates, and a butterfly greenhouse sets hearts of all ages aflutter.

Artis

Joods Historisch Museum (Jewish Historical Museum)

Nieuwe Amstelstraat 1 (531 0310, www. jhm.nl). Tram 9, 14/Metro Waterlooplein. **Open** 11am-5pm daily. **Admission** (includes Hollandsche Schouwburg & Portuguese Synagogue) €12; free-€6 reductions; MK. **Map** p109 B3 ⑥

Housed since 1987 in four synagogues in the old Jewish quarter, the Jewish Historical Museum is full of religious items, photographs and paintings detailing the history of religious practice and Dutch Jewish culture in the Netherlands. There's a real sense of warmth here, especially in the interactive children's section. Temporary exhibitions are also generally excellent, such as the recent Superheroes and Schlemiels, exploring the relationship between comics and Jewish memory.

Portuguese Synagogue

Mr Visserplein 3 (624 5351, guided tours 531 0380, www.portuguese synagogue.nl). Tram 9, 14/Metro Waterlooplein. **Open** *Apr-Oct* 10am-5pm Mon-Thur, Sun; 10am-4pm Fri. *Nov-Mar* 10am-4pm Mon-Thur,

Sun; 10am-2pm Fri. **Admission** (includes Joods Historisch Museum & Hollandsche Schouwburg) €12; free-€6 reductions; MK. **No credit cards**. **Map** p109 B3 ⑦

Architect Elias Bouwman's mammoth synagogue, one of the largest in the world and reputedly inspired by the Temple of Solomon, was inaugurated in 1675. It's built on wooden piles and surrounded by smaller annexes (offices, archives, the rabbinate and one of the world's oldest libraries). A renovation in the 1950s restored the synagogue to its original form, and interesting tours of its noteworthy interior can be organised through the Jewish Historical Museum. The synagogue holds occasional concerts and candlelit events.

Rembrandthuis

Jodenbreestraat 4 (520 0400, www.rembrandthuis.nl). Tram 9, 14/Metro Waterlooplein. **Open** 10am-6pm daily. **Admission** (incl audio guide) €12.50; free-€10 reductions; MK. **Map** p109 A2/3 ⑧

You can't help but admire the skill and effort with which craftsmen have tried to re-create this house, purchased by Rembrandt in 1639 for 13,000 florins

The Hermitage on the Amstel

From Russia with love.

Hermitage Amsterdam

An outpost of St Petersburg's Hermitage museum (see p110) opened in Amsterdam in 2009 with a star-studded, 30-hour ceremony, attended by Queen Beatrix and the Russian president, Dmitri Medvedev.

Set in a former 19th-century hospital complete with 17th-century courtyard, the building has two vast exhibition spaces, a concert hall and a restaurant. The museum mounts two exhibitions a year, borrowing items from the three million-strong collection of its prestigious Russian parent. The Hermitage's riches owe much to the collecting obsession of Peter the Great (1672-1725), who came to Amsterdam to learn shipbuilding and the art of building on waterlogged ground – he applied his knowledge of the latter to his pet project, St Petersburg.

Peter befriended local doctor Frederik Ruysch, perhaps the greatest ever anatomist and preserver of body parts and mutants in jars. Ruysch enjoyed constructing ghoulish collages with gall and kidney stones piled up into landscapes, dried veins woven into lush shrubberies and testicles crafted into pottery. The scenes were animated with dancing foetus skeletons. After kissing the head of a preserved baby, Peter paid Ruysch 30,000 florins for the lot. (Much of it is still on display in St Petersburg's Kunstkammer collection.)

Some of Peter's other prized souvenirs – including Rembrandts – came for a visit in 2013 during an exhibition dedicated to the great man. Other exhibitions have included 'Gauguin, Bonnard, Denis', 'Greek Gold' and 'Nicolas and Alexandra'.

(about €6,000), a massive sum at the time, and occupied by the artist until bankruptcy forced him to move out in 1656. The presentation is, however, dry and unengaging on the whole. Nagging at you is the knowledge that this isn't actually Rembrandt's house, but rather a mock-up of it – which lends an unreal air that's alleviated only when guest artists are allowed to use the studio. There's a remarkable collection of Rembrandt's etchings, which show him at his most experimental, but if it's his paintings you're after, head to the Rijksmuseum (see p134).

Tropenmuseum

Linnaeusstraat 2 (568 8200, www. tropenmuseum.nl). Tram 9, 10, 14/ bus 22. **Open** 10am-5pm Tue-Sun. **Admission** €12; free-€8 reductions; MK. **Map** p109 E2 ❸
Visitors to this handsome building get a vivid glimpse of daily life in the tropical and subtropical parts of the world (a strange evolution for a museum originally erected in the 1920s to glorify Dutch colonialism), including Southeast Asia, Oceania, West Asia, North Africa, Latin America and a series called Man and Environment. Exhibits – from religious items and jewellery to washing powder and vehicles – are divided by region. Temporary exhibitions, covering everything from Bollywood to Death, are consistently excellent. Subsidy cuts might threaten its operation beyond 2013.

Verzetsmuseum (Museum of Dutch Resistance)

Plantage Kerklaan 61 (620 2535, www.verzetsmuseum.org). Tram 9, 14/Metro Waterlooplein. **Open** 11am-5pm Mon, Sat, Sun; 10am-5pm Tue-Fri. **Admission** €8; free-€4.50 reductions; MK. **No credit cards**. **Map** p109 C2 ❿
The Verzetsmuseum tells the story of the Dutch Resistance during World War II through a series of artefacts: false ID papers, clandestine printing presses and illegal newspapers, spy gadgets and an authentic secret door behind which Jews hid. The exhibits explain how the Dutch people survived Nazi occupation, and are interspersed with moving personal testimonies. Regular temporary exhibitions investigate wartime themes and modern-day forms of oppression, and there's a small research room too. Although a lot of the information is in Dutch, staff are often only too happy to give you a personalised tour.

Eating & drinking

Beter & Leuk

NEW *Eerste Oosterparkstraat 91 (767 0029, http://beterenleuk.nl). Tram 3.* **Open** 10am-5pm Mon-Sat. €€.
Breakfast/café.
A breakfast/lunch/boutique café with a mission summed up in its name, which means 'Better and Nice'. Decoration is minimal and the kitchen open. The menu is scribbled on a blackboard and on brown paper; it offers eggs, croissants, home-made granola, sandwiches, salads and cakes.

Brouwerij 't IJ

Funenkade 7 (320 1786, www. brouwerijhetij.nl). Tram 10, 14/ bus 22. **Open** 2-8pm daily. **Bar**.
Map p109 E1 ⓫
The famous tasting house at the base of the Gooyer windmill, where wares from award-winning local brewery 't IJ can be sampled. Inside is bare (still retaining the look of the municipal baths it once was) and seating is minimal, so if the weather permits, plonk down on the pavement and picnic tables outside. Its standard range of tipples is available for sampling behind the bar, from pale Plzen to the darker, head-poppingly strong brew known as Columbus.

Café de Sluyswacht

Jodenbreestraat 1 (625 7611, www.sluyswacht.nl). Tram 9, 14/

Metro Nieuwmarkt. **Open** 12.30pm-1am Mon-Thur; 12.30pm-3am Fri, Sat; 12.30am-7pm Sun. **Bar. Map** p109 A2 **⑫**

Listing precariously, the building housing this wooden-framed bar has been around since 1695, when it began life as a lock-keeper's cottage. Inside it's snuggly and warm, whereas outside you can enjoy great views of Oude Schans. A spacious smoking area attracts a lot of students.

Coffee Gallery

Jodenbreestraat 94 (06 5352 5929, www.thecoffeegallery.nl). Tram 9, 14/Metro Waterlooplein. **Open** 9am-3pm daily. **Café. No credit cards. Map** p109 A3 **⑬**

Remember *Seinfeld*'s Soup Nazi? Well, meet the Coffee Nazi. There are many rules to follow here and the proprietor will not be rushed, but it's all a small price to pay for some of the city's best coffee – and for just over a euro for a takeaway cappuccino. You might want to samples his sandwiches, pastas and risottos too.

Distilleerderij 't Nieuwe Diep

NEW *Flevopark 13 (465 0222, www.nwediep.nl). Tram 7, 14.* **Open** *Apr-Aug* 3-8pm Tue-Fri; noon-8pm Sat, Sun. *Sept-Mar* Hours vary & are shorter. **Bar. No credit cards.**

In the far east in the utterly pleasant Flevopark, this old mill now houses a distillery and tasting house pumping out Dutch jenever and other more fruity liquors. With views over a pond from the picnic tables and a nice selection of bar snacks, this is the perfect place to stop and smell the flowers – and the fermenting grains.

Hiding In Plain Sight

NEW *Rapenburg 18 (06 2529 3620, http://hpsamsterdam.com).* **Open** 6pm-1am Mon-Thur; 6pm-3am Fri, Sat. **Cocktail bar. Map** p109 A12 **⑭**

The house speciality here, the Walking Dead, is appropriately named, given the bar's proximity to the ancient docks where sailors would snog their goodbyes before embarking on treacherous journeys. Based on the potent Zombie, the secret recipe is served (and then set on fire) in a giant glass skull. Bar-imposed limit: one per night. Reservations recommended.

Rijsel

NEW *Marcusstraat 52b (463 2142, www.rijsel.com). Tram 3.* **Open** 6-10pm Tue-Sat. **Dutch/French. €€.**

Housed in a former *huishoudschool*, one of the domestic science institutions blamed for the decline of the Dutch kitchen, you'll find frugality only in terms of the decor at Rijsel. The busy dining room is overseen by an amiable staff. Specialising in the best rotisserie chicken, like, ever, Rijsel has established itself as another delicious reason to head east.

Woo Bros.

NEW *Jodenbreestraat 144 (428 0488, www.restaurantwoobros.nl). Tram 9, 14/Metro Waterlooplein.* **Open** 4pm-1am Tue-Sun. **€€. Asian. Map** p109 A3 **⑮**

With a small-dish menu that seamlessly switches from Japanese to Indonesian cuisine, from Vietnamese to Thai, to Chinese and back (Peking duck sits alongside sushi), Woo Bros. offers fusion perfection in quirky low-lit surroundings.

Shopping

290 Square Meters

Houtkopersdwarsstraat 3 (419 2525, www.290sqm.com). Tram 9, 14/Metro Waterlooplein. **Open** 11am-6pm Tue-Sat. **Map** p109 A3 **⑯**

In its former space, this shop/agency/gallery's claim to fame was that it was the first place in the world where people could purchase customised Nikes. Now, in a more spacious former bank

16cc

vault, it offers a spectrum of goods, ranging from bikes to fashion, limited-edition books and scents.

Dappermarkt

Dapperstraat (694 7495, www. dappermarkt.nl). Tram 3, 7, 9. **Open** 9am-5pm Mon-Sat. **No credit cards. Map** p109 E2 ⑰
Voted best market of the Netherlands, Dappermarkt is a locals' market, which means that prices don't rise along with visitor numbers. It sells all the usual market fodder, plus plenty of cheap clothes.

Out of the Closet

NEW *Jodenbreestraat 158 (620 6261, www.outofthecloset.org/nl). Tram 9, 14/Metro Waterlooplein.* **Open** 10am-7pm Mon-Sat; noon-6pm Sun. **Map** p109 A3 ⑱
This is the first outlet in Europe of the American chain of thrift shops that donates all its profits to providing healthcare for AIDS patients. Besides clothes and furniture, the store offers free advice and HIV tests.

Waterlooplein

Waterlooplein (552 4074, www. waterloopleinmarkt.nl). Tram 9, 14/ Metro Waterlooplein. **Open** 9am-5pm Mon-Sat. **No credit cards. Map** p109 A3 ⑲
Amsterdam's top bazaar is basically a huge flea market with the added attraction of loads of brand new clothes stalls (although gear can be a bit pricey and, at many stalls, a bit naff). Bargains can be found too, but they may be well hidden.

Nightlife

See box p116.

Arts & leisure

16cc

NEW *Kadijksplein 16 (627 0236, www.16cc.nl). Bus 22, 42, 43.* **Open** 4pm-1am Mon-Thur; 4pm-2am Fri-Sat; 1.30pm-1am Sun. **Map** p109 B1 ⑳
On a scenic square with many other eating and drinking options, 16cc is a small café – with small cinema – that

Eastern block parties

Breaking news: the city's hottest clubs make themselves at home in two former newspaper offices in Amsterdam Oost. The **Volkskrantgebouw** (Wibautstraat 150, www.volkskrantgebouw.nl) was launched in 2007 as a new concept, with a group negotiating to take over the building and fill it with creative industries and artists. The icing on the cake is **Canvas op de 7e** (www.canvasopde7e.nl, open 11am-1am Mon-Thur, Sun, noon-3am Fri-Sat), a rooftop café/restaurant/cocktail bar/club on the seventh floor, with a stellar view of the city. Plans are now in the works to convert half the studios into a hotel.

However, Canvas is merely the lo-fi little brother when compared to the operation across the street. **Trouw Amsterdam** (Wibautstraat 131, 463 7788, www.trouwamsterdam.nl, times vary) continues to combine progressive programming and good food – plus it's just been given a 24-hour licence; the bad news is that this is only valid until 1 January 2015 when it has to find a new location. The restaurant (open 5.30-11pm Tue-Sat) serves Mediterranean food in an industrial garden setting.

For a real foodie treat, go next door to the equally temporary – and acclaimed – **Baut** (Wibautstraat 125, 465 9260, www.bautamsterdam.nl) under chef Michiel van der Eerde, a true culinary globetrotter.

looms large with its quirky programming of alternative film, photography, music, art and literature.

ARCAM

Prins Hendrikkade 600 (620 4878, www.arcam.nl). Bus 22, 42, 43. **Open** 1-5pm Tue-Sat. **Admission** free. **No credit cards. Map** p109 B1 ㉑
The gallery here at the Architecture Centrum Amsterdam is focused on the promotion of Dutch contemporary architecture – from the early 20th-century creations of the world-famous Amsterdam School to more modern designs. There are forums, lectures, its own series of architecture books and exhibitions in its fresh 'silver snail' location.

Mediamatic Factory

NEW *VOC-kade 10 (638 9901, www.mediamatic.net). Tram 10, 26.* **Open** hours vary.
Located near urban beach Roest (see p120), Mediamatic Factory is a project/exhibition space and hydroponic farm in an old warehouse space. It's one of the homes of an inspired multimedia organisation that seems to pop up everywhere with ever-more inspired projects. Here, it's busy with a *tosti* factory where staff plan to create and sell grilled-cheese sandwiches from scratch. As of time of publication, the grain was growing and the cow was mooing. Who knows what it will get up to next…

Studio K

Timorplein 62 (ticket office 692 0422, restaurant 06 4803 7582, www.studio-k.nu). Tram 14/bus 43. **Open** 11am-1am Mon-Thur, Sun; 11am-3am Fri, Sat. **Map** p109 E1 ㉒
This former school turned cultural centre is, like cinema mother ship Kriterion (www.kriterion.nl), entirely run by students. The place has a distinctive festival feeling as it puts on films, theatre, debates, exhibitions, comedy, club nights, and food and drink. A treat.

Nederlands Scheepvaartmuseum

The Waterfront

Amsterdam's historic wealth owes a lot to the waterfront: it was here that goods were unloaded, weighed and prepared for storage in the local warehouses. At one time, the harbour and its arterial canals formed a harmonious whole with the city itself. But a drop in commerce slowly destabilised this unity and the building of **Centraal Station** in the late 19th century served as a final marker of a change in the city's mindset. This neo-Gothic monument to modernity blocked both the city's view of the harbour and its own past.

Directly south, the Schreierstoren or 'Weeping Tower' is the most interesting relic of Amsterdam's medieval city wall, built in 1847. It was from this point, on 4 April 1609, that English explorer Henry Hudson departed in search of shorter trade routes to the Far East, and when he failed, explored what was to become the Hudson River, laying the foundation for Dutch colonisation of the region and the establishment of New Amsterdam, later Manhattan.

An eye-opener along the way is the Renzo Piano-designed **NEMO**, a science museum whose green structure dominates the horizon. It dwarfs the silver shell-shaped ARCAM architecture gallery as well as the nautically inclined **Nederlands Scheepvaartmuseum**.

One recent success story is the opening of the largest library in the country, the **Openbare Bibliotheek Amsterdam**, just east of Centraal Station.

Equally ambitious is its neighbour, the city's **Music Conservatory**. De Architekten Cie designed the building according to Japanese *engawa* principles: this means that the hallways are placed on the exterior to maximise soundproofing for the practising students, yet create a transparency that invites passers-by in to listen to a recital.

Sights & museums

NEMO

Oosterdok 2 (531 3233, www.e-nemo.nl). Bus 32, 33, 34, 35. **Open** 10am-5pm Tue-Sun. **Admission** €13.50. **Map** p119 B3 ❶

NEMO has built a strong reputation as a child-friendly science museum. It eschews exhibits in favour of hands-on trickery, gadgetry and tomfoolery: you can play DNA detective games, blow mega soap bubbles or explode things in a 'wonderlab'. Its Teen Facts exhibition explores puberty and beyond, and the changes and challenges of teenage life. On top of that, Renzo Piano's mammoth structure (resembling the reflection of the tunnel below) is a true eye pleaser. The outdoor café, DEK5, is a lovely place in which to while away an afternoon reading and relaxing. The roof is generally freely accessible whenever it's not a virtual beach or hosting a jazz festival.

Openbare Bibliotheek Amsterdam

Oosterdokskade 143 (523 0900, www.oba.nl). Metro Centraal Station. **Open** 10am-10pm daily. **Map** p119 A3 ❷

One of Europe's largest public libraries, this city landmark was designed by Jo Coenen. The building treats arriving visitors to a soaring view up to its seventh floor café-restaurant, which, in turn, offers a spectacular view over Amsterdam. With walnut floors and white walls and shelves, the interior is eminently low key; colour comes from the books and the mixed bag of people using the free Wi-Fi – or the study 'pods' (which make an ideal spot for a nap). The place was much praised when it opened, though critics have posed pertinent questions such as, 'Um, where exactly are all the books?'.

Nederlands Scheepvaartmuseum

Kattenburgerplein 1 (523 2222, www.hetscheepvaartmuseum.nl). Bus 22, 48. **Open** 9am-5pm daily. **Admission** €15; free-€7.50 reductions. **Map** p119 B3 ❸

Dutch nautical history is rich and fascinating. So it follows that the country should boast one of the world's finest nautical museums – second only, say experts, to London's National Maritime Museum; this is especially true since the museum reopened in 2011 after renovations. Marvel at the models, portraits, boat parts and other naval ephemera in a wonderful building built 350 years ago by Daniel Stalpaert. Don't miss the huge replica Dutch East India Company ship at the rear.

Openbare Bibliotheek Amsterdam

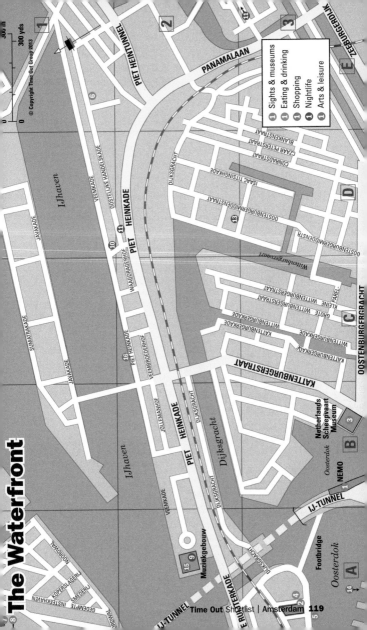

The Waterfront

Sights & museums
Eating & drinking
Shopping
Nightlife
Arts & leisure

PANAMALAAN

PIET HEINTUNNEL

OOSTELIJKE HANDELSKADE

VEEMKADE

PIET HEINKADE

WAAGDRAGERHOF

SUMATRAKADE

JAVAKADE

JAVAKADE

NOORDWAL

GEDEMPTE INSTEEKHAVEN

KOPERSLAGERIJ

IJhaven

IJhaven

DIJKSGRACHT

ISAAC TITSINGHKADE

CONRADSTRAAT
CZAAR PETERSTRAAT
BLANKENSTRAAT

OOSTENBURGERMIDDENSTRAAT

OOSTENBURGERMIDDENSTRA

Wittenburgervaart

GROTE WITTENBURGERSTRAAT
KLEINE WITTENBURGERSTRAAT

KATTENBURGERKADE
WITTENBURGERKADE
KATTENBURGERKADE

OOSTENBURGERGRACHT

KATTENBURGERSTRAAT

Netherlands
Scheepvaart
Museum

Oosterdok

NEMO

IJ-TUNNEL

Oosterdok

PIET HEINKADE

DIJKSGRACHT

VEEMKADE

PIET HEINKADE

VEEMBROEDERHOF

JOLLEMANHOF

DIJKSGRACHT

DIJKSGRACHT

Muziekgebouw

IJ-TUNNEL

E RUITERKADE

Footbridge

ZEEBURGERDIJK

© Copyright Time Out Group 2013

300 m
300 yds

Boats and beaches

Blijburg
Muiderlaan 1001 (416 0330, www.blijburg.nl). Tram 26/bus 359. **Open** varies. **€€€. No credit cards. Global.**
Blijburg beach features bands, barbecues, club nights and festivals. Located on the new artificial islands of residential IJburg, its location shifts – like sand – every few years as construction progresses.

Hannekes Boom
NEW *Dijksgracht 4 (419 9820, www.hannekesboom.nl). Tram 26.* **Open** 11am-1am Mon-Thur, Sun; 11am-3am Fri, Sat. **€€.**
With a huge terrace and its own dock with a harbour view, the Boom rates as one of the city's hottest hotspots – even though it's made of scrap lumber. It's also a treat for kids.

Pont 13
NEW *Haparandadam 50 (770 2722, www.pont13.nl). Bus 22, 48.* **Open** 6-10pm daily. **€€€. Global.**
Simple, hearty fare with genuine flair is served on revamped ferry in the western havens.

REM eiland
NEW *Haparandadam 45-2 (688 5501, www.remeiland.com). Bus 22, 48.* **Open** noon-10pm daily. **€€€. Modern European.**
A former pirate TV station in the North Sea, this ocean platform has been reborn as a restaurant with compelling views that blend well with the *fruits de mer.* It's fine for a drink too.

&Samhoud Places
NEW *Oosterdokskade 5 (260 2094, http://samhoudplaces.com). Metro Centraal Station.* **Open** noon-1am Tue-Fri; 3pm-1am Sat. **€€€.**
International. Map p119 A3 ❹
Moshik Roth is the chef whose cheekily extravagant dishes made his first restaurant in Overveen one of haute Amsterdam's out-of-town favourites. His collaboration with 'caring capitalist' Salem Samhoud brings some rather more 'accessible' options, including a divine eco-friendly tomato burger.

Barco
NEW *Oosterdokskade 10 (626 9383, cafebarco.nl). Metro Centraal Station.* **Open** 4pm-1am Mon-Thur; 4pm-3am Fri, Sat; 4pm-midnight Sun. **Bar.** Map p119 A3 ❺
A repurposed canal barge moored at Oosterdok across from the public library, Barco has 360-degree city views, affordable food, live bands performing in the hold and a sun-trap terrace. That's just about everything, in other words.

Koffiehuis KHL
Oostelijke Handelskade 44 (779 1575, www.khl.nl). Tram 10, 26/bus 359. **Open** noon-10pm Tue-Sun. **No credit cards. Bar.** Map p119 E1 ❻
The beautiful, light-flooded interior harks back to the days in the early 20th century when the Koffiehaus was a canteen serving staff of the Royal Holland Lloyd shipping line. Now it's a café-cum-meeting space. There's art on the walls and regular live music for lifting spirits.

Nevy
Westerdoksdijk 40 (334 6409, www. nevy.nl). Tram 3/bus 48. **Open** noon-1am Mon-Thur, Sun; noon-2am Fri, Sat. **€€€. Bar/Seafood.** Map p119 A1 ❼
Nevy is a sophisticated dining spot, with sleek lines, burnished marbles, a voluptuous lounge and a view over the IJ. The Michelin-starred chef Robert

&Samhoud Places

Kranenborg acts as an adviser to the kitchen, which dedicates itself to cooking wonderful seafood dishes. What more could you ask for?

Open!

Westerdoksplein 20 (620 1010, www.open.nl). Tram 3/bus 18, 21, 22, 48. **Open** noon-10pm Mon-Fri; 5-10pm Sat. **€€. Dutch/French.** **Map** p119 A1 ❽

Set in a box of steel and glass atop an unused railway bridge, this is one of the more attractive restaurants in town. Its open kitchen pumps out simple classics for lunch and dinner, all at reasonable prices: try the bavette of beef with salsa verde or the fish of the day.

Nightlife

Bimhuis

Piet Heinkade 3 (788 2188, www. bimhuis.nl). Tram 25, 26. **Open** most shows start 8.30pm. **Map** p119 A2 ❾

The name Bimhuis is familiar to jazz fans worldwide, and musicians queue up for a chance to grace its stage. Even its move to a bizarre glass box jutting out of the Muziekgebouw complex (see p122) hasn't tarnished its reputation.

Café Pakhuis Wilhelmina

Veemkade 576 (419 3368, www.cafe pakhuiswilhelmina.nl). Tram 10, 26/

bus 42. **Open** Thur-Sat; hours vary. Sometimes open other days. **No credit cards. Map** p119 D1 ❿

Wilhelmina is still often overlooked by casual clubbers. Is it the club's IJ location? The absence of bouncers? Or the cheap bottles of beer? Regardless, don't miss it if your heart lies with today's leftfield music scene.

Harbour Club

`NEW` *Cruquiusweg 67 (767 0421, http:// theharbourclub.nl). Tram 10.* **Open** 11am-1am Mon-Thur, Sun; 11am-2am Fri-Sat. **Map** p119 E2 ⓫

Thousands of square metres of pure glam, in a former wine warehouse on the IJ front, Harbour Club brings Ibiza to these rainy climes. Featuring a restaurant with sushi room, bar, club and terrace, this is *the* place to see and be seen.

Panama

Oostelijke Handelskade 4 (311 8686, www.panama.nl). Tram 10, 26. **Open** 9pm-3am Thur, Sun; 10pm-4am Fri, Sat. **Map** p119 D2 ⓬

Club Panama overlooks the IJ in one of the city's most booming areas. Most nights mix up Dutch DJ talent with big international names, such as Ferry Corsten and Sander Kleinenberg. In the same location, you can eat at the Spanish market-styled Mercat (344 6424, http://mercat.nl).

Roest

NEW *Jacob Bontiusplaats, entry via Czar Peterstraat 213 (308 0283, http://amsterdamroest.nl). Tram 10, 26/bus 43.* **Open** 4pm-1am Wed, Thur; 4pm-3am Fri; 11am-3am Sat; 11am-1am Sun. **Map** p119 D2 ⑬

Named 'rust' as a nod to its industrial setting, Roest has plenty of graffiti-covered cred, and its line-up of theme parties – not to mention the expansive terrace and beach – keep even the most fickle trendsters entertained.

Arts & leisure

De Appel

NEW *Prins Hendrikkade 142 (625 5651, deappel.nl). Metro Centraal Station.* **Open** noon-8pm Tue-Sat, noon-6pm Sun. **Admission** €7; free-€4.50 reductions; MK. **Map** p119 A3 ⑭

The De Appel arts centre prefers not to comply with labels like 'museum' or 'gallery'. Its glamorous premises showcase highly conceptual work by promising artists such as Allard van Hoorn whose glowing *Skies over Snaefell* installation is a treat in itself. Don't miss the café or the courtyard at the back.

Muziekgebouw

Piet Heinkade 1 (788 2010/tickets 788 2000, www.muziekgebouw.nl). Tram 25, 26. **Map** p119 A2 ⑮

Designed by the internationally renowned Danish architectural practice 3xNielsen, the Muziekgebouw is one of the most innovative musical complexes anywhere in Europe. Never afraid to take risks, the centre's weekly schedule bustles with delights ranging from cutting-edge multimedia works to celebrations of composers from the last 150 years. The Muziekgebouw is also home to the Klankspeeltuin (www.klankspeeltuin.nl), where seven- to 12-year-olds can play with an inspired selection of musical machines, installations and computers.

Pakhuis de Zwijger

Pakhuis de Zwijger, Piet Heinkade 179 (624 6380, www.dezwijger.nl). Tram 25, 26. **Map** p119 C2 ⑯

Welcome to a hip cultural venue. Pakhuis de Zwijger is a former warehouse that has been refitted to house various media organisations. It also hosts a cutting-edge array of events, including readings, workshops and gatherings of the design, new media and creative industries; the place is all about innovation. Particularly inspired are VJ visionaries Beamlab (www.beamlab.nl) as well as street fashion guerrillas Streetlab (www.streetlab.nl). There's also a great IJside café that is open weekdays from 9am to 11pm.

Roest

I want to ride my fietsicle

Restored Bicycles

Fietscafe

Bicycles may be taken for granted, but as 'iron horses that need no feeding' they are functional and proud creatures whose invention has transformed modern life as much as the commercial flight. *Fiets*, as the Dutch call bicycles, have democratised personal movement in an affordable way. Thanks to their mechanical nudity – the artist Saul Steinberg called the bike an 'X-ray of itself' – they are easy to maintain. And did we mention their eco-friendly nature?

The Dutch love the humble bike; they buy 1.5 million annually and then, in Amsterdam alone, steal 150,000 of them. It has been calculated that if the 540,000 bikes in the city were lined up, they would cover the Vondelpark twice. To learn how rich the history of cycling is in Amsterdam pick up a copy of Pete Jordan's obsessively researched and excellently written *In the City of Bikes: The Story of the Amsterdam Cyclist* (2013, Harper Perennial).

The city is full of cycling visionaries. VMX Architect has built a shed for 2,500 bicycles, on concrete piles in a canal just west of Centraal Station. Local squatters have invented 'tall bike jousting', a recreation using bikes made of spare parts and welded together to reach dizzying heights. Perhaps you can convince **Recycled Bicycles** (Spuistraat 84a, www.recycledbicycles.org) to build you one.

Visiting parties may want to hire a Fietscafe (www.fietscafe.nl), a mobile pub, which allows up to 17 people to drink beer and pedal in synchrony – but be warned that you will be despised by locals. And the **Fietsfabriek** (Sarphatistraat 141, www.fietsfabriek.nl) continues its quest to bring cargo bikes to the world. For a trendier tone, check out the stripped-down and minimal street bikes of **Vanmoof** (www.vanmoof.com) or check out the bamboo bikes available from **Restored** (Haarlemmerdijk 3, www.restored.nl).

Amsterdam cyclists are rightfully proud, or perhaps even a little smug, about their rights to the road. So they should be, since bikes play a key role in achieving the long-term sustainability of our planet. Happy pedalling!

AMSTERDAM BY AREA

North has risen

EYE Film Institute

There was a time when Amsterdam North was called the Siberia of the city. Even in centuries past, the land on the other side of that body of water called the IJ was known for being little more than the spot that even the Romans overlooked, and where, in later years, the remains of freshly executed criminals were hung for public display. There was little of interest to draw visitors northwards – except perhaps cycling routes towards such painfully scenic fishing villages as Volendam and Marken.

But this is changing quickly and radically. The **EYE Film Institute** (IJPromenade 1, 589 1400, http://eyefilm.nl) and its cinemas were reincarnated in 2012 in a new building directly across from Centraal Station. You won't miss it: it's white and it looks as if it might take flight. If you still haven't taken the free ferry from behind Centraal Station (it takes

all of three minutes), please do so immediately. The view from the café alone is worth your while. Exhibitions cover such directors as Stanley Kubrick or local hero Johan van der Keuken. Downstairs there are pods in which you can surf through the history of Dutch film. EYE is also the new home for other noble filmic initiatives, such as the KLIK! Animation Festival (www.klikamsterdam.nl).

Just west of EYE, in a pavilion next to the Shell Tower, and the surrounding grounds, **Tolhuistuin** (www.tolhuistuin.nl) is a new cultural destination opening in early 2014 for festivals, exhibitions, dining and music.

A 15-minute ferry ride west from behind Centraal Station will take you to **NDSM** (TT Neveritaweg 15, 330 5480, www.ndsm.nl). This former shipping yard has been transformed into a huge creative space with artists' studios, galleries and a slew of singular spaces. Its wonderful post-apocalyptic vibe is ideal for parties, concerts and wacky theatre festivals like Over het IJ (see p43). It has a surrounding district of student container dwellings, a 'clean energy' exhibition, a restaurant/café (www.noorderlichtcafe.nl), and an urban beach hotspot, **Pllek** (www.pllek.nl) – also built up out of shipping containers. This ground zero for Dutch subculture is also home to the Benelux headquarters of the MTV network, in a wildly revamped former woodwork factory. NDSM also hosts a huge flea market (www.ijhallen.nl) every first weekend of the month. So just do it: head north.

Noodermarkt p130

The Jordaan

The Jordaan emerged when the city was extended in the 17th century. It was originally designated as an area for the working classes and industrial enterprises, and it also provided a haven for victims of religious persecution, such as the Jews and Huguenots. However, despite such proletarian origins, its properties are now highly desirable. While many residents are fiercely community spirited, the *nouveaux riches* have moved in to gentrify the area.

The Jordaan has no major sights; it's a place in which you stumble across things. The area north of the shopping-dense **Rozengracht**, the Jordaan's approximate mid-point, is picturesque, whereas the area to the south is more commercial. As you explore, you may chance upon some of Amsterdam's more unusual galleries (see box p131).

Between scenic coffee breaks and decadent daytime beers, browse in the specialist shops tucked away on these adorable side streets. You'll find many outdoor markets nearby: Monday morning's Noordermarkt and Saturday's organic foodie paradise Boerenmarkt take place around the **Noorderkerk**, the city's first Calvinist church, built in 1623. Adjacent to the Noordermarkt lies the Westermarkt, and another general market fills Lindengracht on Saturdays.

Between Brouwersgracht and the postcard-pretty Westelijk Eilanden, quirky shops can be found on Haarlemmerstraat and its westerly extension Haarlemmerdijk, where you'll see Haarlemmerpoort city gate, built in 1840. Behind it lies the wonderful **Westerpark**, which in turn connects to the arts park **Westergasfabriek** (see box 128).

Eating & drinking

Café Chris
*Bloemstraat 42 (624 5942,
www.cafechris.nl).* Tram 10, 13, 17.
Open 3pm-1am Mon-Thur; 3pm-2am
Fri, Sat; 3-9pm Sun. **No credit cards.**
Bar. Map p127 C4 ❶
Not much has changed since 1624 at
the oldest bar in town, where builders
from the Westerkerk would come to
receive their pay. It remains popular
among local workers as an unpretentious place to unwind, surrounded by
charming bric-a-brac.

Foodware
*Looiersgracht 12 (620 8898, www.
foodware.nl).* Tram 7, 10, 17. **Open**
noon-9pm Mon-Sat. **€€. No credit
cards. €. Café.** Map p127 C5 ❷
This takeaway (with a few chairs)
offers soups, sandwiches, salads and
meals; ask for a fork and make for a
canalside bench. Order an Italian
bollen and you are likely to come back
for more.

[NEW] G&T's Really, Really Nice Place
*Goudsbloemstraat 91 (06 1183 7382,
www.reallyniceplace.com).* Tram 3, 10.
Open 11am-3pm Thur, Fri; 10.30am-
4pm Sat, Sun. **No credit cards. €€.**
European/Bar. Map p127 B2 ❸
The former bankers behind G&T's host
quirky pop-up events, serve superlative
brunches on weekends and mix a crack-
ing Bloody Mary – a food group in itself,
according to co-owner Tanya. The place
looks like a Hipstamatic version of a
brown café (all letter-press fonts and
vintage crockery). Hours can vary and
extra events can pop up spontaneously,
so check ahead.

La Oliva Pintxos y Vinos
*Egelantiersstraat 122-124 (320 4316,
www.laoliva.nl).* Tram 3, 10. **Open**
noon-10pm Mon-Wed, Sun; noon-
11pm Thur-Sat. **€€€. Spanish.**
Map p127 B4 ❹

There's much praise for La Oliva's
authentic food and tapas, as well as the
rich selection of wines by the glass. If
it's too full (and there's a good chance
it will be), there are plenty of other
options along this strip, recently nick-
named 'Little Italy'.

Moeders
*Rozengracht 251 (626 7957, www.
moeders.com).* Tram 3, 12. **Open** 5pm-
1am daily (kitchen closes at 10.30pm).
€€. Dutch. Map p127 B5 ❺
A Dutch eaterie-cum-shrine to moth-
erhood, Moeders is a sincere gesture
towards all things maternal. While
focusing on traditional Dutch comfort
food, including *suddervlees* (stewed
beef), *hachée* (minced meat) and a traditional Dutch rice dish prepared for
two, Moeders also features some
international dishes, courtesy of international mothers. The comfy setting
and homespun decor will make you
feel as if you're being held close to
someone's bosom.

Semhar
*Marnixstraat 259-261 (638 1634,
www.semhar.nl).* Tram 3, 10. **Open**
4-10pm Tue-Sun. **€€. African.**
Map p127 B5 ❻
A great spot to tuck into the *injera*
(tasty sourdough pancake) and veg-
friendly food of Ethiopia (best washed
down with a cold beer).

Small World Catering
*Binnen Oranjestraat 14 (420 2774,
www.smallworldcatering.nl).* Tram
3/bus 18, 21, 22. **Open** 10.30am-7pm
Tue-Sat; noon-6pm Sun. **No credit
cards. €€. Café.** Map p127 B2 ❼
The base for this catering company is
a tiny deli. Besides the superb coffee
and fresh juices, you can enjoy a range
of salads, lasagnes and sandwiches.

't Smalle
*Egelantiersgracht 12 (623 9617,
www.t-smalle.nl).* Tram 3, 10, 13,
14, 17. **Open** 10am-1am Mon-Thur,

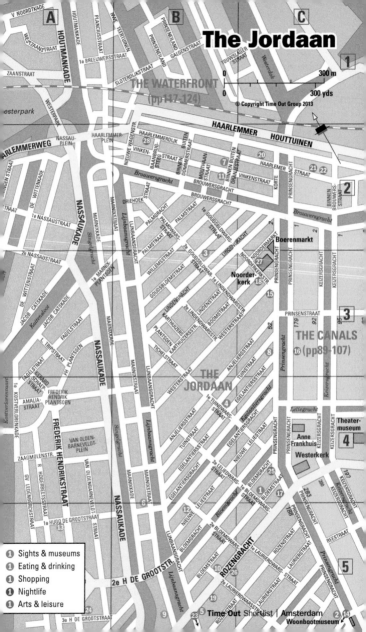

Spotlight on Westerpark

North Sea Jazz Club

A few short decades ago the Westerpark neighbourhood was known for its squatters and drugs. It's now an alluring 'hood, close to the Jordaan, that's unified by the monumental **Westergasfabriek** (Haarlemmerweg 8-10, 586 0710, www.westergasfabriek.com), a former gas works turned arts park.

Designed by American landscape architect Kathryn Gustafson, the Westergasfabriek has thrived, with walking and running trails, a babbling brook, a wading pool for kids and large lawns for both sports and picnicking. The buildings have been turned into cultural destinations: performance venues, galleries, dance clubs and a slew of restaurants, bars and cafés. And the most surprising reuse of space? The giant former gas tank, the Gashouder, is occasionally transformed into a rollerblading rink.

The new **North Sea Jazz Club** (Pazzanistraat 1, 722 0980, northseajazzclub.com) is an initiative from the organisers of the world-renowned North Sea Jazz Festival. For something more urban, there's **MC Theatre** (www.mconline.nl) and its soul food restaurant **Toko MC** (Polonceaukade 5, 475 0425, tokomc.nl). If it's more rock'n'roll you're after, try **Pacific Parc** (Polonceaukade 23, 488 7778, www.pacificparc.nl).

For edgy eats in the area, try **Proef** (Gosschalklaan 12, 682 2656, http://proefamsterdam.nl). It's home to 'eating designer' Marije Vogelzang, who serves up sharing plates, presented with a whimsy that will make you smile. Salads are served in teacups and soup in mason jars. For something more down to earth, check out the sun-friendly patios of **WestergasTerras** (Klönneplein 4-6, 684 8496, http://westergasterras.nl). Or, if it's the third Sunday of the month, you can cure your hangover at one of the stalls of the excellent **NeighbourFood Market** (www.neighbourfoodmarket.nl).

There are also some outstanding hotspots in the adjoining neighbourhood: the Italian restaurant and deli **Bella Storia** (Bentinckstraat 28, 488 0599, bellastoria.info), or the friendly neighbourhood rock'n'roll cocktail bar **Jet Lounge** (Groen van Prinstererstraat 41, 684 1126, www.jetlounge.nl), which also features DJs and live music. And don't miss **Amsterdam** (Watertorenplein 6, 682 2666, www.cradam.nl). This spacious monument to industry pumped water from the coast's dunes for around a century. Now it pumps out honest Dutch and French dishes – from kroketten to caviar – under floodlights rescued from the old Ajax football stadium.

Sun; 10am-2am Fri, Sat. **No credit cards. Bar**. Map p127 C3 ❽
This charming bar boasts one of the most scenic terraces along one of the prettiest canals in the city, so it's hardly surprising that waterside seats are snared early in the day. Its gleaming brass and candles hark back to the 18th century, when it functioned as the Hoppe distillery.

Soundgarden
Marnixstraat 164-166 (620 2853, www.cafesoundgarden.nl). Tram 10, 13, 17. **Open** 3pm-1am Mon-Thur, Sun; 1pm-3am Fri; 3pm-3am Sat. **No credit cards. Bar**. Map p127 B5 ❾
A dirty old rockers' bar where musos, journos and everyone else who refuses to grow up gets smashed in one big, sloppy mêlée. The soundtrack is composed from the entire back catalogue of classic alternative rock, often from DJs and bands. At the back is a surprisingly restful terrace where boats can moor. There's also pool, pinball and a good range of beer.

Struik
Rozengracht 160 (625 4863). Tram 10, 13, 14, 17. **Open** 5pm-1am Mon; 11am-1am Tue-Thur; 11am-3am Fri, Sat; noon-1am Sun. **No credit cards. Bar**. Map p127 B5 ❿
A chilled bar for creatives who like their music cool and their design street. The friendly neighbourhood café feeling is enhanced by econo daily dinner specials. Later on, the DJ kicks in. There is also now a larger sister operation up the street, Brandstof (Marnixstraat 357, 422 0813, www.bar-brandstof.nl).

Vesper Bar
Vinkenstraat 57 (846 4458, www.vesperbar.nl). Bus 18, 22. **Open** 8pm-1am Tue-Thur; 8pm-3am Fri, Sat. **Cocktail bar**. Map p127 B2 ⓫
You know you're in the hands of a good bartender when he simply asks, 'What do you feel like?' Vesper's talented

team serves up old-fashioned classics, modern interpretations or anything you fancy in classy and charming surroundings. Wine and beer take a back seat to the hard stuff here, but, like everything at this intimate bar, both are sourced from small-scale, carefully selected producers.

De Vliegende Schotel
Nieuwe Leliestraat 162-168 (625 2041, www.vliegendeschotel.com). Tram 10, 13, 14, 17. **Open** 4-9.30pm daily. **€€. Vegetarian**. Map p127 B5 ⓬
The 'Venerable Flying Saucer' serves up a splendid array of meat-free dishes in a buffet format. If the restaurant is full, try nearby De Bolhoed (Prinsengracht 60-62, 626 1803) for tasty vegan dishes.

Yam-Yam
Frederik Hendrikstraat 88-90 (681 5097, www.yamyam.nl). Tram 3, 10. **Open** 6-10pm Tue-Sat; 5.30-10pm Sun. **€€. Italian**. Map p127 A5 ⓭
With tasty, inexpensive pastas and pizzas served in a hip atmosphere, it's no wonder that Yam-Yam is a favourite among locals and pre-clubbers from outside the neighbourhood.

Shopping

Antiek Centrum Amsterdam
Elandsgracht 109 (624 9038). Tram 7, 10, 17. **Open** 11am-6pm Mon, Wed-Fri; 11am-5pm Sat, Sun. **Map** p127 C5 ⓮
Mainly antiques, with plenty of collectors' items. It's easy to get lost in the quiet premises and find yourself standing alone by a stall crammed with antiquated clocks ticking eerily away.

Boerenmarkt
Westerstraat/Noorderkerkstraat (no phone, www.boerenmarkt amsterdam.nl). Tram 3, 10. **Open** 9am-4pm Sat. No credit cards. **Map** p127 C3 ⓯

Every Saturday, the Noordermarkt turns into an organic farmers' market. Groups of singers or medieval musicians can make a visit feel more like a day trip than a grocery shop.

I Love Vintage

Prinsengracht 201 (330 1950, www.ilovevintage.nl). Tram 13, 14, 17. **Open** *9.30am-6pm Mon-Sat.* **Map** p127 C3 **16**

There are few vintage stores that combine class (the silk Escada blazers are divine) with affordability (€1.99 for a pair of 1980s pearl earrings) and bang-on service. All in all, it's like stepping into your mum's dressing-up box, but everything fits and you won't resemble a bag lady on exiting.

Kitsch Kitchen

Rozengracht 8-12 (462 0051, www.kitschkitchen.nl). Tram 13, 14, 17. **Open** *10am-6pm Mon-Sat; noon-5pm Sun.* **Map** p127 C4 **17**

Mexican Mercado with a twist. Even the hardiest denouncers of tat will love the colourful culinary and household objects, wacky wallpapers included.

Noordermarkt

Noordermarkt (no phone). Tram 3, 10. **Open** *7.30am-1pm Mon.* **No credit cards.** **Map** p127 C3 **18**

North of Westermarkt, the painfully scenic Noordermarkt is frequented by serious flea market shoppers. The stacks of (mainly second-hand) clothes, shoes, jewellery and hats need to be sorted with a grim determination, but there are real bargains to be had.

SPRMRKT

Rozengracht 191-193 (330 5601, www.sprmrkt.nl). Tram 10, 13, 14, 17. **Open** *noon-6pm Mon; 10am-6pm Tue, Wed, Fri, Sat; 10am-8pm Thur; 1-6pm Sun.* **Map** p127 B5 **19**

A whopping 450 square metres of cool threads. The prize is the shop-within-the-shop, SPR+, which features picks from Silent, Tigha and Helmut Lang. There's also a selection of 1960s and '70s furniture.

NEW Store Without A Home

Haarlemmerdijk 26 (no phone, www.storewithoutahome.com). Tram 1, 2, 4, 5, 9, 13, 17, 24, 25, 26. **Open** *1-6pm Mon; 10am-6pm Tue-Sat.* **No cash.** **Map** p127 C2 **20**

It must bode well for the local economy: 2012 was a year for pop-ups putting down permanent roots (see also the Collector p146). From whimsical birdy clocks to recycled Killim-brand cushions, everything in this interiors trove will make your apartment happier.

Store Without a Home

Crossing a River of Jordaan Art

Galerie Fons Welters

You could easily fill a holiday by trawling through the 40-odd Jordaan galleries. Since they occupy former homes or shops, they are pleasantly compact spaces. The best time to visit is during the afternoons between Wednesday and Saturday, when most galleries are open. **Galerie Gabriel Rolt** (Elandsgracht 34, 785 5146, www.gabriel rolt.com) is currently one of the more respected galleries in town, with an international selection of intriguing artists such as Abner Preis and photography duo Adam Broomberg and Oliver Chanarin.

Torch (Lauriergracht 94, 626 0284, www.torchgallery.com) has built up a quirky reputation by exhibiting the likes of Jake & Dinos Chapman, Anton Corbijn and Richard Kern. And the **Stedelijk Museum Bureau Amsterdam** (Rozenstraat 59, 422 0471, www. smba.nl) is often hipper than its mothership, with subversive shows by locally based rising stars.

Across Rozengracht is **Galerie Fons Welters** (Bloemstraat 140, 423 3046, www.fonswelters.nl). Doyen of the local art scene Fons Welters likes to 'discover' local talent and has shown remarkable taste in the fields of photography and installation, showing Dutch artists Jennifer Tee and Berend Strik. A visit here is worth it for the Atelier van Lieshout entrance alone.

For straightforward iconography, go to **Rockarchive** (Prinsengracht 110, 423 0489, www.rockarchive. com), owned by photographer Jill Furmanovsky, where there is usually a savvy selection of rock prints. Then there's the curious **KochxBos Gallery** (1e Anjeliersdwarsstraat 36, 681 4567, www. kochxbos.nl), which specialises in art from the dark sides of 'lowbrow' artists such as Ray Caesar. And, for some street art action, head to **Go Gallery** (Prinsengracht 64, 422 9580, www.gogallery.nl), which shows local legends such as Ottograph, Juice and The London Police (a huge mural of theirs graces the streetcorner).

If you are fascinated by what lies behind closed doors, then visit **Open Ateliers Jordaan** (www.open ateliersjordaan.nl) in May, when around 70 artists' studios open their doors to the public.

Unlimited Delicious

Haarlemmerstraat 122 (622 4829, www.unlimiteddelicious.nl). Tram 3/ bus 18, 21, 22. **Open** 9am-6pm Mon-Sat. **Map** p127 C2 ㉑

Known for such twisted but delicious treats as a caramel-balsamic-chocolate pie with a brownie bottom, Unlimited Delicious also offers courses in bonbon-making.

Vlaamsch Broodhuis

Haarlemmerstraat 108 (528 6430, www.vlaamschbroodhuys.nl). Tram 3/ bus 18, 21, 22. **Open** 8am-6.30pm Mon-Fri; 8am-6pm Sat; 9.30am-6pm Sun. **No credit cards. Map** p127 C2 ㉒

The name might be a bit of a mouthful, but it's worth a visit to wrap your gums around the tasty sourdough breads, fine French pastries and fresh salads, among other treats.

Nightlife

Maloe Melo

Lijnbaansgracht 163 (420 4592, www.maloemelo.com). Tram 7, 10, 13, 14, 17. **Open** 9pm-3am Mon-Thur, Sun; 9pm-4am Fri, Sat. **Map** p127 B5 ㉓

Well, I woke up this morning, feeling Maloe Melowed. Yes, you've guessed it, this small, pleasantly pokey little juke joint is Amsterdam's native house of the blues. Quality rockabilly and roots acts play here on a regular basis, so shed your gloom and enjoy the tunes.

De Nieue Anita

Frederik Hendrikstraat 111 (no phone, www.denieueanita.nl). Tram 3, 12. **Open** times vary. **Admission** varies. No credit cards. **Map** p127 A5 ㉔

A fixture in Amsterdam's subculture, DNA has become a sparkling promoter of fresh talents in the world of independent rock and electronica. It may keep itself to itself, just west of the Jordaan, but for those in the know it's the place to be. Programming is sporadic and based on good relations with

understanding neighbours; check the website first before heading out.

Arts & leisure

Bibliotheca Philosophica Hermetica

Bloemstraat 15 (625 8079, www. ritmanlibrary.nl). Tram 3, 10. **Open** 1.30-5pm Mon; 10am-12.30pm, 1.30-5pm Tue-Fri. **No credit cards. Map** p127 C4 ㉕

This library holds more than 20,000 manuscripts and volumes of works in the Christian-Hermetic tradition. You'll find that it's the perfect place for factchecking *The Da Vinci Code* or discovering the library's small but illuminating exhibitions.

Boom Chicago

Rozentheater, Rozengracht 117 (217 0400, www.boomchicago.nl). Tram 7, 10, 13, 14, 17. **Open** hours vary. **Map** p127 B5 ㉖

This American improv troupe is one of Amsterdam's biggest success stories. With several different shows running nightly (except Sundays in winter), all in English, the group offers a mix of improvisation and sketches.

Noorderkerk

Noordermarkt 44 (ticket reservations 620 4415, www.noorderkerkconcerten. nl). Tram 3, 10. **No credit cards. Map** p127 C3 ㉗

Although the wooden benches in this early 17th-century church are a little on the hard side, all is soon forgiven thanks to its programme of recitals. Reservations recommended.

The Movies

Haarlemmerdijk 161 (638 6016, www.themovies.nl). Tram 3/bus 18, 21, 22. **Map** p127 B2 ㉘

The oldest cinema in the city continues to exude a genteel atmosphere. The adjoining Wild Kitchen serves decent set dinners costing between €24 and €37; prices include a ticket for a film.

Museumplein

The Museum Quarter, Vondelpark & the South

The heart of the late 19th-century Museum Quarter lies in **Museumplein**, the city's largest square, bordered roughly by the **Concertgebouw**, the **Rijksmuseum**, the **Stedelijk Museum of Modern Art** and the **Van Gogh Museum**. The three museums have all had major refurbishments and as of 2013 have all reopened – so the square's pulse is again as strong as ever (see boxes p137 and p138). Museumplein itself is actually not really an authentic Amsterdam square, but it does have plenty of grass, a wading pool that turns into a skating ramp and a pleasant café.

As you would expect in such cultural surroundings, property doesn't come cheap and the affluence is apparent. Housing comes in the form of elegant 19th-century mansions, and Van Baerlestraat and PC Hooftstraat are as close as Amsterdam gets to Rodeo Drive, their boutiques offering solace to ladies who might otherwise lunch alone with their poodles. Further south around Cornelius Schuytstraat and Jacob Obrechtstraat there are more high-end shopping opportunities.

Vondelpark is the city's largest and most central park, and the last few years have witnessed much renovation as the park has sunk two to three metres since it was first built – some of the larger trees are, in fact, 'floating' on huge blocks of styrofoam, or are slyly reinforced with underground poles. There are several ponds and lakes, along with play areas and cafés, the most pleasant of which is **'t Blauwe Theehuis**. Vondelpark gets fantastically busy on sunny days and Sundays, when bongos abound, dope is toked and football games take up any space that happens to

Stedelijk Museum of Modern Art

be left over. Films, plays and public concerts are also staged, with a festival of free open-air performances taking place in summer. The park is also the starting point of Friday Night Skate (www.fridaynight skate.com) which sees hundreds of skating fanatics snaking through the city for 20 kilometres.

Stretching out in the shape of a ring beneath Vondelpark is a fairly indeterminate region known as **Nieuw Zuid** (New South), which is itself bordered to the north by Vondelpark, to the east by the Amstel and to the west by the 1928 Olympisch Stadion (www.olympisch-stadion.net).

Sights & museums

House of Bols
Paulus Potterstraat 14 (570 8575, www.houseofbols.nl). Tram 2, 3, 5, 12. **Open** (last tickets 1hr before closing) noon-6.30pm Mon-Thur, Sun; noon-10pm Fri; noon-8pm Sat. **Admission** €14.50. **Map** p135 D2 ❶
The Bols were among the first producers of fine *jenever* – the original gin – and began it all in 1575. Besides its World of Bartending, the centre also features a Hall of Taste, which promises a fun, synesthetic experience. You may even get a free cocktail and a couple of shots in the Mirror Bar after the tour. It's too bad that it doesn't serve absinthe – that might combine nicely with a visit to the Van Gogh Museum across the street.

Rijksmuseum
Museumstraat 1 (0900 0745, www. rijksmuseum.nl). Tram 2, 5, 7, 10, 12. **Open** 9am-5pm daily. **Admission** €15; free-€7.50 reductions; MK. **Map** p135 D2/E2 ❷
Reopening to much fanfare in 2013 after a decade of renovation (see box p137), the Rijksmuseum was originally designed by PJH Cuypers and opened in 1885. The nation's 'treasure house' hosts its largest collection of art and artefacts, including 40 Rembrandt and four Vermeer paintings. The building holds up a mirror to Centraal Station, built by the same architect. You can also check out its outpost at the Schiphol Airport, and the website is excellent too. Book your tickets online to avoid the queues.

Stedelijk Museum of Modern Art
Museumplein 10 (573 2911, www.stedelijk.nl). Tram 2, 3, 5, 12.

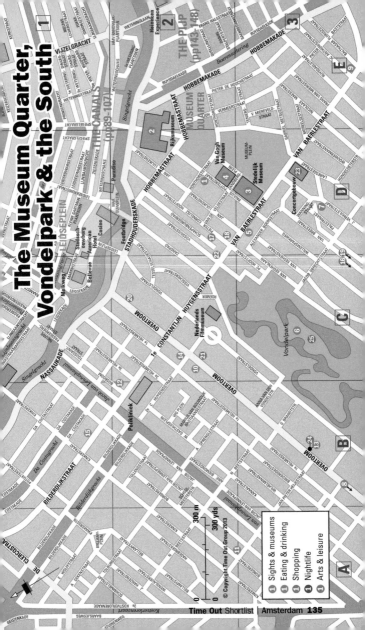

The Museum Quarter, Vondelpark & the South

1

THE PIJP (pp143-148) **2**

3

THE CANALS (pp89-107)

MUSEUM QUARTER

Sights & museums
Eating & drinking
Shopping
Nightlife
Arts & leisure

© Copyright Time Out Group 2013

300 m
300 yds

Open 10am-6pm Mon-Thur, Sat, Sun; 10am-10pm Thur. **Admission** €15; free-€7.50 reductions; MK. **Map** p135 D3 ❸

After roaming homeless for years, the Stedelijk Museum returned to its revamped haunt in 2012 (see box 138). The museum has an amazing and diverse collection to draw from. Pre-war highlights include works by modern masters Cézanne, Picasso, Matisse and Chagall, plus a collection of paintings and drawings by the Russian constructivist Kasimir Malevich. Among post-1945 artists here are Minimalists Donald Judd, Barnett Newman and Frank Stella, Pop artists Roy Lichtenstein, Sigmar Polke and Andy Warhol, Abstract Expressionists Karel Appel and Willem De Kooning, and conceptual artists Jan Dibbets, Jeff Koons and Bruce Nauman.

Van Gogh Museum

Paulus Potterstraat 7 (570 5200, www.vangoghmuseum.nl). Tram 2, 3, 5, 12. **Open** *May-Aug* 9am-6pm Mon-Thur, Sat, Sun; 9am-10pm Fri. *Sept-Apr* 9am-5pm Mon-Thur, Sat, Sun; 9am-10pm Fri. **Admission** €15; free-€2.50 reductions; MK. *Temporary exhibitions* prices vary. **Map** p135 D2 ❹

An excellent collection of more than 200 paintings and 500 drawings by everyone's favourite troubled genius occupies the Gerrit Rietveld-designed building on a permanent basis. The relatively new wing by Japanese architect Kisho Kurokawa is usually home to temporary exhibitions that focus on Van Gogh's contemporaries and his influence on other artists. These shows are assembled from both the museum's own extensive archives and private collections. Try to visit around noon (from 11am) or late afternoon (around 4.30pm): the queues at other hours can be frustratingly long, and the gallery unbearably busy. It's worth noting that there's a programme of lectures, concerts and films on Friday evenings. You can book online to avoid the queues.

Eating & drinking

Bagels & Beans

Van Baerlestraat 40 (675 7050, www.bagelsbeans.nl). Tram 2, 3, 5, 12. **Open** 8am-5.30pm Mon-Fri; 9am-6pm Sat, Sun. **Café**. **Map** p135 D3 ❺

An Amsterdam success story, this branch of B&B also boasts a wonderfully peaceful back patio. Perfect for an economical breakfast, lunch or snack; sun-dried tomatoes are a speciality, always employed with particular skill.

't Blauwe Theehuis

Vondelpark 5 (662 0254, www.blauwe theehuis.nl). Tram 1, 2, 3, 5, 12. **Open** 9am-5pm Mon-Fri; 9am-8pm Sat, Sun (hours extended on sunny weekends). **Bar**. **Map** p135 C3 ❻

One of the few local landmarks that allows you to nestle inside with a beer, HAJ Baanders' extraordinary 1930s teahouse – a sort of UFO-hat hybrid – is a choice spot for fair-weather drinking. In summer, there are DJs and barbecues, although it's a romantic spot for dinner and drinks all year round.

Café Welling

Jan Willem Brouwerstraat 32 (662 0155, www.cafewelling.nl). Tram 2, 3, 5, 12, 16. **Open** 4pm-1am Mon-Thur; 4pm-2am Fri; 3pm-2am Sat; 3pm-1am Sun. **Café/bar**. **Map** p135 D3 ❼

Just behind the Concertgebouw, brownish Welling offers plenty of choice in the beer department – plus locally produced jenever – and a welcoming, relaxed atmosphere in contrast to many of the other overpriced posh spots near here. Be charmed by the regulars – who often come in carrying their instruments.

Caffe Oslo

Sloterkade 1a (669 9663, www.caffe oslo.nl). Tram 1. **Open** 9am-1am Mon-Thur; 9am-3am Fri; 10am-3am Sat; 10am-1am Sun. **Café/bar**. **Map** p135 A3 ❽

'Museum of the Netherlands'

The Rijksmuseum rebuilt.

The numbers are impressive: 2,500 visitors per hour come and try to absorb the 8,000 works of art spread over 80 rooms that cover 12,000 square metres of exhibition space dedicated to the Netherlands' cultural history since 1100 AD. The only drawback is that it took the **Rijksmuseum** (see p134) ten years of rebuilding to make this happen. But since it reopened in 2013, the locals have (mostly) stopped their quibbling. After all, in addition to Rembrandt's *Nightwatch* and an impressive selection of Vermeers, the museum also has a badass biplane from 1917 suspended from its ceiling.

The €375 million renovation was undertaken by Spanish architects Cruz y Ortiz, who united the museum's two halves with an underground passage linking the two courtyards. A century of whitewash was removed and original 19th-century frescoes painstakingly recreated. The end result is simply stunning.

The British historian Simon Schama waxed lyrical: 'What has been done with the museum is less a restoration with some fancy contemporary design than the inauguration of a curatorial revolution. When you see those early Rembrandts or the great Mannerist *Massacre of the Innocents* of Cornelis van Haarlem, with its ballet of twisting rumps, you will also encounter, as would those who would first have seen them, the silver, weapons and cabinets that were the furniture of the culture that made those pictures possible.'

While most visitors are as impressed as Schama, the media hype around the museum seems to suggest that the city is going through an arts renaissance, when, in fact, smaller and more grassroots operations – the ones that may produce the Rembrandts and Vermeers of the future – have recently experienced massive cutbacks (see box p141).

Stedelijk takes the spotlight

A world-class collection and a brand new extension.

Stedelijk

Eight years is a long time to wait for a bath, in anyone's book. In 2012, the **Stedelijk Museum of Modern Art** (see p134) reopened to give the city back its world-class modern art collection that covers everything from Mondrian to Emin. It came with a world-class 'bathtub' – as the locals soon dubbed it – made of shiny composite fibres more commonly used for the hulls of yachts.

The bathtub is the eye-catching new extension by architects Benthem Crowel, which now dominates the rather ho-hum original building from 1895. It also provides a very grand entrance that now faces the Museumplein square instead of the street. Once inside, the contrasting halves come together in presenting the best of the Stedelijk's collection of 90,000 objects.

The highlights are a very mixed bag indeed: Roy Lichtenstein's *As I Opened Fire*, Gilbert&George's *Shit Pictures*, Henri Matisse's *La perruche et la sirene*, Christian Friedrich's *Untitled* video art,

Jean Tinguely's kinetic sculptures, Jeff Koons' *Ushering in Banality*, Kazimir Malevich's *Suprematist Composition (with eight red rectangles)*, Anselm Kiefer's *Innenraum*, Diane Arbus's *A Jewish Giant at home with his parents in the Bronx, NY*. And more…

There are also works by local heroes such as video artist Aernout Mik and painter Marlene Dumas. And as to be expected, there is also an excellent display of 2,000 design objects – including a complete bedroom of Gerrit Rietveld from 1926 – that help explain why the Netherlands remains in the vanguard of international design.

With American curator Anne Goldstein at the helm, the museum hopes to be able to play with the big boys of international art now, such as the London Tate Modern, Bilbao's Guggenheim and Paris's Pompidou Centre. But their annual budgets dwarve that of the Stedelijk. Even so, it's still a world-class collection worth immersing oneself in. Happy bathing!

So slick a bar comes as a surprise plonked canal-side in an unremarkable residential area not far from the Vondelpark. Inside it's all blond wood, cool, creamy colours and a beautiful crazy-paving floor. The punters are slightly older, style-hungry locals who come for breakfast and stay late for the fashionable menu and inimitable laid-back atmosphere.

Eetcafé I Kriti

Balthasar Floriszstraat 3 (664 1445, www.ikriti.nl). Tram 3, 5, 12, 24. **Open** 5pm-midnight daily. €€€. **Greek**. Map p135 E3 ❾
Eat and party Greek style in this evocation of Crete. On a lucky night, the owner and chef Yannis steps out of the kitchen between squid grillings to sing and play guitar for guests, sometimes boosted by plate-lobbing antics.

Gollem's Proeflokaal

Overtoom 160-162 (612 9444, www.cafegollem.nl). Tram 1, 3, 12. **Open** 4pm-1am Mon-Thur; noon-3am Fri, Sat; noon-1am Sun. **Bar**. **No credit cards**. Map p135 C2 ❿
A simply outstanding place to get sozzled, this dark and cosy Belgian beer specialist offers more than 150 bottled brews – including 42 abbey beers and 14 trappist – and 14 on tap, from easy drinkers to demonic head-pounders such as Delirium Tremens. The helpful menu lists the strengths of the suds for those erring on the side of caution. There's another branch at Raamsteeg 4, on the New Side.

Kashmir Lounge

Jan Pieter Heijestraat 85-87 (683 2268, www.kashmirlounge.com). Tram 7, 17. **Open** 10am-1am Mon-Thur; 10am-3am Fri, Sat; 11am-1am Sun. **No credit cards**. **Coffeeshop**. Map p135 A3 ⓫
Illuminated with candlelight, Kashmir may seem too dark at first, but once your eyes adjust, you'll discover an opulent cavern of Indian tapestries, ornate tiles, hand-carved walls and cushions swathed in zebra and cheetah prints. With a multitude of obscure corners and partially enclosed tables, you can feel like a VIP at no extra charge. With a terrace and regular DJs and live music, this is a gem of a coffeeshop.

Pastis

🆕 *1e Constantijn Huygensstraat 15 (616 6166, www.pastisamsterdam.nl). Tram 1, 3, 12.* **Open** 9am-1am Mon-Thur; 9am-2am Fri, Sat; 10am-1am Sun. €€€. **Brasserie**. Map p135 B2 ⓬
Not to be confused with its New York namesake, Pastis may not be in the Meatpacking District, but this neighbourhood favourite sure packs a punch when it comes to brasserie classics from caesar salads to crème brûlée. Generous opening hours make this the perfect choice for a very easy Sunday morning indeed.

De Peper

Overtoom 301 (412 2954, www.depeper.org). Tram 1. **Open** 6pm-1am Tue, Thur, Sun; 6pm-3am Fri. €. **No credit cards**. **Vegetarian**. Map p135 B3 ⓭
This purveyor of the cheapest and best vegan food in town is a collectively organised, non-profit project mingling culture with an awesome kitchen – well, depending on who's volunteering that night. Book ahead between 4pm and 6.30pm, and dinner is served between 7pm and 8.30pm. It's part of OT301 (see p142).

Peperwortel

Overtoom 140 (685 1053, www.peperwortel.nl). Tram 1, 12. **Open** noon-9pm daily. €€. **No credit cards**. **Global**. Map p135 C2 ⓮
You could survive for weeks on takeaways from Pepper Root (which, if you follow the name's Jewish Amsterdam roots, translates into 'Horseradish'), with its range of dishes embracing everything from Dutch to Middle Eastern, as well as Asian and Spanish cuisines.

FOUR

Riaz

*Bilderdijkstraat 193 (683 6453,
www.riaz.nl). Tram 3, 7, 10, 12, 17.*
Open 1am-9.30pm Mon-Fri, Sat; 2-9pm
Sun. **€€. No credit cards. South
American**. Map p135 B1 ⑮
A Surinamese joint where you might
be lucky enough to bump into Ruud
Gullit; it's where he scores his rotis
when he's in town.

Ron Gastrobar

NEW *Sophialaan 55 hs (496 1943,
www.rongastrobar.nl) Tram 1, 2.* **Open**
noon-10.30pm Mon-Fri (kitchen closed
2.30-5.30pm); 3-10.30pm Sat; noon-
10.30pm Sun. **€€. International**.
Near the south edge of Vondelpark, this
restaurant is named after local celebrity
chef Ron Blaauw, who is not afraid to
shake things up. In 2013 he put his two
Michelin stars on the line by coming up
with a simpler and more affordable concept. The menu is made of 25 no-
nonsense back-to-basics mains at €15
each. But the costs add up quickly if you
do wine with your dine. Michelin may
very well let him keep his stars.

Shopping

2

NEW *Cornelis Schuytstraat 27 (845
2626, http://2-amsterdam.nl). Tram 2.*
Open noon-6pm Mon; 10am-6pm Tue-
Sat; noon-5pm Sun. Map p135 C3 ⑯
If Cornelis Schuytstraat were on the
Monopoly board, the Ferillis would be
taking it over, probably with that natty
hat as their avatar. After the massive
success of their menswear mecca, 1,
(no.19, http://1-amsterdam.nl) on the
same strip, 2 marks the family's foray
into womenswear, serving up chic
brands like American Retro and Lala
Berlin in this former florist's.

Azzurro Due

*PC Hooftstraat 138 (671 9708,
www.azzurofashiongroup.nl). Tram 2,
3, 5, 12.* **Open** 1-6pm Mon; 10am-6pm
Tue, Wed, Fri, Sat; 10am-9pm Thur;
noon-5pm Sun. Map p135 D2 ⑰
If you've got to splurge on cutting-edge
fashion, this is as good a spot as any.
Saucy picks from Marni, Chloé and
Stella McCartney attract the usual
hordes of big spenders.

FOUR

NEW *PC Hooftstraat 127 (679 2244,
http://f-o-u-r.com). Tram 2, 3, 5, 12.*
Open 1-6pm Mon; 10am-6pm Tue, Wed,
Fri, Sat; 10am-9pm Thur; 1-6pm Sun.
Map p135 D2 ⑱
The first clothing store in Amsterdam
that can be transformed into a pop-up
club complete with monster sound

system, this fourth venture from the Azzurro Fashion Group – stocking everything from street style to Louboutins for men – has raised the bar for experiential shopping.

Marlies Dekkers

Cornelis Schuytstraat 13 (471 4146, www.marliesdekkers.nl). Tram 2. **Open** 1-6pm Mon; 11am-6pm Tue-Fri; 11am-5pm Sat. **Map** p135 C3 ⑲
Amsterdam's globally acclaimed lingerie designer has her own store on the posh shopping strip of Cornelis Schuytstraat. She also has a boutique in the Nine Streets area (Berenstraat 18).

Marqt

Overtoom 21 (422 6311, www.marqt.com). Tram 1, 3, 12. **Open** 9am-9pm daily. **Map** p135 C2 ⑳
This sleek health supermarket stocks local and organic products. The whole set-up, including the minimalist milk packaging, comes across as a fine piece of branding. You may even have trouble paying by cash – it's that futuristic. There are other locations in Jordaan (Haarlemmerstraat 165) and in the Eastern Canal Ring (Utrectsestraat 17).

Pied-à-Terre

Overtoom 135-137 (627 4455, www.jvw.nl). Tram 1, 3, 12. **Open** 1-6pm Mon; 10am-6pm Tue, Wed, Fri; 10am-9pm Thur; 10am-5pm Sat. **No credit cards**. **Map** p135 C2 ㉑
In this store, you can find travel books, guides and maps for active holidays. Adventurous walkers can seek advice from helpful staff for out-of-town trips.

Rivièra Maison

Van Baerlestraat 2-4 (471 1699, http://amsterdam.rivieramaison.com). Tram 1, 2, 3, 5, 12. **Open** 1-6pm Mon; 10am-6pm Tue, Wed, Fri, Sat; 10am-9pm Thur; noon-5pm Sun. **Map** p135 C2 ㉒
At this two-storey concept store, cool interiors collide with stylish lifestyle products – right up to the latest design

Subsidy slash

The Netherlands has long had a generous attitude towards subsidising cultural initiatives. But in 2011 the then right-leaning cabinet slashed arts funding by €200 million.

Of course there are arguments that subsidies breed a certain laziness and mediocrity. And certainly there were many cases where the fat could be trimmed. However, the cuts came with much rhetoric about the elitist and parasitic ways of the arts world (aka 'the hobbies of the left'). This rhetoric echoed the thoughts of the anti-Muslim Freedom Party leader and failed filmmaker Geert Wilders, who then enjoyed veto power over a frail coalition government under PM Mark Rutte. There was also little time for 40 arts organisations – including four orchestras, a dozen dance and theatre companies, and a range of art galleries – to react and find alternative funding.

Many believe that these cuts will be permanently damaging to the country's much-lauded cultural scene. While the established institutions generally kept their funding and the smaller initiatives are often driven by goodwill anyway, it was those in the intermediate range that suffered the most. And it's these organisations that play a vital role in connecting popular culture with high culture.

But what's done is done and now organisations are scrambling to come up with new, more entrepreneurial, paradigms in which they can continue to exist. Stay tuned…

books, fragrances and candies. Where IKEA offers a cheap breakfast to lure its punters, here you'll find complementary coffee and a wine bar instead.

Rosa Rosas

[NEW] *Rietwijkerstraat 33 (617 5148, www.rosarosas.nl). Tram 2.* **Open** 11am-6pm Tue, Wed, Sat; 11am-7pm Thur, Sat. **No credit cards**.
If you can manage to ignore the penetrating stares of the retro mannequins, which wouldn't look out of place in *Dawn of the Dead*, new boutique Rosa Rosas is a fruitful stomping ground for vintage lovers. The eclectic mix of clothes – there's a healthy ratio of tea dresses, paisley shawls and granny beads – are all carefully chosen. The style pedigree is also apparent in everything from the lilac walls to the vintage sweet jar at the counter.

Arts & leisure

Concertgebouw

Concertgebouwplein 2-6 (reservations 671 8345, www.concertgebouw.nl). Tram 2, 3, 5, 12, 16, 24. **Map** p135 D3 ㉓
With its beautiful architecture and crystal-clear acoustics, this is a favourite venue of many of the world's top musicians, and is home to the world-famous Royal Concertgebouw Orchestra. As you would expect, the sound in the Grote Zaal (Great Hall) is excellent. The Kleine Zaal (Recital Hall) is perhaps less comfortable for the audience, but is the perfect size for chamber groups and soloists. The Concertgebouw celebrated its 125th anniversary in 2013.

OT301

Overtoom 301, (779 4913, www.ot 301.nl). Tram 1, 6. **No credit cards**. **Map** p135 B3 ㉔
The former Dutch film academy building has been transformed by squatters into a cultural 'breeding ground', which includes a club, a radio station, a vegan restaurant (De Peper, see p139) and an arthouse cinema. Not far away is the equally alternative OCCII (Amstelveenseweg 134, www.occii.org).

Vondelpark Openluchttheater

Vondelpark (428 3360, www.open luchttheater.nl). Tram 1, 2, 3, 12. **No credit cards**. **Map** p135 C3 ㉕
Theatrical events have been held in Vondelpark since 1865, and the tradition continues each summer on Fridays, Saturdays and Sundays. Lunchtime concerts, mid-afternoon children's plays, theatre performances and bands regularly fill the stage. The theatre gets packed, but with recent funding problems, it may be forced to cut back further on its programming.

Concertgebouw

Sarphatipark

The Pijp

You don't come to the Pijp for historical sites; this area is rooted firmly in the present. Well over 150 different nationalities keep its global village alive, and many upmarket restaurants and bars have flourished here in recent years. The gentrification process is firmly under way as the construction of the Metro's controversial Noord-Zuidlijn (see box p68) continues pretty much directly beneath bustling Ferdinand Bolstraat.

The Pijp is the best known of the working-class quarters built in the late 19th century. Harsh economic times necessitated a plan of long, narrow streets, leading to its apt nickname, 'the Pipe'. High rents forced tenants to sublet rooms to students and artists, lending the area its bohemian character.

Today, the Pijp is home to a mix of halal butchers, Surinamese, Spanish and Turkish delicatessens, and restaurants offering authentic Syrian, Moroccan, Thai, Pakistani, Chinese and Indian cuisine. This makes the Pijp one of the best spots in town for quality snacking treats, the many ingredients for which are almost always bought fresh from the single largest daily market anywhere in the Netherlands: Albert Cuypmarkt. The market attracts thousands of customers every day to the junctions of Sweelinckstraat, Ferdinand Bolstraat and 1e Van der Helststraat, north into the lively Gerard Douplein, and also south towards Sarphatipark. Another pretty street, which is rich with cafés and bars, is Frans Halsstraat.

Sights & museums

Heineken Experience
Stadhouderskade 78 (523 9222, www.heinekenexperience.com). Tram 7, 10, 16, 24, 25. **Open** 11am-7.30pm

Mon-Thur (last entry 5.30pm); 11am-8.30pm Fri-Sun (last entry 6.30pm).
Admission €18. **Map** p145 A4 ❶
If you're after green hoodies emblazoned with logos of your favourite beer, this is the place to come (or head straight to the Heineken store; Amstelstraat 31, www.heinekenthecity.nl). As one might expect, it's all very light-hearted – where else could you take a virtual reality ride from the perspective of a Heineken bottle? And you get two bonus beers.

Eating & drinking

Bazar

Albert Cuypstraat 182 (675 0544, www.bazaramsterdam.nl). Tram 4, 16, 24, 25. **Open** 11am-1am Mon-Thur; 11am-2am Fri; 9am-2am Sat; 9am-midnight Sun. €€. **North African**. **Map** p145 B4 ❷
This imposing former church on the Albert Cuyp market is always bustling, and it's imperative to book ahead in the evening. We recommend starting the day here, though. The breakfast, served on an enormous fretwork tray, consists of a hard-boiled egg, assorted Turkish breads, marinated feta, spicy beef sausage, a 'thousand hole' crêpe, fresh fruit, yoghurt and honey, orange juice and coffee. A truly religious awakening.

Butcher

NEW *Albert Cuypstraat 129 (470 7875, http://the-butcher.com). Tram 4, 16, 24, 25.* **Open** 11am-midnight daily (sometimes open later). €€. **Burgers**. **Map** p145 B4 ❸
Never mind the hush-hush 'invitation only' club upstairs, it's all about the burgers at this chic-but-spare joint. There are around a dozen versions on the menu, from the aptly titled Big Daddy (with 250g of Aberdeen Angus beef) to the Veggie Delight. Nearby is Burgermeester (Albert Cuypstraat 48, www.burgermeester. eu), an outlet of a citywide healthful burger chain.

Café Krull

Sarphatipark 2 (662 0214, www.cafekrull.com). Tram 3, 4, 16, 24, 25. **Open** 9am-1am Mon-Thur, Sun; 9am-3am Fri, Sat. **Bar**. **Map** p145 B4 ❹
Light from the windows floods this delightful locals' café, which is busy at all hours with laptop holders taking advantage of Wi-Fi, parents treating their offspring to a hot chocolate, and – later on – evening imbibers of every stripe. The outdoor picnic tables are a dream in summer.

French Café

NEW *Gerard Doustraat 98 (470 0301, www.thefrenchcafe.nl). Tram 16, 24.* **Open** 5-10pm Tue-Sat. €€€. **French**. **Map** p145 B4 ❺
This charming and highly lauded brasserie in the heart of the Pijp offers upscale French fare, such as a terrine of guinea fowl and duck liver and *côtes de boeuf* with *pommes fondante*. *Bon appétit.*

Little Collins

NEW *Eerste Sweelinckstraat 19 (673 2293, www.littlecollins.nl). Tram 3, 4, 25.* **Open** 9am-10pm Wed-Sat; 9am-4pm Sun. €€. **Brunch**. **Map** p145 B3 ❻
Dishes at this Aussie-run brunch hero range from wholesome home-made muesli to a gut-busting 'big one': home-made sausage with bacon, eggs and all the trimmings. Whichever you choose, wash it down with a spicy bloody mary.

Renato's Trattoria

Karel du Jardinstraat 32 (673 2300). Tram 3, 12, 25. **Open** 6-10pm daily. €€. **No credit cards**. **Italian**. **Map** p145 B5 ❼
Dropping in here is like briefly stepping into Italy itself, with hearty hospitality and raw kitchen action to match. Pizza – heavily loaded but with a delicious crispy crust – is the house speciality, popular with all ages, but a real hit with kids.

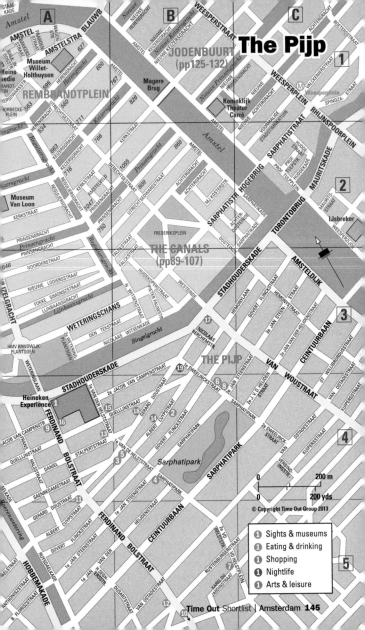

The Pijp

A **B** **C**

Amstelkade
Amstel
AMSTELSTRAAT
BLAUWB
Nieuwe Heerengracht
WEESPERSTRAAT
Achtergracht

JODENBUURT
(pp125-132)

Museum Willet-Holthuysen

Magere Brug

Koninklijk Theater Carré

REMBRANDTPLEIN

Keizersgracht
Prinsengracht
Amstel

Museum Van Loon

THE CANALS
(pp89-107)

FREDERIKSPLEIN

Sarphatistraat
HOGEBRUG

TORONTOBRUG

IJsbreker

WEESPERPLEIN
Weesperplein
RHIJNSPOORPLEIN

SARPHATISTRAAT

MAURITSKADE

AMSTELDIJK

STADHOUDERSKADE

WETERINGSCHANS

Singelgracht

NICOLAAS BERCHEMSTR

17

THE PIJP

VAN WOUSTRAAT

CEINTUURBAAN

STADHOUDERSKADE

Heineken Experience 1

19 1e SWEELINCKSTRAAT

6 8
1e JAN STEENSTRAAT

FERDINAND BOLSTRAAT

16
9
15

2e JACOB VAN CAMPENSTRAAT

18
14

ALBERT CUYPSTRAAT

GOVERT FLINCKSTRAAT

SARPHATIPARK

Sarphatipark

SARPHATIPARK

2e SWEELINCK STRAAT

OSTADESTRAAT

200 m

200 yds

© Copyright Time Out Group 2013

FERDINAND BOLSTRAAT

CEINTUURBAAN

11

HOBBEMAKADE

12

1 Sights & museums
1 Eating & drinking
1 Shopping
1 Nightlife
1 Arts & leisure

Le Restaurant

2e Jan Steenstraat 3 (379 2207, www. le-restaurant.nl) Tram 3, 4, 25. **Open** 7-10pm Tue-Sat. €€€€. **No credit cards. French. Map** p145 B4 **8**

Acclaimed chef Jan de Wit returned home after a two Michelin star restaurant adventure in Vreeland. His formula is simple: five courses inspired by French cuisine and what's in season, changing on a monthly basis. It earned him the first 10/10 review from feared local critic Johannes van Dam.

De Taart van m'n Tante

Ferdinand Bolstraat 10 (776 4600, www.detaart.com). Tram 3, 12, 25. **Open** 10am-6pm daily. **No credit cards. Café. Map** p145 A4 **9**

The café – affectionately named My Aunt's Cake – began its existence as a purveyor of over-the-top cakes (which it still produces) before becoming the campest tearoom in what can be a very camp town.

Twenty Third Bar

Ferdinand Bolstraat 333 (678 7111, www.okura.nl). Tram 16, 24. **Open** 6pm-1am Mon-Thur, Sun; 6pm-2am Fri, Sat. **Bar. Map** p145 B5 **10**

On the 23rd floor of Hotel Okura (see p177), this cocktail bar offers fantastic views of the Pijp and the compact Amsterdam School architecture (see box p147) of the Rivierenbuurt. Be prepared to pay for the view – and the 17 different varieties of champagne on offer.

Volt

NEW *Ferdinand Bolstraat 176-178 (471 5544, www.restaurantvolt.nl).* Tram 16, 24. **Open** 4-10pm daily. €€€. **French. Map** p145 B5 **12**

This De Pijp newbie offers a French fusion menu from chef Rick van der Meer with hearty offerings such as roast partridge, and a succulent and tender *diamanthaas*, a Dutch-kosher cut of beef from between the shoulder blades. Minimalist decor in toffee

colours, reasonable prices and unpretentious vibe complete the picture.

Warung Spang-Makandra

Gerard Doustraat 39 (670 5081, www.spangmakandra.nl). Tram 16, 24. **Open** 11am-10pm Mon-Sat; 1-10pm Sun. €. **Global. Map** p145 A4 **11**

An Indonesian-Surinamese restaurant serving tasty and addictive Javanese *rames* (mixed plates). The decor is very simple, but the relaxed vibe and beautifully presented dishes will make you want to linger for a while over your meal, rather than take it away.

Wijnbar Boelen & Boelen

1e Van der Helststraat 50 (671 2242, www.wijnbar.nl). Tram 7, 10, 16, 24, 25. **Open** 4pm-midnight Tue-Thur, Sun; 4pm-1am Fri, Sat. **Bar. Map** p145 A4 **13**

Many of the regulars come here just to sample the Frenchified food but, as the name implies, the wine's the real star at this compact yet airy bar, located on the edge of the Pijp's main nightlife strip. The emphasis is on old world tipples, but there are also well-edited selections from the new world.

Shopping

Albert Cuypmarkt

Albert Cuypstraat (no phone, www. albertcuypmarkt.com). Tram 3, 12, 16, 24, 25. **Open** 9am-6pm Mon-Sat. **No credit cards. Map** p145 B4 **14**

The country's largest general market sells all kinds of things, from pillows to prawns, at great prices. The clothes tend to be run-of-the-mill cheap threads. In 2013, a new organic food market began on side street 1e Sweelinckstraat every Wednesday.

Collector

NEW *1e van der Helststraat 1d (623 3229, www.thecollector.com).* Tram 7, 10, 16, 24. **Open** 10am-6pm Wed-Fri; noon-6pm Sat. **Map** p145 A4 **15**

The sign at the back of the Collector, Suzette van Dam's cavern of boho

The Amsterdam School

The city's own modernist moment.

Scheepvaarthuis

Amsterdam's architectural monuments are not the products of imperial minds, but rather the living homes of merchants and working men and women.

Many were designed by members of the expressionist Amsterdam School, who imbued their Gaudí-esque buildings with a socialist vision during the interwar years of the early 20th century.

It was Hendrik Berlage who pioneered the architectural movement. He rejected the ornate styles that had defined 19th-century Dutch homes, and facilitated an experimental era of building in the shape of the urban development Plan Zuid, built between 1917 and 1925, which provided much-needed housing for the working classes.

Although the Amsterdam School was short-lived due to its lack of funding, stylistic examples remain liberally dotted around the city. Located along the waterfront, the epic **Scheepvaarthuis** (Prins Hendrikkade 108-114), built as a shipping house, is usually considered to be the school's

first work; it is now the Grand Hotel Amrâth (see p165).

For **Plan Zuid**, take Josef Israelkade, between 2e Van der Helststraat and Van Woustraat – a pleasant stretch just off the Amstel River. Enter PL Takstraat and then circle Burg Tellegenstraat, popping into the Cooperatiehof courtyard on the way, to see the school's work at its best.

If you backtrack and cross the Amstelkanaal, then walk down Waalstraat, you'll find that later examples of the school's work exhibit greater restraint. Enjoy Amsterdam School views from bar Café Wildschut (Roelof Hartplein 1-3, 676 8220). It's also worth visiting the Spaarndammer neighbourhood. The unusually shaped apartment building on the Spaarndammerplantsoen, known as the Ship, is home to the **Museum Het Schip** (Spaarndammerplantsoen 140, 418 2885, www.hetschip.nl, open 1-5pm Tue-Sun). The museum operates Amsterdam School boating and walking tours, and has an exhibition space devoted to its architectural legacy.

womenswear and trinkets in a former photographer's studio, reads 'F*ck it, Let's Go To New York', but she actually draws her style inspiration from time spent at London's College of Fashion, and she's the first Dutchie to stock bags from Anya Hindmarch. For another well curated fashion store hit nearby Charlie + Mary (Gerard Doustraat 84, www.charliemary.com) and its excellent in-house café the Proud Otter.

Dirk van den Broek

Marie Heinekenplein 25 (673 9393, www.lekkerdoen.nl). Tram 10, 16, 24. **Open** 8am-9pm Mon-Sat; 10am-8pm Sun. **Map** p145 A4 ⓰

No run-of-the-mill supermarket, for a time Dirk van den Broek was extraordinarily fashionable: its red bags were must-haves for Amsterdam's designer lemmings and have even been spotted on the arms of the fashion ratpack overseas. Dirk remains cheaper than its supermarket competitor Albert Heijn, while its choice has improved.

Hutspot Amsterdam

NEW *Van Woustraat 4 (223 1331, www.hutspotamsterdam.com). Tram 4, 25.* **Open** 10am-7pm Mon-Sat, noon-6pm Sun. **Map** p145 B3 ⓱

A new concept: a permanent place for pop-ups. Hutspot brings together 50 creatives in 800sq m, covering everything from furniture to sausage. Everything is for sale and the selection changes every month. So go on, browse and snack happy!

Poptasi

NEW *Gerard Doustraat 103 (06 5734 4911, http://poptasi.com). Tram 4, 16, 24, 25.* **Open** 10am-5pm Tue-Sat. **Map** p145 B4 ⓲

All extravagant wallpaper and cartoon-punk iconography, Amsterdam's only macaroon specialist looks like what might have resulted had Tim Burton and David LaChapelle co-directed the movie *Chocolat*. Inventive flavours such as salted caramel, liquorice and Bounty (chocolate and coconut) mean the place tastes as good as it looks.

Nightlife

Badcuyp

1e Sweelinckstraat 10 (675 9669, www.badcuyp.nl). Tram 3, 4, 12, 16, 24, 25. **Open** noon-1am Mon-Thur, Sun; 1pm-3am Fri, Sat. **Map** p145 B3 ⓳

Small and friendly, this popular nightspot focuses on playing world music and jazz. Besides the intriguing range of international talents in the main hall, the cute café plays host to regular salsa, African, jazz and open jam evenings. The café/restaurant downstairs is also quite nice.

Albert Cuypmarkt p146

Rotterdam p157

Day Trips

There's more to the Netherlands than just the capital city, of course, and for a relatively compact country it boasts an astonishing variety of landscapes, from sandy beaches and windswept dykes to thick woods and leafy forests, along with real urban jungles. Amsterdam itself is part of one of the world's most densely populated areas: no fewer than 40 per cent of the country's entire population inhabit the built-up sprawl known as the Randstad or 'Edge City' – which is named for its coastal location on the Netherlands' western edge.

This region is made up of Delft, Haarlem, the Hague, Leiden and Utrecht, as well as bitter urban rivals Amsterdam and Rotterdam. The area's road, rail and waterway networks are impressive, making for a pleasant journey from the city to the countryside. All the destinations in this chapter can easily be explored on day trips, but they also stand up to more leisurely and sustained exploration.

Delft

Imagine a miniaturised Amsterdam, with canals reduced to dinky proportions, bridges narrowed and merchants' houses in miniature, and you have the essence of Delft. Even though it's small and often scoffed at for its sleepiness, Delft is a student town with plenty going on. Its bars and cafés may give the impression to outsiders of being survivors of a bygone era – white-aproned waiters attend to your beck and call in high-ceilinged interiors – but that's the norm in Delft. While other cities offer hot chocolate finished with aerosol cream, cafés here use dollops of real cream in the cocoa and accompany it with a fancier brand of biscuit.

All the sites of interest can be found in the old centre. As soon as you cross over the road from the station towards the city centre, you encounter an introduction to Delft's past: a representation of Vermeer's famous Milkmaid in stone. Delft was traditionally a centre for trade, producing and exporting butter, cloth and beer – at one point in the distant past, 200 breweries could be found alongside its canals – and, later, 'Royal Blue' pottery attracted many admirers from abroad.

The city's subsequent loss in trade has been Rotterdam's gain, but Delft holds on firmly to the artistic heritage of its rich past, which can be observed in the centuries-old gables, humpback bridges and shady canals. To appreciate just how little has changed, take a stroll to the end of Oude Delft, the city's oldest canal, cross the busy road to the harbour and compare the view with Vermeer's *View of Delft*, now on display in the Mauritshuis in the Hague (see p154).

Sights & museums

De Delftse Pauw

Delftweg 133 (015 212 4920, www.delftsepauw.com). **Open** *Apr-Oct* 9am-4.30pm daily. *Nov-Mar* 9am-4.30pm Mon-Fri; 11am-1pm Sat, Sun. **Admission** free.
Delft is famous for its blue-and-white tiles and pottery, known as Delft Blue (and internationally as Royal Blue). This is one of the few factories open to visitors.

Het Prinsenhof Municipal Museum

Sint Agathaplein 1 (015 260 2358, www.prinsenhof-delft.nl). **Open** 11am-5pm Tue-Sun. **Admission** €8.50; free-€6 reductions. Ticket also valid for Museum Lambert van Meertan.

This castle-like structure in the former convent of St Agatha hosts temporary exhibitions, and displays on William of Orange, who was assassinated here in 1584. The bullet holes are visible on the stairs.

Museum Lambert van Meerten

Oude Delft 199 (015 260 2358). **Open** 10am-5pm Tue-Sat; 1-5pm Sun. **Admission** €6.50; free-€5.50 reductions. Ticket also valid for Het Prinsenhof Municipal Museum.
This museum offers an overview of the Delft Blue industry and its collection includes a huge range of tiles, with everything from battling warships to randy rabbits.

Nieuwe Kerk

Markt 80 (015 212 3025, www.oudeennieuwekerkdelft.nl). **Open** *Jan, Nov, Dec* 11am-4pm Mon-Fri; 10am-5pm Sat. *Feb-Mar* 10am-5pm Mon-Sat. *Apr-Oct* 9am-6pm Mon-Sat. *Nov-Dec* 11am-4pm Mon-Fri; 10am-5pm Sat. **Admission** €3.50; free-€3 reductions. Ticket also valid for Oude Kerk. *Tower* €3.50; free-€3 reductions.
The 'New Church' took almost 15 years to construct and was finished in 1396. It contains the mausoleums of lawyer-philosopher and founder of 'natural law' theory Hugo de Groot and William of Orange (interned alongside his dog, who faithfully followed him into death by refusing food and water), in a black and white marble mausoleum by Hendrick de Keyser. De Keyser also designed the epic 1620 Stadhuis across the Markt.

Oude Kerk

Heilige Geestkerkhof 25 (no phone, www.oudeennieuwekerkdelft.nl). **Open** *Nov-Jan* 11am-4pm Mon-Fri; 10am-5pm Sat. *Feb, Mar* 10am-5pm Mon-Sat. *Apr-Oct* 9am-6pm Mon-Sat. **Admission** €3.50; free-€3 reductions. Ticket also valid for Nieuwe Kerk.

Day Trips

Schiermonnikoog
Ameland
Terschelling

Vlieland
WADDEN ISLANDS
Hoogebeintum
Dokkum
LEEUWARDEN
GRON-
INGEN
Harlingen
Grouw
Drachten
Texel
Sneek
FRIESLAND
Terherne
Heerenveen
Heeg
Den Helder
Sloten
Lemmer
DRENTHE
Anna
Paulowna
Steenwijk
Uffelte
Schagen
Opperdoes
IJSSELMEER
Blokzijl
Giethoorn
NOORD
Medemblick
Emmeloord
Meppel
Broek-op-
Langedijk
Twisk
Enkhuizen
Urk
Vollenhove
OVER-
IJSSEL
Heiloo
HOLLAND
Hoorn
Zwartsluis
Kampen
Alkmaar
MARKERMEER
Ketelhaven
ZWOLLE
Limmen
Pumerend
Edam
Lelystad
Beverwijk
Volendam
Oostvaardersplassen
Flevohof
Raalte
Kennemer
Duinen Nat.Pk.
IJmuiden
Zaanstad
Broek in W.
FLEVOLAND
Deventer
HAARLEM
AMSTERDAM
Almerestad
Harderwijk
Zandvoort
Muiden
APELDOORN
Bennebroek
Naarden
Bussum
Vogelenzang
Hillegom
Fort
Loenen
Bunschoten-
Spakenburg
Hoge Veluwe
Nat. Park
Zutphen
Keukenhof
Aalsmeer
Vreeland
Hilversum
Lisse
Noordwijk
Rijnsburg
Loenen
Soestdijk
Katwijk
2 3
Sijpestein
Amersfoort
ZUID-
Oudaen
Castle
De Haar
Castle
Austerlitz
LEIDEN
Alphen
Scheveningen
HOLLAND
Gouda
UTRECHT
Ede
Oosterbeek
DEN HAAG
Zoetermeer
UTRECHT
GELDERLAND
Naaldwijk
DELFT
Oudewater
Wijkbij
Duurstede
Hoek van Holland
Culemborg
Rhenen
ARNHEM
Europoort
ROTTERDAM
Tiel
Vlaardingen
Gorinchem
NIJMEGEN
Voorne
Putten
Oss
GERMANY
Stellendam
De Biesbosch
Nat. Park
Alblasserdam
DORDRECHT
'S-HERTOGENBOSCH
Schouwen
Brouwershaven
Goeree-
Overflakkee
Hoeke-Waard
Geertruidenberg
Drunen
Uden
terscheldedam
Delta Expo
Oudenbosch
Oosterhout
Waalwijk
Overloon
De Groote Peel
Nat. Reserve
Zierikzee
Noord
Beveland
Tholen
BREDA
Kaatsheuvel
delburg
Veere
TILBURG
Nuenen
Helmond
elande
Goes
Yerseke
Roosendaal
NOORD - BRABANT
singen
Kapelle
Bergen op
Zoom
EINDHOVEN
Venlo
Kruiningen
ZEELAND
LIMBURG
Terneuzen
Zeeuws -
Vlaanderen
ANTWERPEN
ANVERS
Weert
Thorn
Roermond

GENT
GAND
B E L G I U M
Sittard
GERMANY
Geleen
Valkenburg
Heerlen
Schin
AACHEN
MAASTRICHT

1. Oud-Loosdrecht
2. Breukeleveen
3. Westbroek

N O R T H   S E A

50 km
30 miles

© Copyright Time Out Group 2013

The town's other splendid house of worship, the Gothic 'Old Church' (c1200), is known as 'Leaning Jan' because its tower stands 2m (over 6ft) off-kilter. Art-lovers should note that it's the final resting place of Vermeer.

De Porceleyne Fles

Rotterdamseweg 196 (015 251 2030, www.royaldelft.com). **Open** *Apr-Oct* 9am-5pm daily. *Nov-Mar* 9am-5pm Mon-Sat. **Admission** €12.

Another look behind the scenes of a Delft Blue pottery factory.

Getting there

Delft is 60 kilometres (37 miles) south-west of Amsterdam along the A4. Trains from Amsterdam Centraal Station take just under an hour.

Tourist information

Toeristen Informatie Punt (Tourist Information Point)

Kerkstraat 3 (015 215 4051, www.delft.nl). **Open** *Apr-Sept* 10am-5pm Mon, Sat; 9am-6pm Tue-Fri; 10am-4pm Sun. *Oct-Mar* 11am-4pm Mon; 10am-4pm Tue-Sat; 10am-3pm Sun.

Haarlem

Although Amsterdam is located in Noord-Holland, Haarlem – 15 minutes away by train – is the provincial capital. A cycle ride away from the beaches of Zandvoort-aan-Zee and Bloemendaal-aan-Zee, Haarlem is a smaller, gentler and perhaps even older version of Amsterdam. All traces of the city's origins as a tenth-century inland sea settlement disappeared when the Haarlemmermeer was drained in the 19th century. But it hasn't lost its appeal: the city centre,

with its lively square, canals and charming almshouses, is beautiful.

Sights & museums

Frans Halsmuseum

Groot Heiligland 62 (023 511 5775, www.franshalsmuseum.nl). **Open** 10am-5pm Tue-Fri; 11am-6pm Sat-Sun. **Admission** €13; free-€11 reductions; MK.

Housed in what were an elderly men's almshouses and an orphanage (well worth a visit in themselves), this museum has a magnificent collection of 16th- and 17th-century portraits, still lifes, genre paintings and landscapes. The highlight is a group of eight portraits of militia companies and regents from the brush of Frans Hals. The museum also holds vast collections of period furniture, Haarlem silver and an 18th-century apothecary with Delftware pottery.

De Hallen

Grotemarkt 16 (023 511 5775, www.dehallen.nl). **Open** 11am-5pm Tue-Sat; noon-5pm Sun. **Admission** €6; free-€5 reductions; MK.

De Hallen is a genuinely up-to-the-minute modern art museum housed in two interesting old buildings, the Verweyhal (a 19th-century gentleman's club) and the atmospheric Vleeshal or 'meat hall', which was originally a 17th-century butcher's market. Exhibitions focus on cutting-edge artists, such as Joseph Beuys, Roger Hiorns and Sarah Lucas.

St Bavo

Grotemarkt (023 553 2040, www.bavo.nl). **Open** *Winter* 10am-4pm Mon-Sat. *Summer* 10am-5pm Mon-Sat. **Admission** €2.50; free-€1.25 reductions.

This truly enormous church, dominating Grotemarkt, the main square, provides an excellent point to begin exploring Haarlem's long history. Built around 1313, it suffered fire damage in 1328 and reconstruction lasted a further 150 years. It's surprisingly bright inside: cavernous white transepts stand as high as the nave and make a stunning sight. The floor is made up of 1,350 gravestones, including one featuring only the word 'Me' and another long enough to hold a famed local giant. In the interests of balance, there's also a dedication to a local midget who died of injuries from a game of dwarf-tossing. Ironic really, as it was a sport that he had invented. The centrepiece is the famous Müller organ (1738) – the most photographed organ in the world. An extraordinary gold and red instrument, it boasts an astonishing 5,068 pipes. In its time it was played by Handel, as well as the ten-year-old Mozart, who squeezed out a few tunes in 1765 while he was on a tour of the Netherlands with his family.

Teylers Museum

Spaarne 16 (023 516 0960, www.teylersmuseum.eu). **Open** 10am-5pm Tue-Sat; noon-5pm Sun. **Admission** €11; free-€8.50 reductions; MK.

Although it lies somewhat in the shadow of the Frans Halsmuseum, the Teylers is a good example of an Enlightenment museum, with an encyclopedic collection. Founded in 1784, it's the oldest museum in the Netherlands. Fossils and minerals rest beside antique scientific instruments, and there's a superb collection, spanning the 16th to the 19th centuries, of more than 10,000 drawings by Old Masters, including Rembrandt, Michelangelo and Raphael. A new wing hosts temporary art and science exhibitions.

Getting there

By car, Haarlem lies ten kilometres (six miles) west of Amsterdam on the A5. Trains from Amsterdam Centraal Station have a journey time of roughly 15 minutes.

Tourist information

VVV

Verwulft 11 (0900 616 1600 premium rate, www.haarlemmarketing.nl). **Open** *Oct-Mar* 1-5.30pm Mon; 9.30am-5.30pm Tue-Fri; 10am-5pm Sat. *Apr-Sept* 9.30am-6pm Mon-Fri; 9.30am-5pm Sat; noon-4pm Sun.

The Hague

Beginning life in the 13th century as a hunting ground for Dutch counts, the Hague's full name, 's Gravenhage, means 'the Count's Hedge'. But the Hague ('Den Haag') is not in fact officially a city. In days of yore, the powers that be did not want to offend its more ancient neighbours, Leiden and Utrecht, and so never granted the Hague a status beyond that of a mere town. Nevertheless, it is a hub of power and centre for international justice.

Sights & museums

Binnenhof

Hofweg 1 (070 364 6144, http://english.prodemos.nl). **Open** 9.30am-5pm Mon-Sat; 11am-4pm Sun. **Admission** €7.50.

The Hague's history begins right here, where, in 1248, William II built a castle. Now parliament buildings occupy the site, and every September the monarch arrives in a golden coach for the state opening of parliament. Tours are organised daily around the Knights' Hall, where the ceremony takes place.

Escher in Het Paleis

Lange Voorhout 74 (070 427 7730, www.escherinhetpaleis.nl). **Open** 11am-5pm Tue-Sun. **Admission** €9; free-€8 reductions.

The Gemeentemuseum's sister museum, Escher in het Paleis, is filled with further examples of Escher's wonderfully expressive art.

Haarlem p152

Gemeentemuseum Den Haag

Stadhouderslaan 41 (070 338 1111, www.gemeentemuseum.nl). **Open** 11am-5pm Tue-Sun. **Admission** €14.50; free-€12.50 reductions; MK.

The star of this gallery is Piet Mondrian's Victory Boogie Woogie, bought for €36 million in 1998. The museum also holds the world's largest collection of Mondrians, plus several pieces by MC Escher – not to mention one of the ever best fashion collections.

Madurodam

George Maduroplein 1 (070 416 2400, www.madurodam.nl). **Open** *Jan, Feb* 9am-6pm daily. *Mar, Sept, Oct* 9am-7pm daily. *Apr-Jun* 9am-8pm daily. *Jul, Aug* 9am-9pm daily. *Nov-Dec* 9am-6pm daily. **Admission** €15; free-€13.50 reductions.

An incredibly detailed miniature city that serves up every Dutch cliché in the book: windmills turn, ships sail and trains speed around the world's largest model railway. If you visit the Madurodam on a long summer's evening, when the models are illuminated from within by 50,000 miniature lamps, you should be prepared for your sceptical appreciation to evaporate completely and be replaced by unalloyed, child-like wonder.

Mauritshuis

Korte Vijverberg 8 (070 302 3456, www.mauritshuis.nl). **Open** *Sept-Mar* 10am-5pm Tue-Sat; 11am-5pm Sun. *Apr-Aug* 10am-5pm Mon-Sat; 11am-5pm Sun. **Admission** €10.50 incl audio tour; free reductions; MK.

Once a home for local counts, like much of the Hague, the Mauritshuis now opens its doors to the public. It houses one of the most famous art collections in the world, displaying works by Rubens, Rembrandt and Vermeer. Mauritshuis is closed until mid- 2014 with the exhibition 'Masterpieces from the Mauritshuis' running in the meanwhile at the Gemeentemuseum Den Haag. (see p154).

Panorama Mesdag

Zeestraat 65 (070 310 6665, www.mesdag.nl). **Open** 10am-5pm Mon-Sat; noon-5pm Sun. **Admission** €8,50; free-€7.50 reductions; MK.

This building houses the largest painting in the Netherlands, measuring 120m (400ft) in circumference, from which the museum takes its name.

zPainted by Hendrik Willem Mesdag (and with the assistance of the great Amsterdam painter George Hendrik Breitner, then still a student), it presents a depiction of the landscape of Scheveningen, which visitors can examine from an observation platform. The Panorama Mesdag also displays works by artists belonging to the Barbizon School and the Hague School; and its collection features seascapes by Roelofs and Mauve, as well as genre paintings by Alma-Tadema.

Getting there

By car, the Hague is situated 50 kilometres (31 miles) south-west of Amsterdam on the A4, then the A44. Trains from Amsterdam Centraal Station to Den Haag station take 50 minutes; you may need to change at Leiden, Hoofddorp or Duivendrecht.

Tourist information

VVV

Spui 68 (www.denhaag.nl). **Open** noon-8pm Mon; 10am-8pm Tue-Fri; 10am-5pm Sat; noon-5pm Sun.

Leiden

Canal-laced Leiden derives a good deal of its picturesque charm from the fact that it's home to the Netherlands' oldest university. It was founded here in 1575 and was the place of study of such notable alumni as the French philosopher René Descartes, sixth president of the United States John Quincy Adams and many members of the Dutch royal family. The old town teems with students, bikes and bars, and features the highest concentration of historic monuments anywhere in the

The Hague

Leiden

country, so it's the perfect destination for a charming weekend of sightseeing.

Sights & museums

Hortus Botanicus Leiden
Rapenburg 73 (071 527 7249, www.hortusleiden.nl). **Open** *Apr-Oct* 10am-6pm daily. *Nov-Mar* 10am-4pm Tue-Sun. **Admission** €6; free-€3 reductions.

More than 6,000 species of flora are represented at one of the world's oldest botanical gardens, including descendants of the country's first tulips. First, you have to walk down an alley to discover this peaceful oasis.

Molenmuseum de Valk
2e Binnenvestgracht 1 (071 516 5353, molendevalk.leiden.nl). **Open** 10am-5pm Tue-Sat; 1-5pm Sun. **Admission** €4; free-€3 reductions; MK.

If Dutch clichés are what you came here to see, head straight to the 'Falcon Windmill Museum', an erstwhile mill where you can see the old living quarters, machinery and a picturesque view over Leiden. For an even better panorama, travel to the top of the

Burcht, a 12th-century fort situated on an ancient mound in the centre.

Naturalis
Darwinweg 2 (071 568 7600, www.naturalis.nl). **Open** 10am-5pm daily. **Admission**: €11; free-€8 reductions; MK.

At Holland's main natural history museum, you'll find a staggering ten million fossils, minerals and assorted stuffed animals.

Rijksmuseum van Oudheden
Rapenburg 28 (071 516 3163, www.rmo.nl). **Open** 10am-5pm Tue-Sun. **Admission** €9.50; free-€7.50 reductions; MK.

Perhaps Leiden's most noteworthy museum, the Rijksmuseum van Oudheden houses the largest collection of archaeological artefacts in the Netherlands. Of particular interest is the display of Egyptian mummies and an exhibition of bog finds.

Rijksmuseum voor Volkenkunde
Steenstraat 1 (071 516 8800, www. volkenkunde.nl). **Open** 10am-5pm

Tue-Sun. **Admission** €11; free-€8 reductions; MK.
The National Museum of Ethnology showcases cultures of Africa, Oceania, Asia, the Americas and the Arctic.

Stedelijk Museum de Lakenhal

Oude Singel 28-32 (071 516 5360, www.lakenhal.nl). **Open** 10am-5pm Tue-Fri; noon-5pm Sat, Sun. **Admission** €7.50; free-€4.50 reductions; MK.
In the Golden Age of the late 16th and 17th centuries, Leiden grew fat on textiles and spawned three great painters: Rembrandt van Rijn, Jan van Goyen and Jan Steen. Although few works by these masters remain in Leiden today, this museum does have a Rembrandt, plus works by other Old Masters and fascinating collections of pewter, tiles, silver and glass.

Getting there

By car, Leiden is 40 kilometres (24 miles) south-west of Amsterdam on the A4. Trains from Amsterdam Centraal Station take 35 minutes.

Tourist information

VVV

Stationsweg 41 (071 516 6000, http://portal.leiden.nl). **Open** 8am-5pm Mon-Fri; 10am-4pm Sat; 11am-3pm Sun.

Rotterdam

The antithesis of Amsterdam, this port city – its nickname is the Havenstad or 'harbour city' – brings a touch of urban grit to the Dutch landscape. Almost entirely flattened during World War II, the city has blossomed into a concrete-and-glass jungle, and what it lacks in charm it makes up for with creativity and innovation.

In fact, the city remains in an almost continuous state of regeneration: a fine example of this is Rotterdam Centraal Station, which is currently being rebuilt. Such construction may mean that your entry point into the city is a building site, but the developments promise to be breathtaking – and should be well worth the long wait – when the station and surrounding area is finally complete in 2014.

Culturally on top of its game, Rotterdam's a haven for artists, musicians, designers and cutting-edge architecture. Its citizens love a good party too – among its many festivals, multicultural celebration Summer Carnival (www.zomercarnaval.nl) draws almost a million people each July.

Sights & museums

Euromast

Parkhaven 20 (010 436 4811, www.euromast.nl). **Open** *Apr-Sept* 9.30am-11pm daily. *Oct-Mar* 10am-11pm daily. **Admission** €9.25; €5.90-€8.25 reductions.
A bird's-eye view of the whole city and its dockyards – and way beyond – can be had from this tower, if you can handle the precipitous height of 185m (607ft). Some 100m (330ft) up, there's a café-restaurant and even two hotel suites. There are also three rather vertiginous thrills: Euroscoop is a rotating lift, and the foolhardy can abseil or take a death slide from 100m.

Kijk-Kubus

Overblaak 70 (010 414 2285, www.kubuswoning.nl). **Open** 11am-5pm daily. **Admission** €2.50; free-€2 reductions.
Rotterdam's Oude Haven (Old Harbour) is a work of imaginative modernism, the pinnacle of which lies in the form of Piet Blom's yellow cubic houses. Constructed during the 1970s,

Kijk-Kubus remains a monument to modernims. Some of the houses are private residences; others have been converted into a hostel (www.stayokay.com/nl/hostel/rotterdam).

Kunsthal

Westzeedijk 341 (010 440 0301, www.kunsthal.nl). **Open** 10am-5pm Tue-Sat; 11am-5pm Sun. **Admission** €12.50; free-€8.50 reductions.

Designed by Rem Koolhaas's locally based OMA bureau, the Kunsthal offers over 3,000sq m (32,000sq ft) worth of art, design and photography displays, and features regular travelling shows. The adjoining street, Witte de Withstraat, offers several modern art galleries and a variety of excellent restaurants and bars.

Museum Boijmans van Beuningen

Museumpark 18-20 (010 441 9400, www.boijmans.nl). **Open** 11am-5pm Tue-Sun. **Admission** €12.50; free-€10 reductions. MK.

The city's principal art museum is home to a magnificent collection of traditional and contemporary art, including works by such masters as Bruegel, Van Eyck and Rembrandt.

Netherlands Architecture Institute

Museumpark 25 (010 440 1200, www.nai.nl). **Open** 10am-5pm Tue-Sat; 11am-5pm Sun. **Admission** €10; free-€6.50 reductions. MK.

Favourite city son and starchitect Rem Koolhaas designed Rotterdam's cultural heart, the Museumpark, where you'll find outdoor sculptures and five museums. This one, which opened in 1993, gives an overview of the history and development of architecture, with particular emphasis on the city of Rotterdam itself. It also hosts regular temporary exhibitions on architecture-related subjects and has an extensive archive that will be of interest to experts.

Getting there

By car, Rotterdam is 73 kilometres (45 miles) south of Amsterdam on firstly the A4, and then the A13. Direct trains from Centraal Station in Amsterdam take about one hour.

Tourist information

VVV Rotterdam Info Café

Coolsingel 195 (010 790 0185). **Open** 9am-5.30pm Mon-Sat; 10am-6pm Sun.

Utrecht

Utrecht is one of the oldest cities in the Netherlands, and during the Middle Ages, it was the biggest. A religious and political centre for hundreds of years, the city was once home to 40 places of worship, all with a skyline of towers and spires. From a distance, it must have looked like a holy pincushion. However, there's more to Utrecht than just history: its university is one of the largest in the country – still expanding and employing architects such as Rem Koolhaas (who designed the Educatorium) – and the centre bustles with trendy shops and cafés. Particularly popular are the banks of the Oudegracht, the canal that runs through the centre of the city, with its cafés and shops, excellent places for snacks, drinking beer and boat-watching.

As for the surrounding countryside, Utrecht lies in an area that is rich in castles, forests and arboretums. **Slot Zuylen** (Zuylen Castle, Tournooiveld 1, Oud Zuilen, 030 244 0255, www.slotzuylen.com) overlooks exquisite waterfalls and gardens. Check out the concerts and shows in the gorgeous gardens of **Kasteel Groeneveld** (Groeneveld Castle, Groeneveld 2, Baarn, 035 542 0446, www.kasteelgroeneveld.nl), to the

Windmills, tulips and clogs

These perennial Dutch clichés beguile most visitors, no matter how cool they may think they are. And rightly so. They're part of the Netherlands' DNA: you can stroll into a gallery anywhere in the world and see a Van Gogh, but there aren't many places where you can sip beer beside a windmill.

Painted wooden clogs make fantastic wall-decorations and are even seen on some feet: mostly workmen's (they're EU-recognised safety shoes), children's and occasionally those of hicks from the sticks. The improbably fascinating **Klompenmakerij De Zaanse Schans** (Kraaienest 4, Zaandam, 075 681 0000, www.zaanseschans.nl) is a museum detailing the shoe's history and symbolism. It stands in the middle of a 'living' outdoor museum of green painted houses, warehouses and windmills.

Tulips, meanwhile, are ubiquitous, and play a crucial role in sustaining the economy. The most famous place to buy them is Amsterdam's floating flower market **Bloemenmarkt** (see p103). The place is less dazzling than it sounds, but still looks pretty. For real action, head to Aalsmeer's **flower auction** (Legmeerdijk 313, 0297 392185, www.floraholland.com), which shifts 19 million blooms daily.

Eight windmills still stand in Amsterdam, the most famous of which is **De Gooyer** (Funenkade 5), abutting the award-winning brewery Brouwerij 't IJ (p113). There are also a couple of photogenic examples on Haarlemmerweg: **De 1200 Roe** (No.701) was built in 1632, while De Bloem (No.465) is a mere whippersnapper dating from 1878. Both windmills were in use until the 1950s. Seize the opportunity to see the improbably urban **De Otter** (Gillis van Ledenberchstraat 78), from 1638, in Westerpark while you still can. Its future is being wrangled over by the highest court in the land, which is currently deciding whether it should be moved to a place where wind can actually reach the mill.

north-east of Utrecht. Take a stroll in the **Arboretum von Gimborn** (Velperengh 13, 034 341 2144, www.gimbornarboretum.nl) in Doorne, then pop over to the **Kasteel Huis Doorn** (Doorn Castle, Langbroekerweg 10, 034 342 1020, www.huisdoorn.nl). This will answer a question that's probably been puzzling you for ages: what happened to the Kaiser after World War I? In fact, Wilhelm II lived here in exile for 20 years before eventually passing away in 1941.

Sights & museums

Centraal Museum

Nicolaaskerkhof 10 (030 236 2362, www.centraalmuseum.nl). **Open** 11am-5pm Tue-Sun. **Admission** €11; €5-€9 reductions; MK.
A varied collection, ranging from Van Gogh artworks to modern art and fashion. A house opposite the museum is dedicated to Miffy creator Dick Bruna, who was born and lives in the town.

Domtoren

Domplein (030 236 0010, www. domtoren.nl). **Open** Oct-Mar noon-4pm Mon-Fri, Sun; 11am-4pm Sat. *Apr-Sept* 11am-4pm Tue-Fri; 11am-6pm Sat. **Admission** €7.50; free-€6.50 reductions.
Reaching more than 112m (367ft), the cathedral tower is the highest in the country. The panorama is worth climbing 465 steps to reach: spectacular vistas stretch 40km (25 miles) to Amsterdam. The neighbouring space was once occupied by a huge church, which was destroyed by a tornado in 1674. Inside the Domkerk, you'll see before and after sketches.

Museum Catharijneconvent

Lange Nieuwstraat 38 (030 231 3835, www.catharijneconvent.nl). **Open** 10am-5pm Tue-Fri; 11am-5pm Sat, Sun. **Admission** €9.50; free-€8.50 reductions, MK.

The St Catharine Convent Museum is located in a beautiful late-medieval building. Mainly dedicated to Dutch religious history, it also has a great collection of paintings by Old Masters, including Rembrandt.

Nationaal Museum van Speelklok tot Pierement

Steenweg 6 (030 231 2789, www.museumspeelklok.nl). **Open** 10am-5pm Tue-Sun. **Admission** €9.50; free-€8.50 reductions; MK.
Although it sounds as though it's only for hurdy-gurdy fanciers and organ grinders, this museum – which houses the world's biggest collection of automated musical instruments, is great fun, especially the regular guided tours that bring the street organs, cuckoo clocks and rabbits in hats to life for visitors of all ages.

Rietveld-Schröderhuis

Prins Hendriklaan 50 (030 236 2310, www.rietveldschroderhuis.nl). **Open** 11am-5pm Wed-Sun. *Guided tours* every hr 11am-4pm. Reservations essential. **Admission** €14; €3-€12 reductions; MK.
Another Utrecht-born celebrity in the Centraal Museum's collection is De Stijl architect and designer Gerrit Rietveld, who is best known for his rectangular chairs and houses. His Rietveld-Schröderhuis is located on the outskirts of the city centre.

Getting there

Utrecht is 40 kilometres (25 miles) south-east of Amsterdam. Direct trains from Amsterdam Centraal Station take half an hour.

Tourist information

VVV

Domplein 9 (0900 128 8732 premium rate, www.utrechtyourway.nl). **Open** noon-5pm Mon, Sun; 10am-5pm Tue-Sat.

Essentials

Maison Rika p169

Hotels

Amsterdam has always had a shortage of accommodation. But despite the economic downturn, new luxury hotels seem to have popped up everywhere recently. For example, **Conservatorium** (see p176) is located in a former conservatory and **Sir Albert** (see p177) in a former diamond factory. These two reflect a local pattern whereby existing buildings are revamped rather than new ones built from scratch. These hotels may well have been inspired by the successes earlier in the millennium of former shipping office **Grand Hotel Amrâth Amsterdam** (see p165) and former youth prison **Lloyd Hotel** (see p174). The people behind the latter recently built on their success by opening a fashion hotel, the **Exchange** (see p165), in a prime central location; the decor in each room is the work of a fashion designer. Late 2013

may also see the opening of the Faralda NDSM Crane Hotel (www.faralda.nl), three luxury suites atop a shipping crane at the former NDSM docks in North.

The economy sector has been just as creative, in the face of fierce competition from the likes of homestay websites Airbnb and Couchsurfing, which have both proved popular in this town where residents are both relaxed and hospitable. **CitizenM** (see p175) – local folks with global ambitions – came up with their own unique solution: just stack up some shipping containers and rent them out as 'budget luxury' accommodation. Meanwhile in neighbouring Sloterdijk to the west a hostel, **Meineger Hotel** (Orlyplein 1, 808 0502, www. meininger-hotels.com) has been built in an abandoned office building.

ESSENTIALS

The best way to experience the local version of Dutch hospitality is to stay in a B&B. Far from the dowdy seaside associations that the term conjures up, B&Bs are often designed to their stylish owners' high specifications. However, be warned: if you're on a budget, then bed-and-breakfasting is seldom the most economical option.

Hotels cluster around particular districts of Amsterdam: the Museum Quarter and the Canals district have plenty, whereas the Pijp and Jordaan, alas, contain only a few hotels. A general rule is to avoid those near the station or Red Light District.

If you're looking for a houseboat to rent, check out www.house boats.nl. If you prefer to camp then head to the relaxed but happening Camping Zeeburg (www.camping zeeburg.nl) just east of the city.

Money matters

Credit card payment isn't always accepted in this quaint old city, particularly in smaller places, so check first. A rate may or may not include the city tax of five per cent, which could be added on to your final bill. Most hotels have Wi-Fi, but you may be charged extra for it. Before booking, it's always worth checking for special deals on hotels' own websites, or on more commercial hotel websites – www.tripadvisor.com or www. booking.nl (also in English) are good places to start.

The Old Centre

Barbizon Palace

Prins Hendrikkade 59-72 (556 4564, www.nh-hotels.com). Centraal Station Metro/tram 1, 2, 4, 5, 9, 13, 16, 17, 24, 26. €€€.
This flash branch of the reliable home-grown NH chain is opposite Centraal Station, and so it's ideal if you're

---

SHORTLIST

Best newcomers
- Conservatorium (p176)
- Andaz Amsterdam (p168)

Contemporary design
- Sir Albert (p177)
- Andaz Amsterdam (p168)

Local flavour
- Greenhouse Effect (p165)
- Canal House (p168)
- Van Ostade Bicycle Hotel (p177)

Best nests for culture vultures
- Ambassade Hotel (p168)
- Hotel 717 (p171)
- Lloyd Hotel (p174)

Rooms with a view
- Dikker & Thijs Fenice Hotel (p171)
- Hotel Okura Amsterdam (p177)
- Doubletree by Hilton (p174)
- Maison Rika (p169)

Cheap and cheerful
- Hotel Leydsche Hof (p171)
- Hotel Prinsenhof (p171)
- Stayokay Amsterdam Zeeburg (p173)

Sophisticated style
- Dylan (p168)
- Grand Hotel Amrâth Amsterdam (p165)
- InterContinental Amstel Amsterdam (p172)
- Sofitel the Grand Amsterdam (p166)

Central location
- The Exchange (p165)
- RHO (p166)

Quirky interiors
- Lloyd Hotel (p174)
- The Exchange (p165)
- Seven Bridges (p173)

ESSENTIALS

Inspiration wherever you are

REVIEWS
TICKETS
BOOKINGS

Our FREE apps do it all

making an early start. Public areas are decked out in sleek monochrome, making the rooms themselves (in bland hotel beige) a little disappointing. That said, facilities include conference rooms in a 15th-century chapel and a Michelin-starred restaurant.

Exchange

NEW *Damrak 50 (523 0080, http://exchangeamsterdam.com). Centraal Station Metro.* €€-€€€.
A simple hallway leads back to a red gift-box of a reception, offering just a peek of the statement seating in the mezzanine above. Each of the 61 unique rooms has been exquisitely designed by Amsterdam fashion graduates, and it shows. Don't miss the adjoining mini department store Options! (see p77) for designer gifts.

Flying Pig Downtown

Nieuwendijk 100 (420 6822, group bookings 428 4934, www.flyingpig.nl). Tram 1, 2, 5, 13, 17. €.
A stalwart of the backpacking scene. Young (it doesn't accept guests over 40 or under 18) travellers flock here from around the world and staff organise walking tours and in-line skating for free. There are also branches near to the Vondelpark and on the beach at Noordwijk-aan-Zee; the latter comes into its own in the summer, with watersports, beach activities and barbecues.

Grand Hotel Amrâth Amsterdam

Prins Hendrikkade 108 (552 0000, www.amrathamsterdam.nl). Tram 1, 2, 5, 9, 13, 17, 24. €€€€.
The Amrâth nods handsomely to historic Dutch seafaring supremacy and the birth of an architectural movement. Considered to be the first example of the work of the Amsterdam School, this century-old shipping office bursts with creative brickwork and sculpture. It sports 137 rooms, 26 suites and a pool. A deluxe classic.

Grand Hotel Krasnapolsky

Dam 9 (554 9111, www.nh-hotels.com). Tram 1, 2, 4, 5, 9, 13, 14, 16, 17, 24, 25, 26. €€€€.
Bang in the centre of Amsterdam, right opposite the Royal Palace, facilities here are really excellent: restaurants, bars, a ballroom, masseur and a winter garden for a relaxing weekend brunch. Options range from suites to compact rooms at the back.

Greenhouse Effect

Warmoesstraat 55 (624 4974, www.greenhouse-effect.nl). Tram 4, 9, 24, 25. €.
If you're planning to disappear in a cloud of cannabis smoke, this place above a coffee shop (see p71) is where to rest your addled head. Some rooms feature shared facilities, several are kitted out in trippy styles and others have good canal views. Breakfast is served until noon and there's also a bar.

Hotel de l'Europe

Nieuwe Doelenstraat 2-14 (531 1777, www.leurope.nl). Tram 4, 9, 14. €€€€.
Another landmark hotel with views across the Amstel, this is the place for indulgent splurges or honeymoon hideaways: think marble bathrooms, Bulgari toiletries and a jacuzzi in the bridal suite. A 2010 restoration added a 'Dutch Master Wing' of suites, complete with heated pool. The hotel is also home to the highly rated restaurant Bord'Eau.

Le Maroxidien

Prins Hendrikkade 534 (400 4006, www.lemaroxidien.com). Tram 1, 2, 5, 9, 13, 17, 24. €€€.
This floating B&B in a historical houseboat has a charming hostess, three guest rooms (themed around Morocco, India and Mexico) two shared bathrooms and a living room. Great organic breakfast.

Nova

Nieuwezijds Voorburgwal 276 (623 0066, www.novahotel.nl). Tram 1, 2, 5. €€.

The five charming townhouses that make up Nova are comfortably and plainly furnished (good-looking in an IKEA sort of way). Located in the more chilled 'New Side', the hotel is near a nightlife zone as well as the main cultural sights.

Renaissance Amsterdam

Kattengat 1 (621 2223, www.marriott.com). Tram 1, 2, 4, 5, 13, 17. €€€.

An upmarket option for exploring the bohemian charms of the Jordaan and Harlemmerstraat, this 400-roomed place compensates for its flowery decor with luxuries like in-house movies, interactive videos and a fitness area, making it a good bet for flush families with recalcitrant kids. There's also a babysitting service. High-tech conference facilities also make it a favourite with business travellers.

Residence Le Coin

Nieuwe Doelenstraat 5 (524 6800, www.lecoin.nl). Tram 4, 9, 14, 16, 24, 25. €€.

On a quiet, café-lined street between the Old Centre and the central shopping district, this medium-sized hotel arranged across seven buildings has spacious, very stylish rooms in muted colours. Rooms are drenched in light thanks to big windows, and furnishings are a classy mix of old and new, with designer chairs and lots of shiny wood. The attic rooms are particularly full of character, and many come with kitchenettes, making this a good bet for families.

RHO Hotel

Nes 5-23 (620 7371, www.rhohotel.nl). Tram 1, 2, 4, 5, 9, 13, 16, 17, 24, 25. €€.

If your budget doesn't stretch as far as the swankier and more expensive hotels on and around Dam square, this hotel matches on location, if not on interior design or style. Set on a back-street bustling with bars, restaurants

and theatres, the hotel has an art deco lobby that harks back to the days when it was a gold merchant's, although the rooms themselves are surprisingly plain.

Sofitel the Grand Amsterdam

Oudezijds Voorburgwal 197 (555 3111, www.thegrand.nl). Tram 4, 9, 16, 24, 25. €€€€.

It's probably the centuries of history in this luxurious courtyard hotel – once Amsterdam's City Hall – that attracts visiting royals and politicians. Guestrooms are spacious and airy, thanks to big windows; bathrooms are embellished with Roger & Gallet smellies; and the suites range from junior to royal. The highly regarded restaurant, Bridges, was once the City Hall canteen. There's also a raw bar, serving the likes of oysters and lobster sandwiches.

Victoria

Damrak 1-5 (623 4255, www.parkplaza.com/amsterdamnl_victoria). Centraal Station Metro/tram 1, 2, 4, 5, 9, 13, 16, 17, 24, 25, 26. €€.

The public areas of this 300-roomed hotel opposite Centraal Station, decked out in browns, creams and reds, look dapper. Rooms are a good size, and come with all the trappings. The excellent health club and pool are open to guests and non-guests alike – fees vary.

Winston

Warmoestraat 129-131 (623 1380, www.winston.nl). Tram 4, 9, 16, 24, 25. €.

The legendary Winston, now part of St Christopher's Inns, has a youthful, party-loving atmosphere. Rooms, ranging from 'Monochrome' to 'Latex' to 'Tranquillity', are decorated in eccentric, eclectic style. Cheaper dorm beds are available too, but are much less fun. There's also a bar and club (see p78).

Andaz Ams Prinsengracht

A touch of Dutch.

The lovechild of Dutch design maestro Marcel Wanders and hospitality super-group Hyatt, the **Andaz Amsterdam** (see p168) is stuffed with playful references to Amsterdam and 'Dutchness'. However, with its lush worldliness, it is also positively un-Dutch. And with giant tulips and Wanders' 'airborne snotty vases' also on display, Andaz can also come across as purely surreal.

Renowned for his Knotted Chair and as initiator of Moooi (see p51), Wanders has managed to transform a notoriously ugly public library into something entirely worthy of Hyatt's 'luxury boutique' category. The location is ace: along the canal, in the middle of the Nine Streets quirky shopping district and a few doors away from design mecca Frozen Fountain (see p96).

The bright, modern rooms feature 'screaming' clogs mounted on the wall and Delftware-style washbasins. To reflect the building's bibliophile past, rooms come with an excellent selection of books about design and

Amsterdam – the five luxury rooftop suites have their own mini-libraries.

The public spaces feature carpeting emblazoned with world maps suggestive of Golden Age exploration; the wallpaper is built up with Delft blue motifs that tell the story of Amsterdam's long relationship with the arts, and video monitors in the hallways beam the very latest in video art.

The in-house restaurant Bluespoon, under Chef Julien Piguets, uses fresh produce – strictly sourced from between the north of the Netherlands to the north-western coast of France – to build up seasonal dishes that have already set the local culinary scene swooning. And the portions are huge. The lounge, with a decor that changes with the season, serves such treats as rillettes and oysters, along with micro-brewery beers, champagne and cocktails.

A gym, spa and a selection of flexible meeting spaces round out this true tribute to the city. Even if you don't stay here, it's certainly worth dropping by to have a look.

Western Canal Belt

Ambassade Hotel

Herengracht 341 (555 0222, www. ambassade-hotel.nl). Tram 1, 2, 5. €€€.

Staff in this literary hotel are discreet and attentive, and rooms – from single to suite to apartment – are decorated in eclectic yet opulent style. There's also a library, the many shelves of which are loaded with signed tomes written by illustrious former guests, which residents are free to peruse at their leisure.

Amsterdam Wiechmann

Prinsengracht 328-332 (626 3321, www.hotelwiechmann.nl). Tram 1, 2, 5, 7, 10, 17. €€.

From a suit of armour in reception to teapots and toasters in the breakfast room, retro touches adorn this long-established Jordaan hotel. Decor errs on the chintzy side, but the place is cosy nevertheless, and costlier rooms look on to the canal.

Andaz Amsterdam

Prinsengracht 587 (523 1234, http:// amsterdam.prinsengracht.andaz. hyatt.com). Tram 1, 2, 5. €€€. See box p167.

Canal House

NEW *Keizersgracht 148 (622 5182, www.canalhouse.nl). Tram 13, 17.* €€€.

It's not exactly new, but after a three-year renovation, these three 17th-century canal houses are certainly fresh in the way they combine old (ornate chimneys, heavy ceiling beams and a tasteful array of knick-knacks) and new (plush modern furnishings and obsessive but not intrusive service). After reopening in 2012, Canal House was acclaimed as one of Europe's greatest hotels by such heavy hitters as *Condé Nast Traveller* and the *New York Times*.

Dylan

Keizersgracht 384 (530 2010, www. dylanamsterdam.com). Tram 1, 2, 5. €€€€.

Outrageous elegance and an obsession with detail mark the Dylan's raspberry, turmeric or coal rooms. The restaurant, Vinkels, boasts chef Dennis Kuipers' French-inspired menu. Everything, from the alignment of the cushions to the service, is well thought out.

Estherea

Singel 303-309 (624 5146, www. estherea.nl). Tram 1, 2, 5. €€€.

Spread over several elegant houses at the spectacular epicentre of the canals,

Canal House

this hotel has been run by the same family for decades. The emphasis is on understated luxury: rooms are swathed in Fortuny-style fabrics and have DVD players (on request) and marble bathrooms. For those hot summer days (and nights), air-conditioning has recently been installed.

't Hotel

Leliegracht 18 (422 2741, www.thotel.nl). Tram 1, 2, 5, 13, 14, 17. €€.
A stylish bolthole on a beautiful canal in the Jordaan, this prosaically named place is fitted throughout in 1920s-inspired style. Photographic prints of Amsterdam streetscapes adorn the walls, the colour scheme is muted and the armchairs are design classics. All rooms have great views on to the canal or the rear garden and all are spacious. Split-level room eight, tucked away up in the eaves of the building, is especially characterful.

Hotel Brouwer

Singel 83 (624 6358, www.hotel brouwer.nl). Tram 1, 2, 5, 13, 17. €.
These eight neat, en suite rooms all look on to the Singel canal, but it's not the place for extras. However, if you're after well-priced accommodation in a longstanding family hotel, you're in for a treat. Unusually for budget class, there's a lift, plus TVs in the doubles.

Hotel Pulitzer

Prinsengracht 315-331 (523 5235, www.hotelpulitzeramsterdam.com). Tram 13, 14, 17. €€€€.
Sprawling across 25 canal houses, rooms are big and stylish in this glamorous hotel. There's a lovely garden and, in August, the classical music Grachtenfestival takes place in and around the grounds, making it an excellent choice for music fans.

Maison Rika

NEW *Oude Spiegelstraat 12 (330 1112, http://rikaint.com). Tram 2, 13, 14.* €€€.

Dylan

ESSENTIALS

A chic two-bedroom canal house across the way from Ulrika 'Rika' Lundgren's Nine Streets fashion emporium, where the Swedish fashion maven provides a carefully curated to-do list so guests can experience Amsterdam like a local – albeit a very well-heeled one.

Singel Hotel

Singel 13-17 (626 3108, www.singel hotel.nl). Tram 1, 2, 5, 13, 17. €.
This medium-sized, 32-roomed hotel is ideally located for canal and Jordaan hikes, and for arrival and departure by train (it's a five-minute walk from Centraal Station). Inside its solid 17th-century walls, rooms are plain and furnished in a modern, basic style; they are generally clean and tidy, and all en suite. But be warned that the street-facing rooms can be noisy.

Toren

Keizersgracht 164 (622 6352, www.thetoren.nl). Tram 13, 14, 17. €€€.
This building has been a Golden Age mansion, a prime minister's home, a university and even a hiding place for persecuted Jews during World War II. Now it's a family-run hotel and comes with all the usual upmarket trappings: opulent fabrics, grand public rooms and attentive staff. Some of the guestrooms are cramped, but deluxe rooms have jacuzzis, and the bridal suites even come with elegant double whirlpool baths.

Southern Canal Belt

American Hotel

Leidsekade 97 (556 3000, www.edenamsterdamamerican.com). Tram 1, 2, 5. €€€€.
This dazzling art nouveau monument looks extra spruce now that a fountain has been added to its terrace, and its public areas – like the buttressed Café Americain – are all eye-pleasing. Rooms (not including suites) are pretty cramped, although they do enjoy views

of the canal or square below. The decor is smart-but-bland hotel standard.

Banks Mansion

Herengracht 519-525 (420 0055, www.banksmansion.nl). Tram 4, 9, 14, 16, 24, 25. €€€.
Once you check into this grand hotel in a former bank building, everything is for free – yep, drinks in the lounge, movies in your room, and even the minibar. This classy form of an all-inclusive holiday also involves a pillow menu, cascade showerheads, sound system and plasma TVs. Needless to say it's hardly bargain basement stuff, but look out for deals on the website.

Bridge Hotel

Amstel 107-111 (623 7068, www.the bridgehotel.nl). Tram 4, 9, 14. €€.
Gloriously isolated on the eastern bank of the Amstel, this hotel in a former stonemason's workshop is just a few minutes from the bright lights of Rembrandtplein, and well situated for the Plantage and Jodenbuurt. Rooms are simple and bright; river views cost extra. There are apartments and a studio for stays longer than three days.

Kamer01 p172

Dikker & Thijs Fenice Hotel

Prinsengracht 444 (620 1212, www.dtfh.nl). Tram 1, 2, 5. €€€
This well-established place is owned by a publisher, so authors often drop in. Set in an 18th-century warehouse near Leidseplein, rooms are plain but smart, while the glamorous penthouse has glass walls for unsurpassed views over the rooftops. In the morning, the breakfast room is bathed in jewel-coloured light from the stained-glass windows.

Hotel 717

Prinsengracht 717 (427 0717, www.717hotel.nl). Tram 1, 2, 5. €€€€
The epitome of understated glamour, this small, flower-filled place emphasises searching the globe for the best accoutrements: linens from the USA, bespoke blankets from Wales, spring mattresses from London. There is afternoon tea daily and a garden. Guests are the type who shed euros on antiques in the Spiegelkwartier.

Hotel Leydsche Hof

Leidsegracht 14 (638 2327, www.free webs.com/leydschehof). Tram 1, 2, 5. €€.
A hidden gem on a genteel canal just minutes from Leidseplein; the Piller family lovingly cares for the seven bright, simply decorated rooms in their charming 17th-century house. All are done out in dark wood, and the high-ceilinged breakfast chamber boasts a striking marble fireplace.

Hotel de Munck

Achtergracht 3 (623 6283, www.hotel demunck.com). Tram 4, 7, 10. €€.
This higgledy-piggledy place in an old Dutch East India Company captain's house is perched on a secluded little canal near the river. Rooms here are plain and basic (and some are looking rather tired), though they are clean and neat. The breakfast room is a delight, however, with a 1950s jukebox and walls plastered with old album covers.

Hotel Prinsenhof

Prinsengracht 810 (623 1772, www.hotelprinsenhof.com). Tram 4. €.
This dinky, ten-room hotel is near the nightlife and foodie Utrechtsestraat and has helpful staff. Rooms themselves (some have canal views) are simple, some share facilities, and they're

ESSENTIALS

all clean and tidy. Those physically less able should note that the stairs are very steep.

Hotel V

Weteringschans 136 (662 3233, www.hotelv.nl). Tram 4, 12, 25. €€

Hotel V is just outside the Canal Ring but only a short hike away from the Pijp. The boutique B&B-style hotel is ideal for both business travellers sick of sterility and clubbers who want to to be led by the hip staff to where the action is. There's sleek decor in all rooms and a lovely lounge with a pebbly fireplace. A second, more central location opened in 2013 (www.hotel vnesplein.nl) along the theatre street Nes in the Old Centre.

InterContinental Amstel Amsterdam

Professor Tulpplein 1 (622 6060, www.amsterdam.intercontinental.com). Tram 7, 10. €€€€.

They don't come much posher than this: if movie stars or royalty are in town, they almost always lay their heads in one of the huge, soundproofed rooms or luxury suites here. Staff are liveried, the restaurant is Michelin-starred (now with chef Roger Rassen), and every service imaginable is present, pool included. If money is no object or it's a once-in-a-lifetime splurge, this is the place for you.

Kamer01

Singel 416 (06 5477 6151, www. kamer01.nl). Tram 1, 2, 5. €€€.

A very stylish, gay-friendly B&B that exhibits warm hospitality, plus huge showers, circular beds, iMacs and flatscreen TVs. There are only two rooms: one red, the other blue. Minimum two-night stay.

Mercure Hotel Arthur Frommer

Noorderstraat 46 (622 0328, www. mercure.com). Tram 4, 16, 24, 25. €€€.

On a residential street within walking distance of the sights and the local nightlife, this courtyard hotel is in one of the nicest locations in town by far, near Amstelveld and with restaurant-lined Utrechtsestraat also very close at hand. Rooms are spacious and smart, though not overburdened with fancy extras. There's also a bar that's popular with guests and non-guests.

Doubletree by Hilton p174

Nicolaas Witsen

Nicolaas Witsenstraat 4 (626 6546, www.hotelnicolaaswitsen.nl). Tram 4, 7, 10, 25. **€€**.

One of the few hotels to fill the gap between museums and the Pijp, this place, though plain, functional (and a tad overpriced), is well placed for both serious culture vultures and hedonistic fun-seekers. Ground-floor rooms can get noisy but plusses include free Wi-Fi and a lift. The excellent deli on the corner encourages in-room midnight feasting.

Seven Bridges

Reguliersgracht 31 (623 1329, www.sevenbridgeshotel.nl). Tram 4, 16, 24, 25. **€€**.

The ideal destination for hermits who want a luxury hidey-hole far from the madding crowd, this hotel is also convenient for the museums and trips into the city centre. There are no public spaces, just eight antique-packed rooms. Breakfast is served in bed on Villeroy and Boch crockery. One of Amsterdam's best-kept secrets.

Jodenbuurt, the Plantage & the Oost

Eden Lancaster

Plantage Middelaan 48 (535 6888, www.edenhotelgroup.com). Tram 9, 14. **€€**.

If you're planning on taking the kids to the excellent Artis zoo, this hotel is a good bet as it's just across the road and its triple and quad rooms are very much aimed at families. Although it is a little way from the more central sights, the main railway station is a short tram ride or 20-minute walk away, and there are several good cafés in the immediate vicinity.

Hotel Adolesce

Nieuwe Keizersgracht 26 (626 3959, www.adolesce.nl). Trams 9, 14/Metro Waterlooplein. **€**.

You won't get any breakfast at this unfussy place near the Skinny Bridge, but guests can help themselves to a buffet with sandwiches, drinks, fruit and chocolate in the lounge. Rooms are pretty plain – the attic room is nicest – but it's close to both the Hermitage Amsterdam (see p110) and the Waterlooplein flea market (see p115).

Hotel Arena

's Gravesandestraat 51 (850 2400, www.hotelarena.nl). Tram 3, 7, 10. **€€**.

A hotel, restaurant and club in an old orphanage, a ten-minute tram ride from town, Arena is the one-stop shop of food, booze and boogie. Standard and larger rooms are a bit boring, but pricier, extra-large rooms and suites are kitted out by leading local designers.

Stayokay Amsterdam Zeeburg

Timorplein 21 (551 3190, www.stayokay.com). Trams 3, 7, 10, 14. **€**.

This new branch of the reliable hostel chain in a grand old school building is aimed at families and discerning hostellers. Rooms sleep two to six. Designed in warm reds with mosaic floors and sleek furniture, a hostel never looked so good. It's attached to happening cinema and club Studio K (see p116).

The Waterfront & North

Amstel Botel

NDSM Werf Pier 3 (626 4247, www.amstelbotel.nl). Ferry from Centraal Station. **€**.

Housed on a large boat, Amstel Botel is a 15-minute free ferry ride from behind the station. You have a choice of pier-side or water-side rooms. This is good, clean accommodation with a few added frills such as in-house movies. The bar (9am-1am) has pool, pinball and a jukebox.

Doubletree by Hilton

NEW *Oosterdoksstraat 4 (530 0800, http://doubletree3.hilton.com). Centraal Station Metro.* €€€€.
Just east of Centraal Station near the new public library, Doubletree is one of the largest hotels in the country – with spectacular urban and harbour views from its rooftop terrace. Rooms feature floor-to-ceiling windows, iMacs, and free Wi-Fi. Corporate clients are particularly well served with a business centre and convention facilities.

Lloyd Hotel

Oostelijke Handelskade 34 (561 36 04, www.lloydhotel.com), Tram 10, 26. €.
This former youth prison has been re-invented as hotel accommodation, complete with a new 'cultural embassy', a space presenting Dutch culture to visitors. Fitting in nicely in a harbour neighbourhood that has always been famed for its modern residential architecture, the Lloyd features the work of hotshot Dutch designers Atelier van Lieshout and Marcel Wanders. The hotel's founders went on to develop the fashion hotel the Exchange (see p165).

Mövenpick Hotel Amsterdam City Centre

Piet Heinkade 11 (519 1200, www.movenpick-hotels.com). Tram 25, 26. €€€.
A glamorous multi-storey branch of the Swiss chain recently opened on the banks of the IJ. Rooms are decorated in muted modern greys and woods. The more expensive ones include access to an executive lounge and have great views over the water and the city.

The Jordaan

Frederic Rentabike

Brouwersgracht 78 (624 5509, www.frederic.nl). Bus 18, 21, 22, 348, 353. No credit cards. €€.
This bike shop also does a nice sideline in renting out six houseboats, located all around town, from sleek vessels to more homely numbers. Houseboat no.3, on the Prinsengracht, is big, stylish, central and has internet access.

Truelove Guesthouse

Prinsenstraat 4 (320 2500, 06 248 056 72 mobile after 6pm, www.truelove.be). Tram 1, 2, 5. €€.

Movenpick Hotel Amsterdam City Centre

Truelove Guesthouse

Above an antiques shop (now the hotel reception), this dinky place is decorated with the odd quirky piece from the selection downstairs. The attic room is best, but all come with TV, fridge and kettle. There's also an apartment located on Langestraat.

The Museum Quarter, Vondelpark & South

Between Art and Kitsch
Ruysdaelkade 75 (679 0485, www.between-art-and-kitsch.com). Tram 16, 24. **€**.
This B&B has just two rooms: one is decorated in mock art deco with authentic period knick-knacks; the other in faux baroque. Both rooms live up to the name's promise, making it a quirky accommodation option. On a nice canal, it's great for culture vultures keen to get out there and explore.

Bilderberg Jan Luyken
Jan Luykenstraat 58 (573 0730, www.bilderberg.nl). Tram 2, 3, 5, 12. **€€**.

One of the city's most stylish secrets, this place – complete with spa and wine bar – is just a skip from the upmarket shops along PC Hooftstraat. Rooms feature designer touches and are something of a bargain for a place with these looks and facilities.

CitizenM
NEW *Prinses Irenestraat 30 (811 7090, www.citizenm.com). Tram 5.* **€€**.
Welcome to the future of hotels: the shipping container. Due to the housing shortage, local students have long been living in these humble units, but CitizenM is utilising them as the basis for a 'budget luxury' designer hotel chain. The 14sq m rooms are created and assembled off-site, and have wall-to-wall windows, a shower pod, a toilet pod, a king-size bed with luxury linens and a flatscreen TV. Refreshments are available 24/7 from the 'canteen'. Second location: Schiphol Airport.

College Hotel
Roelof Hartstraat 1 (571 1511, www. thecollegehotel.com). Tram 3, 5, 12, 24. **€€€**.

ESSENTIALS

CitizenM p175

College Hotel is part of the city's hotel and catering college and thus staffed by students. Boutique styling and some glamorous touches – including an award-winning washroom – ensure that prices here are far from pocket money. Some rooms, though lovely, are small; pay top dollar to get oodles of space, though most of the suites have now been converted into units with two or three separate spaces, ideal for families. There's a bar and an ambitious modern Dutch restaurant. Perhaps because of the hotel's educational function, service can be unpredictable.

Conscious Hotel

NEW *De Lairessestraat 7 (671 9596, www.conscioushotels.com). Tram 2, 3, 5, 12.* €-€€.
This relatively new, budget and sustainable Dutch chain considers itself a practitioner of 'eco design' while being careful not to come across as hippyish. Think design furniture made of recycled coffee mugs and upside-down plants over the bed. There's a second location near Vondelpark.

Conservatorium

NEW *Van Baerlestraat 27 (570 0000, http://conservatoriumhotel.com). Tram 1, 2, 3, 5, 12, 16, 24.* €€€€.
With a prestigious location on the Museumplein, and set in the hallowed former Sweelinck music conservatory that's been transformed by Italian architect Piero Lissoni, the 129-room Conservatorium has exquisite architecture that embraces Amsterdam's rich historical heritage while looking to the future. With its über-luxe suites, unique spa facilities and seasonal dining options, the Conservatorium is already a centre of Amsterdam's rich cultural heritage and bustling daily life.

Hotel Vondel

Vondelstraat 26 (515 0453, www.hotel vondel.nl). Tram 1, 2, 3, 5, 7, 10, 12. €€€.

A well-hidden gem near the museums and Amsterdam's more upmarket shopping district, this chic little number made up of seven 19th-century homes is covered with art and boasts a lovely decked garden. Rooms, including junior and family suites, are designer driven, with Burberry-check blankets, chandeliers and nice swanky bathrooms. Unusually for such a trendy hotel, families are welcome.

The Pijp

Hotel Okura Amsterdam

Ferdinand Bolstraat 333 (678 7111, www.okura.nl). Tram 12, 25. €€€€.
This multi-storey, multi-tasking, very smart business-class stopover has everything captains of industry need: a top-floor cocktail bar, a full-size pool and health club; and sushi bars. Rooms are done up in suitably masculine style and range from small standards to the huge (and hugely expensive) presidential suite on the 21st floor. The French restaurant Ciel Bleu is truly the tops, situated scenically on the 23rd floor. Servers buzz about you all evening, presenting one astounding creation after the next, whether it's lobster

wrapped in gold leaf, scallops topped with black truffle or Waterland veal served with sweetbreads.

Sir Albert Hotel

NEW *Albert Cuypstraat 2-6 (305 3020, www.siralberthotel.com). Tram 16, 24.* €€€.
Once a diamond factory, Sir Albert is a new 'luxury boutique' featuring the interior stylings of BK Architects, with high-ceilinged rooms inspired by the great design movements of the past. The hotel balances old-school service with all the mod cons. The Japanese pub-style restaurant, Izakaya, has already been embraced by local foodies – but with the Albert Cuyp market nearby, other dining options also abound.

Van Ostade Bicycle Hotel

Van Ostadestraat 123 (679 3452, www.bicyclehotel.com). Tram 3, 12, 16, 24, 25. €.
This staging post for pedal-pushers was one of the first places to stay in the Pijp. Staff can suggest trips and rent out bikes. Rooms are comfy and there are loads of excellent places nearby to refuel for the day ahead or wind down after a long, hard ride around town.

College Hotel p175

Getting Around

Arriving & leaving

By air

Schiphol Airport

0900 0141 premium rate, www.schiphol.nl.
Amsterdam's airport lies 18 kilometres (11 miles) south-west of the city. There's only one terminal building, but within that there are four departure and arrival halls.

Connexxion Airport Hotel Shuttle

Connexxion desk, Schiphol Plaza, near Arrivals hall 4, Schiphol Airport (038 339 4741, www.airporthotelshuttle.nl). Buses leave from plaform A7, immediately outside the Arrivals hall.
This bus from Schiphol to Amsterdam departs at least every 30 minutes between 6am and 9pm daily. Anyone who buys a ticket (€16.50 single/(€26.50 return) can use the service; it isn't restricted to hotel guests. Drop-off points are at 100-odd hotels; see the website for schedules, destination hotels and booking services.

Airport trains

Trains leave approximately every ten minutes between 5am and midnight (after which they depart hourly). The journey to Centraal Station takes about 20 minutes. Buy your ticket (€3.90 single) before you board, or you're highly likely to incur a €35 fine. You are also charged an extra €0.50 if you buy your ticket from a counter; instead, use the machines, which have instructions in English as well as Dutch.

Airport taxis

A fixed fare from the airport to the south and west of the city costs around €40, and to the city centre about €50. Bear in mind that there are always plenty of licensed taxis beside the main exit. You can also book your taxi ahead on the Schiphol website (www.schiphol.nl).

By bus

Long-distance international Eurolines coaches (088 076 1700, www.eurolines.nl) stop at Amstel station, Julianaplein 5, in the south-east of the city, connected to Centraal Station by Metro and train.

By train

A range of national trains operated by NS (www.ns.nl, where e-tickets can be bought), as well as international services, stop at Centraal Station in the city centre or, in some cases, Schiphol airport.

In town

Getting around Amsterdam is very easy: there are efficient, cheap and integrated trams, Metros and buses, and in the centre most places can be reached on foot. Locals tend to get around by bike, and there are also boats and water taxis. Public transport provision for those with disabilities, however, is dire.

The best way to travel is by tram, with a network of routes through the centre (buses and the Metro are more for outlying suburbs).

GVB

Stationsplein CS, Old Centre: New Side (0900 8011 premium rate, http://en.gvb.nl). Tram 1, 2, 4, 5, 9, 13, 16, 17, 24, 25, 26. **Open** *Phone enquiries 9am-7pm Mon-Sat. In person 9am-7pm Mon-Sat.*

The GVB runs Amsterdam's Metro, bus and tram services, and can also provide detailed information and departure and arrival times on all of them, as well as sell tickets.

Fares & tickets

An **OV-chipkaart** ('chip card') system operates across trams, buses and Metros. An OV-chipkaart has a one-time cost of €7.50 and can be purchased at ticket vending machines at stations, various tobacco shops, at many supermarkets and at GVB Tickets & Info (see p178). The card is valid for four to five years. You can load the card in the ticket vending machine, paying with cash or a debit card, and use it immediately. You can also load the card in the yellow 'add value' machine you'll find at tobacco shops and various other shops.

An unlimited 24-hour chip card for one day costs €7.50. You can also buy unlimited 48-, 72-, 96-, 120-, 144- and 168-hour cards (ranging from €12 to €32). A 24-hour OV-chipkaart is now available that will take you to out-of-town destinations too for €13.50.

With any type of OV-chipkaart, you have to check in or check out when boarding or disembarking a tram, bus or Metro, using the card readers in the trams and buses, at the entryway to Metro stations or on the Metro platform. Hold your card in front of the reader and wait for a beep and green light to flash. Follow the same procedure on the way out.

An alternative to the OV-chipkaart is the **I Amsterdam City Card**, which includes unlimited use of the public transport system and free entrance to 38 museums and attractions. It can be purchased at several shops and newsagents across Amsterdam, or at one of the Amsterdam Tourist Offices (see p186). It costs €42 (24 hours), €52 (48 hours) or €62 (72 hours).

Don't even think about travelling without a ticket: inspectors make regular checks, and passengers without tickets are hit with €35 on-the-spot fines.

Trams & buses

Trams run from 6am Mon-Fri, 6.30am Sat and 7.30am Sun. Night buses (numbered 348 to 369) take over later (1am-5am Mon-Thur, Sun; 1am-6.30am Fri, Sat) and all go to Centraal Station, except 369, which runs from Station Sloterdijk to Schiphol Airport.

Night bus stops are indicated by a black square with the bus number printed on it. During off-peak hours and at quiet stops, stick out your arm to let the driver know you want to get on. Signs at tram and bus stops show the name of the stop and line number, and boards indicate the full route.

Other road users must remember that a tram will only stop if absolutely necessary. Cyclists should listen for tram warning bells and cross tramlines at an angle that avoids the front wheel getting stuck. Motorists should avoid blocking tramlines: cars are allowed to venture on to them only if turning right.

Metro

The Metro uses the same ticket system as trams and buses (see above) and serves suburbs to the south and east. Three separate lines – 51, 53 and 54 – terminate at Centraal Station (sometimes abbreviated as CS), while line 50 connects West with South-East. Metro trains run from 6am Mon-Fri, 6.30am Sat and 7.30am Sun to around 12.15am daily.

Taxis

Most taxis are operated by the central office TCA. They're hard to hail on the street, but ranks are found around the city; most central are the ones at Centraal Station, by the bus station at the junction of Kinkerstraat and Marnixstraat, on Rembrandtplein and Leidseplein. Cabs can be ordered on 777 7777. Wheelchairs will only be carried in taxis if folded.

Getting a taxi in Amsterdam is relatively straightforward, but check that the meter starts at the minimum charge (€2.80). Even short journeys are expensive (€2.03 per kilometre), and ask the rough cost of the journey before setting out. You can also ask for a flat rate.

If you feel as though you have been ripped off (cases are relatively rare), ask for a receipt and contact the TCA (650 6506, open 24 hours daily) or the police.

You can also look into hiring a Watertaxi (see p181) or a Scooter taxi (0900 8890, www.myhopper.nl)

Driving

If you must bring a car to the Netherlands, join a national motoring organisation beforehand. It should then issue you with booklets that explain what to do in the event of a breakdown. To drive a car in the Netherlands, you need a valid national driving licence, although ANWB (see right) and many car hire firms favour photocard licences (Brits need the paper version as well for this to be legal; the photocard takes a couple of weeks to come through if you're applying from scratch). You'll need proof that the vehicle has passed a road safety test in its country of origin, as well as an international identification disk, a registration certificate and relevant insurance documents.

Car hire

Local car hire (autoverhuur) firms generally expect drivers to be over 21 with at least a year's experience, and a valid national driving licence (with photo) and passport. All require a credit card deposit.

Diks Autoverhuur
662 3366, www.diks.net.

Hertz
612 2441, www.hertz.nl.

Parking

Parking is a nightmare: the centre is metered from 9am until at least 7pm (midnight in many places), setting you back up to €5 an hour; ticketing is very common. Parking passes for daytime (9am-7pm, €30; 24 hours, €45) and weekly passes (9am-7pm, €180; 24 hours, €270) can be bought at Cition service points or online via www.cition.nl or at parking ticket machines (day passes only). Bear in mind that after controlled hours, parking at meters across the city is completely free, and prices can vary between neighbourhoods.

Car parks

Car parks are indicated by a white 'P' on a blue square sign. **ANWB Parking Amsterdam Centraal** (Prins Hendrikkade 20A in the Old Centre, 638 5330) is open 24 hours daily and charges €5 per hour, or €55 per day. Some nearby hotels offer a 10 per cent discount on parking here. **Europarking** (Marnixstraat 250, 0900 446 6880 premium rate) in Oud-West is slightly cheaper, charging €2 per 26 minutes or a part thereof, or €40 per day, but is only open from 6.30am Mon-Wed; 6.30am-midnight Thur; 24 hours Fri-Sun. Both accept payment by credit card. You can also consider **Park and Rides** (see www.bereikbaaramsterdam.nl for locations), which cost €8/day. When leaving your car, empty it of valuables: cars with foreign number plates are particularly vulnerable to break-ins.

Fines

Fines are €49.60 plus the price of one hour of parking in that section of town and can be paid within 48 hours at one of two service points: Daniel Goedkoopstraat 7-9 (open 7am-11pm daily, also acts as car pound) and DeClercqstraat 42-44 (open 8am-4.30pm Mon-Sat). If you suspect your car has been towed away, call 251 2121.

Petrol

There are 24-hour petrol stations (tankstations) at Gooiseweg 10, Sarphatistraat 225, Marnixstraat 250 and Spaarndammerdijk 218.

Water transport

Amsterdam is best seen from the water. Sure, there are canal cruises, but they don't offer the freedom to do your own exploring. You can try to bond with a local boat owner; otherwise your options are limited to the pedal-powered canal bike or pedalo. Upon rental, don't ignore the introductory rundown of the rules of the water (put at its most basic: stick to the right and be very wary of canal cruisers, which always assume that size makes right).

Pedalos

Canal Bike

Weteringschans 24, Southern Canal Belt (626 5574, www.canal.nl). **Open** *Summer* 10am-6pm daily at Leidseplein, Rijksmuseum, Westerkerk and corner Keizersgracht/Leidsestraat.

Winter 10am-5pm daily at Leidseplein, Rijksmuseum and Westerkerk.

Canal buses

Canal Bus

Weteringschans 26, Southern Canal Belt (623 9886, www.canal.nl). Tram 7, 10, 16, 24, 25. **Open** 9am-7pm daily.

Water taxis

Water Taxi Centrale

Prins Hendrikkade 25, at the jetty of Lovers boating company, Old Centre: New Side (535 6363, www.water-taxi.nl). Tram 1, 2, 4, 5, 9, 13, 16, 17, 24, 25, 26. **Open** 8am-midnight daily.

Cycling

There are bike lanes on most roads, marked with white lines and bike symbols. Never leave a bike unlocked, and use two locks. Most Dutch bikes have pedal-backwards brakes (as opposed to handlebar-mounted), which take some getting used to. There are plenty of places to rent bikes, for about €10 a day, but the following two are friendly and recommended. Note that a passport and/or credit card is required.

Rental

Frederic Rentabike

Brouwersgracht 78, Jordaan (624 5509, www.frederic.nl). A 7-minute walk west of Central Station. **Open** 9am-5.30pm daily.
Frederic also rents out houseboats, apartments and guestrooms.

StarBikes Rental

De Ruyterkade 127, The Waterfront (620 3215, www.starbikesrental.com). A 5-minute walk east of Centraal Station. **Open** 8am-7pm Mon-Fri; 9am-7pm Sat, Sun.
Star Bikes also has a nice café overlooking the waters of the IJ.

Resources A-Z

Accident & emergency

In the case of minor accidents, you can just turn up at the outpatient departments of the following city hospitals (*ziekenhuis*). All are open 24 hours a day, seven days a week.

Academisch Medisch Centrum

Meibergdreef 9, Zuid (566 9111, first aid 566 2222). Metro Holendrecht.

Boven IJ Ziekenhuis

Statenjachtstraat 1, Noord (634 6346, first aid 634 6200). Bus 34, 36, 37, 125, 245, 363, 392.

Onze Lieve Vrouwe Gasthuis

's Gravesandeplein 16, Oost (599 9111, first aid 599 3016). Tram 3, 7/bus 37/Metro Weesperplein or Wibautstraat.

St Lucas Andreas Ziekenhuis

Jan Tooropstraat 164, West (510 8911, first aid 510 8164). Tram 13/bus 64/Metro Jan van Galenstraat.

VU Ziekenhuis

De Boelelaan 1117, Zuid (444 4444, first aid 444 3636). Tram 16, 24/ Metro Amstelveenseweg/bus 62, 142, 170, 171, 172, 176, 310.

Banks

There's little difference between the rates of exchange that are offered by banks and bureaux de change, but banks do tend to charge less commission than other places. Dutch banks buy and sell foreign currency and exchange travellers' cheques, but few give cash advances against credit cards.

ATMs

Cash machines are found at banks, supermarkets and larger shops such as HEMA. If your card carries the Maestro or Cirrus symbols, you should be able to withdraw cash from ATMs, although it's worth checking with your bank that it's possible to do so, and what the charges are.

Customs

If you are you entering the Netherlands from another EU country, you may import goods that are for your own use. You are not liable for the payment of import tax. If you enter the country from a non-EU country however, the following limits apply:

- 1 litre of spirits or 2 litres of sparkling wine or 2 litres of fortified wine, such as sherry or port, or a proportional assortment of these products, and 4 litres of non-sparkling wine and 16 litres of beer.
- 200 cigarettes or 250 grams of smoking tobacco or 100 cigarillos or 50 cigars, or a proportional assortment of these products.
- Other goods to the value of €430. For more information on allowances go to the English website of the tax authorities at www.belastingdienst.nl.

Dentists

To find a dentist (*tandarts*), call 0900 821 2230. Operators can put you in touch with your nearest dentist, and telephone lines are open 24 hours for those with more dental emergencies.

Otherwise, you'll need to make yourself an appointment at one of the following.

AOC Tandartsenpraktijk

Wilhelmina Gasthuisplein 167, Oud West (616 1234). Tram 1, 2, 3, 5, 12. **Open** 9am-5pm Mon-Fri.
AOC offers emergency dental treatment and a recorded service: if you call 686 1109, staff will inform you where a walk-in clinic in your area will be open at 11.30am and 9.30pm that day.

TBB

570 9595, 0900 821 2230.
A 24-hour service that can refer callers to a dentist. Bear in mind that calls to the service are charged at a premium rate.

Disabled

Winding, cobbled streets, poorly maintained pavements and steep canal house steps can present real difficulties to the physically less able, but the pragmatic Dutch can generally solve problems quickly. Most large museums, cinemas and theatres have decent disabled facilities. The Metro is accessible to wheelchair users, but most trams are not, due to their high steps. The website www.toegankelijk amsterdam.nl has a list of hotels, restaurants and attractions that cater well for the disabled.

Drugs

See p22.

Electricity

The Netherlands uses standard European 220V, 50-cycle AC voltage via two-pin continental plugs. Visitors from Britain will need an adaptor; American visitors may need a transformer.

Embassies

American Consulate General

Museumplein 19 (575 5330, http://amsterdam.usconsulate.gov). Tram 2, 3, 5, 12, 16, 24/bus 170.

Australian Embassy

Carnegielaan 4, The Hague (070 310 8200, 0800 0224 794 Australian citizen emergency phone, www. netherlands.embassy.gov.au).

British Consulate General

Koningslaan 44 (676 4343, www.britain.nl). Tram 2.

British Embassy

Lange Voorhout 10, The Hague (070 427 0427, www.britain.nl).

Canadian Embassy

Sophialaan 7, The Hague (070 311 1600, www.canada.nl).

Irish Embassy

Dr Kuyperstraat 9, The Hague (070 363 0993, www.irishembassy.nl).

New Zealand Embassy

Eisenhowerlaan 77N, The Hague (070 346 9324, www.nzembassy.com).

Gay & lesbian information

COC Amsterdam

Rozenstraat 14 (626 3087, www. cocamsterdam.nl). Tram 10, 13, 14, 17. **Open** *Telephone enquiries* 10am-4pm Mon-Thur.
The Amsterdam branch of COC deals with the campaigning side of gay life.

Gay & Lesbian Switchboard

Postbus 11573 (623 6565, www. switchboard.nl). **Open** *Telephone enquiries* 2-6pm Mon, Wed, Fri.

ESSENTIALS

General information and advice on safe sex is given by friendly English-speakers.

Helplines

Alcoholics Anonymous
625 6057 (24-hour manned service), www.aa-netherlands.org.
English and Dutch information on the times and dates of meetings, and contact numbers for counsellors. The website is in English, and you can locate meetings by day or by town.

Narcotics Anonymous
06 2234 1050, www.na-holland.nl.
Offers a 24-hour answerphone service in English and Dutch, with counsellors' phone numbers.

Telephone Helpline Amsterdam
675 7575. **Open** 24hrs daily.
A counselling service – comparable to the Samaritans in the UK and Lifeline in the US – for anyone who is suffering emotional problems. English isn't always understood at first, but keep trying and someone will be able to help.

Internet

All global ISPs have a presence here (check websites for numbers). Most hotels are well equipped, with dataports in the rooms, terminals in the lobby, or Wi-Fi throughout, although some hotels will charge to use it. Many cafés and restaurants have Wi-Fi – just ask for their security code.

Internet Café
Martelaarsgracht 11, Old Centre: New Side (no phone, www.internet cafe.nl). Tram 4, 9, 16, 24, 25.
Open 9am-1am Mon-Thur, Sun; 9am-3am Fri, Sat. Rates from €1/30mins. **No credit cards.**

Left luggage

There's a staffed left-luggage counter at Schiphol Airport (795 2843, www.schiphol.nl), where you can store luggage for up to one month, open daily from 6am to 10pm (€7 per item for 24 hours and €6 per item for each day thereafter). It also has automated lockers, accessible 24 hours daily (from €6 per 24hrs). There are more lockers in the arrival and departure halls, and central Amsterdam has plenty of lockers at Centraal Station, with 24-hour access from €3.70 for 24hrs).

Lost property

Centraal Station
Stationsplein 15, Old Centre: Old Side (0900 202 1163 premium rate, www.ns.nl). Tram 1, 2, 4, 5, 9, 13, 16, 17, 24, 25, 26. **Open** 24 hours daily; between 1pm and 5.30pm access only through the eastern entrance.
Items found on trains are kept for four days at the office on the east side of the station (0900 321 2100 premium rate), after which they are forwarded to Centraal Bureau Gevonden Voorwerpen (Central Lost Property Office), 2e Daalsedijk 4, 3551 EJ Utrecht (www.nshi speed.nl, open 8am-5pm Mon-Fri), where they are stored for three months. Fill in the 'tracing' form on the website and have them posted (collecting them personally is not possible) for €15 and upwards.

GVB Lost Property
Arlandaweg 100 (0900 8011). Tram 12. **Open** 9am-6.30pm Mon-Fri. *Phone enquiries* 2-6.30pm Mon-Fri.
Wait at least a day or two before you call and describe what you lost on the bus, metro or tram. If your property has been found, you can pick it up at the GVB head office at Arlandaweg. If you have lost your keys, you don't have to call ahead.

Municipality Lost Property

Korte Leidsedwarsstraat 52 (14 020).
Tram 1, 2, 5, 7, 10. **Open** *In person*
9am-4pm Mon-Fri. *By phone* noon-4pm
Mon-Fri.
If you have lost your passport or ID
card, check the local police station.

Opening hours

Banks are open 9am-5pm Mon-Fri.
Bars are open at various times
throughout the day and close at
about 1am Mon-Thur, Sun; 2am
or 3am Fri, Sat. Shops are open
1-6pm Mon (although many stay
closed on this day), 10am-6pm
Tue-Fri (some until 9pm Thur),
9am-5pm Sat. Many central
shops are open on Sunday.

Pharmacies

Dam Apotheek

Damstraat 2, Old Centre: Old Side
(624 4331). Tram 4, 9, 14, 16, 24, 25.
Open 8.30am-5.30pm Mon-Fri; 10am-
5pm Sat; noon-5pm Sun.
Outside these times, call Afdeling
Inlichtingen Apotheken (694 8709)
for a 24-hour service that will
direct you to your nearest late-
opening chemist.

Police stations

Hoofdbureau van Politie (Police Headquarters)

Lijnbaansgracht 219 (0900 8844
premium rate). Tram 1, 2, 5, 7, 10.
Open 24hrs daily.
For details and contact information
regarding local police stations, go
to www.politie.nl.

Post offices

Following a reorganisation of the
postal services, all but one of the
post offices in Amsterdam have
been closed. Instead, many tobacco
shops, supermarkets and book
shops offer postal services. Look
for the orange illuminated sign
with the PostNL logo. The postal
information line is available on
0900 0990 premium rate. The one
remaining old-fashioned post office
stands at Singel 250, Old Centre:
New Side. It's open 7.30am-6.30pm
Mon-Fri; 7.30am-5pm Sat.

Safety

Amsterdam is a relatively safe city,
but do take care. The Red Light
District is rife with undesirable
characters who, though not violent,
are expert pickpockets; be vigilant,
especially on bridges; and don't
ever make eye contact with anyone
who looks as though they are up to
no good, drug dealers especially.
Be extra careful to watch out
for thieves on the Schiphol train;
if you cycle, lock your bike up
well (two locks are advisable).
Keep valuables in your hotel safe,
don't leave bags unattended, and
ensure your cash and cards are
tucked away, and preferably
zipped up in your bag.

Smoking

In 2008, the Netherlands imposed
a smoking ban in all public indoor
spaces. As for cannabis, locals
have a relaxed attitude, but
smoking it isn't acceptable
everywhere in the city: use your
discretion, and if in doubt, ask
before you spark up.

Telephones

Amsterdam's dialling code is 020;
to call within the city, you don't
need to use the code. If dialling
from outside the Netherlands, use
the country code 31, followed by
the number. Drop the first '0' of
the area code; for Amsterdam,
use 20 rather than 020. US mobile

ESSENTIALS

phone users should make sure they call their phone provider in advance of departure, to check their mobile's compatibility with GSM bands.

Time

Amsterdam is one hour ahead of Greenwich Mean Time (GMT). All clocks on Central European Time (CET) go back and forward on the same dates as GMT.

Tipping

Service charges are included in hotel, taxi, bar, café and restaurant bills. However, it's polite to round up to the closest euro for small bills or the nearest five for larger sums, although tipping 10% is becoming more common (leave the extra in change rather than filling in the credit card slip). In taxis, most people tip 10%.

Tourist information

I amsterdam Tourist Information Centres

Stationsplein 10, Old Centre: New Side (702 6000, www.iamsterdam.com). Tram 1, 2, 4, 5, 9, 13, 16, 17, 24, 25, 26. **Open** 9am-5pm Mon-Sat; 10am-5pm Sun.

The main tourist office stands right outside Centraal Station. English-speaking staff provide up-to-date information on transport, entertainment and day-trips. They can also arrange hotel bookings (for a fee), and excursions or car hire for free. Brochures detail walks and cycling tours; maps and a listings magazine are also available. The information line has an English-language service.

Other locations Leidseplein 1 (10am-5pm daily); Schiphol Airport, arrivals hall 2 (7am-10pm daily).

Translators & interpreters

Amstelveens Vertaalburo

Ouderkerkerlaan 50, Amstelveen (645 6610, www.avb-vertalingen.nl). Bus 142, 149, 165, 166, 170, 171, 172, 175, 186, 187, 199, 215, 216, 300. **Open** 9am-5pm Mon-Fri. **No credit cards.**

Mac Bay Consultants

PC Hooftstraat 15, Museum Quarter (24hr phoneline 662 0501, www.mac bay.nl). Tram 2, 5. **Open** 9am-7pm Mon-Fri.

Visas

EU citizens do not require a visa; citizens of the US, Canada, Australia and New Zealand need a valid passport for stays of up to three months. Otherwise, apply for a tourist visa. EU nationals with a resident's permit can work here; for non-EU citizens, it's hard to get a visa without a job in place.

When to go

Climate

The climate is changeable. January and February are the coldest months, and the summers tend to be humid. If you have a grasp of Dutch, call the weather line on 0900 8003 (€0.70/min), otherwise search for the weather forecast via Google.

Public holidays

Known as Nationale Feestdagen in Dutch, these include New Year's Day, Good Friday, Easter Sunday and Monday, Koningsdag (King's Day, 27 April or 26 April if 27 April is on a Sunday), Remembrance Day (4 May), Liberation Day (5 May), Ascension Day, Whit (Pentecost) Sunday and Monday, Christmas Day and Boxing Day.

Vocabulary

Almost every person you'll come across in Amsterdam will speak good English, and you'll be able to get by without a word of Dutch during your stay. However, a bit of effort goes a long way, and locals are appreciative of those visitors polite enough to take five minutes to learn some basic phrases. Here are a few that might help.

Useful expressions

Hello hallo/dag; **goodbye** tot ziens/dag; **yes** ja; **yes please** ja, graag; **no** nee; **no thanks** nee, dank je; **please** alstublieft; **thank you** dank u; **excuse me** pardon; **do you speak English?** spreekt u Engels?; **sorry, I don't speak Dutch** het spijt me, ik spreek geen Nederlands; **I don't understand** ik begrijp het niet; **I am ill** ik ben ziek; **good** goed; **bad** slecht; **big** groot; **small** klein; **nice** mooi; **tasty** lekker; **open** open; **closed** gesloten/dicht; **entrance** ingang; **exit** uitgang; **the bill** de rekening; **hotel room** hotelkamer; **single/ twin/ double bedroom** eenpersoonskamer/tweepersoonskamer met aparte bedden/ tweepersoonskamer; **I want** ik wil graag; **how much is** wat kost

Getting around

Bus bus; **car** auto; **tram** tram; **train** trein; **ticket/s** kaart/kaarten; **street** straat; **square** plein; **canal** gracht; **left** links; **right** rechts; **straight on** rechtdoor; **far** ver; **near** dichtbij; **here** hier; **there** daar; **where is?** waar is?

Places

Shop winkel; **bank** bank; **post office** postkantoor; **pharmacy** apotheek; **hotel** hotel; **bar** bar; **restaurant** restaurant; **hospital** ziekenhuis; **bus stop** bushalte; **station** station

Time

Now nu; **later** straks; **morning** ochtend; **afternoon** middag; **evening** avond; **night** nacht; **today** vandaag; **yesterday** gisteren; **tomorrow** morgen; **what time is** hoe laat is; **what's the time?** hoe laat is het?; **noon** middag; **midnight** middernacht; **at eight o'clock** om acht uur; **quarter past eight** kwaart over acht; **20 past eight** tien voor half negen; **25 past eight** vijf half negen; **half past eight** half negen; **25 to nine** vijf over half negen; **quarter to nine** kwaart voor negen

Numbers

0 nul; **1** een; **2** twee; **3** drie; **4** vier; **5** vijf; **6** zes; **7** zeven; **8** acht; **9** negen; **10** tien; **11** elf; **12** twaalf; **13** dertien; **14** veertien; **15** vijftien; **16** zestien; **17** zeventien; **18** achttien; **19** negen-tien; **20** twintig; **21** eenentwintig; **22** twee'ntwintig; **30** dertig; **40** veertig; **50** vijftig; **60** zestig; **70** zeventig; **80** tachtig; **90** negentig; **100** honderd; **101** honderd een; **200** tweehonderd; **1,000** duizend; **1,000,000** een miljoen

Days & months

Monday maandag; **Tuesday** dinsdag; **Wednesday** woensdag; **Thursday** donderdag; **Friday** vrijdag; **Saturday** zaterdag; **Sunday** zondag; **January** januari; **February** februari; **March** maart; **April** april; **May** mei; **June** juni; **July** juli; **August** augustus; **September** september; **October** oktober; **November** november; **December** december

Menu Glossary

Basics

Bestek cutlery; **brood** bread; **broodje** bread roll; **glas** glass; **lepel** spoon; **menukaart** menu; **mes** knife; **peper** pepper; **de rekening** the bill; **vork** fork; **wijnkaart** wine list; **zout** salt

Snacks

Bitterballen mini croquettes filled with meat and potato; **borrel/bittergarnituur** platter of snacks to accompany drinks (usually sausage, salami, cheese and *bitterballen*); **borrelnoten** crispy coated nuts; **frikadel** a popular, deep-fried skinless sausage with mysterious ingredients; **kaassouffle** cheese fritter, only tasty when it is served very hot; **kroket** croquette filled with meat and potato; **oliebollen** deep-fried dough balls that are traditionally served around New Year, either plain or supplemented with raisins, currants and/or diced apples; **pannekoek** pancake; **patat** French fries/chips, also called *frites*; **patat met** French fries/chips with mayonnaise; **pindas** peanuts; **saucijzenbroodje** hot sausage roll made with puff pastry; **snert** a thick pea soup, also called *erwtensoep*; **tostis** grilled ham and/or cheese sandwiches; **uitsmijter** cheese and/or ham on bread topped with three fried eggs

Meat

Bal/gehaktbal meatball; **biefstuk** steak; **bio** organic; **eend** duck; **kalf** veal; **kalkoen** turkey; **kip** chicken; **lam** lamb; **rund** beef; **scharrel** free-range; **spek** bacon; **struisvogel** ostrich; **varkensvlees** pork; **vlees** meat; **worst** sausage

Fish

Ansjovis anchovies; **gambas** prawns; **garnalen** shrimps; **gerookte** smoked; **haring** herring; **maatjesharing** first herring of the season; **makreel** mackerel; **mosselen** mussels; **oesters** oysters; **paling** eel; **tong** sole; **tonijn** tuna; **venusschelpen** clams; **vis** fish; **zalm** salmon; **zeeduivel** monkfish; **zeevruchten/zeebanket** seafood

Fruit & vegetables

Aardappel potato; **aardbei** strawberry; **appel** apple; **bosbes** blueberry; **champignons** mushrooms; **citroen** lemon; **druiven** grapes; **framboos** raspberry; **fruit/vruchten** fruit; **groenten** vegetables; **kersen** cherries; **knoflook** garlic; **kruiden** herbs; **limoen** lime; **rauwkost** coleslaw; **rijst** rice; **sinasappel** orange; **zuurkool** sauerkraut

Puddings & cakes

Flensje crêpe; **gember** ginger; **griesmeel** semolina; **hangop** strained thick yoghurt; **honing** honey; **koek** cake; **koekje** biscuit; **roomijs/ijs** ice-cream; **slagroom** whipped cream; **stroop** syrup; **suiker** sugar; **toetje** dessert; **vla** custard

Dairy

Blauwe kaas blue cheese; **boter** butter; **geitenkaas** goat's cheese; **kaas** cheese; **magere/halfvolle/volle melk** skimmed/semi-skimmed/full milk; **oud/extra belegen** mature; **roomkaas** cream cheese; **schapenkaas** cheese made from sheep's milk

Index

ESSENTIALS